AF600742

Affect Me.
Social Media Images in Art

Lara Baladi
Irene Chabr
Forensic Architecture
Lynn Hershman Leeson
Thomas Hirschhorn
Randa Maroufi
Rabih Mroué
Thomas Ruff
D. H. Saur

Kuratiert von / Curated by
Julia Höner
Kerstin Schankweiler

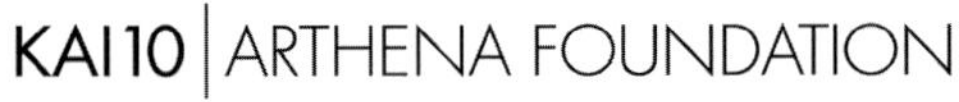

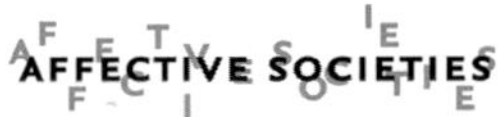

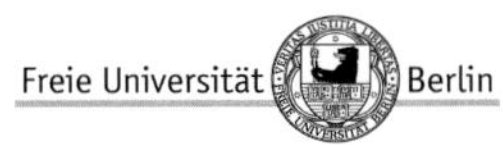

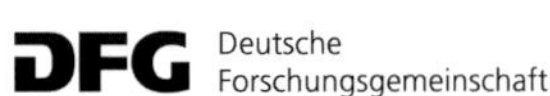

Content

Inhalt

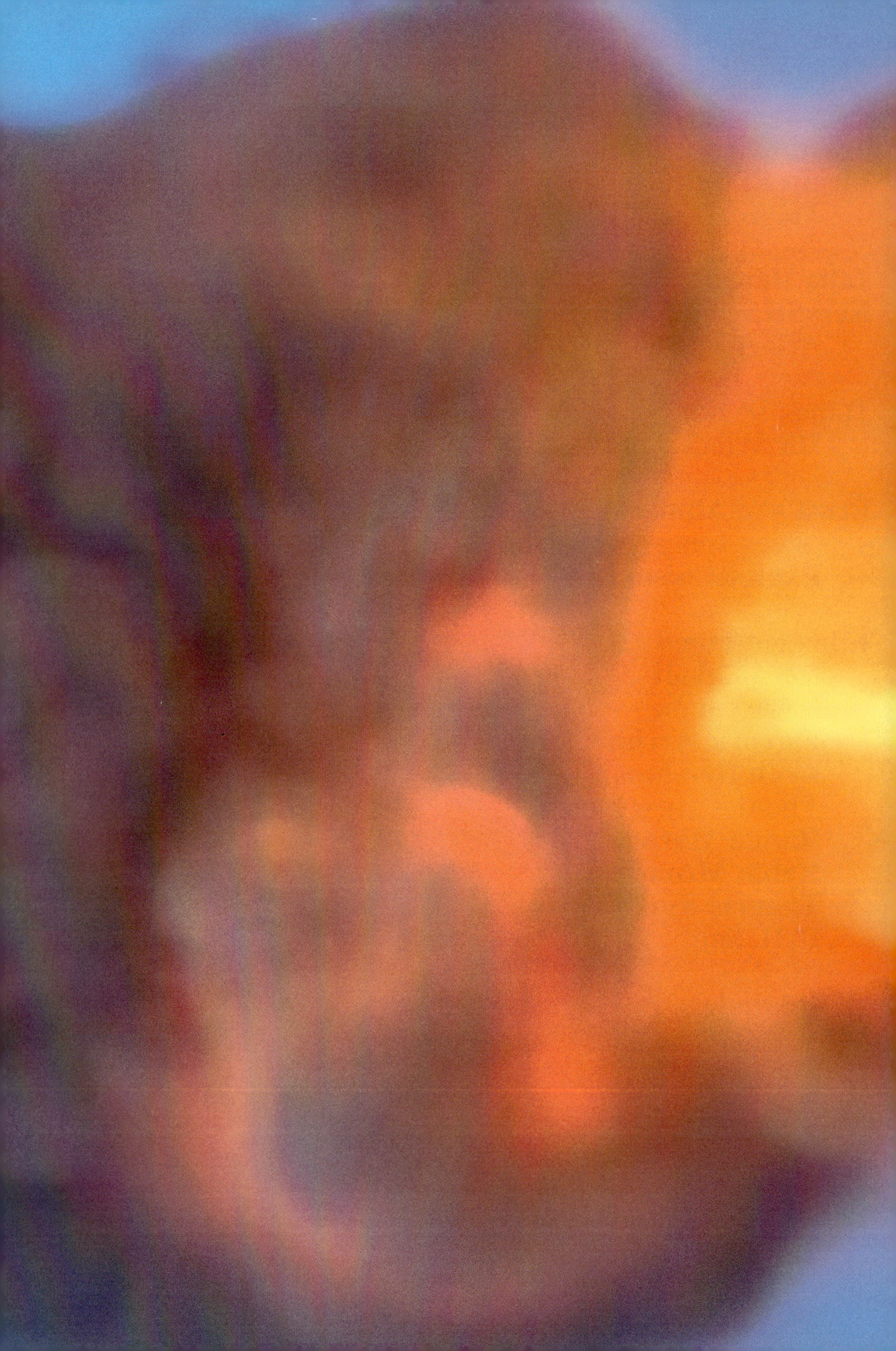

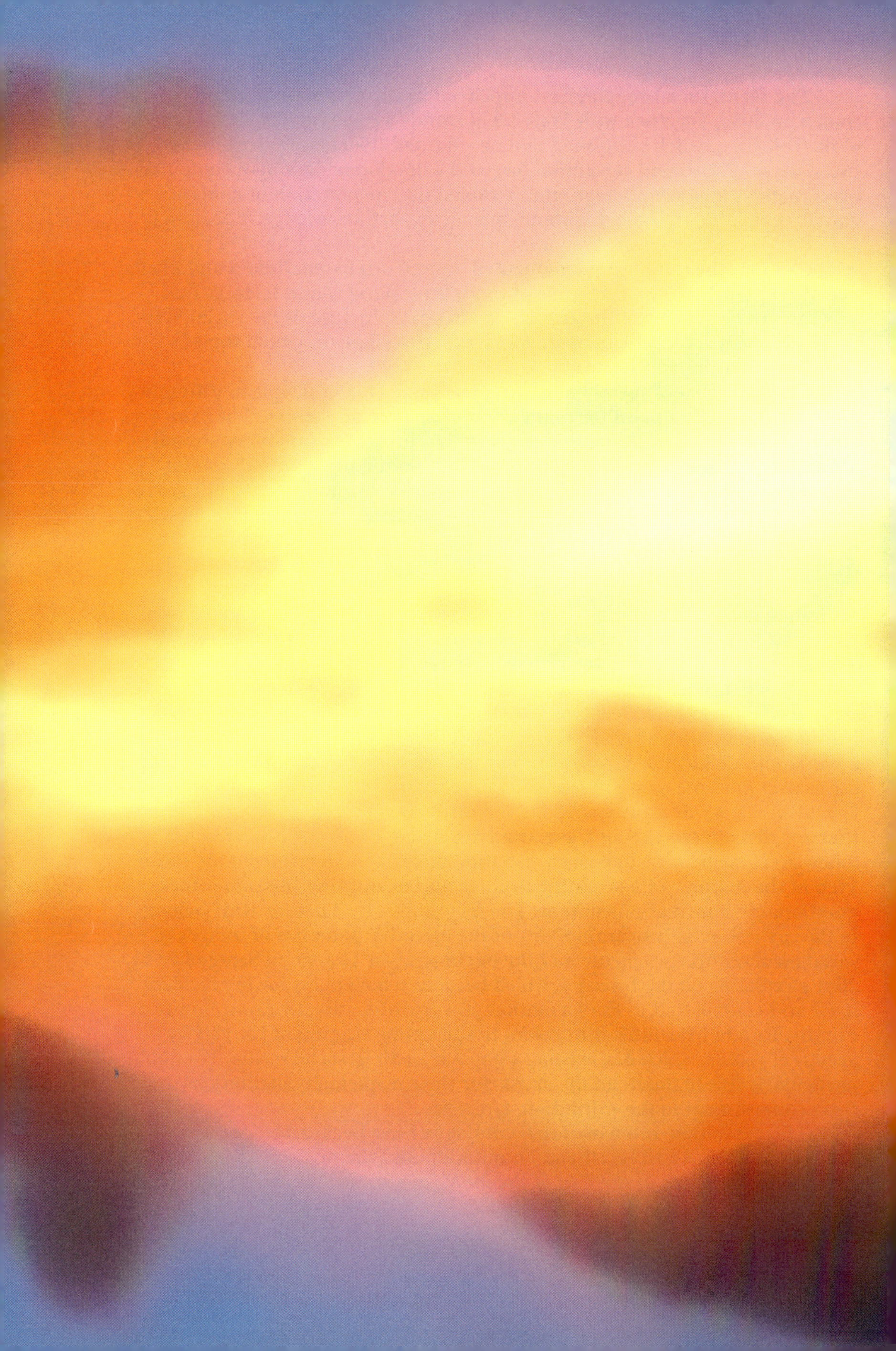

Foreword

The term, social media, first appeared in the German dictionary, Duden, in 2013. Together with Web 2.0, it stands for the further development of the Internet, which simplified and accelerated the communication between users. The digital revolution forced the development of new, computer-based algorithms, which have since enabled user production of content and its uploading to the net without specific expert knowledge. The data is available for all citizens of the online world and provides a topic of conversation for others by being commented on and discussed, linked and liked. Social relationships, the exchange of thoughts, opinions and feelings find new ways to be organised through the dialogical structure of the social Web. The Internet has thereby become an interactive stage on which images play an increasingly important role.

This potential of social media to affect and connect people in different places is the starting point for many current artistic discourses. The exhibition, *Affect Me. Social Media Images in Art*, presents nine international artists' works that refer to images of mainly politically charged events circulating online. For the first time, an exhibition examines these images in terms of their affective potential. This new relationship between images, the witnessed events and the actors involved is to be characterised by the term, affect, which runs like a leitmotif through the whole exhibition project. The artists facilitate reflection on new image phenomena, which in the exhibition are quite consciously not presented alongside visual practices of users and activists—even if artists often alternate today between art and activism and borders become increasingly blurred.

Artists such as Thomas Hirschhorn or Lynn Hershman Leeson access images of extreme violence, and thus particularly affective material, on the Internet and amplify them in their work. In contrast, the installations of Lara Baladi and Rabih Mroué combine recent mobile phone videos of political protest movements with images from other sources, for example, popular culture. Both artists expand the pictorial rhetoric and power of images that are distributed through social media. Irene Chabr and D. H. Saur follow an encyclopaedic approach, collating pictorial material from the social Web in the manner of a scientific archive and examining the sometimes questionable information content. The *jpeg* series, by Thomas Ruff belongs to the earliest artistic examinations of the affective potential of images in social media. Ruff uses pictures of the burning Twin Towers on September 11, 2001 circulating on the Internet, which became synonymous for the incident itself and contributed to the formation of worldwide affective communities. Finally, Randa Maroufi's film refers to the online staging of the self by groups of youths, which has become a popular motif in social media. We would particularly like to thank all the artists for their inspiring contributions and their commitment to the exhibition *Affect Me*.

The exhibition and associated catalogue have been developed in close cooperation of KAI 10 | Arthena Foundation and the project, *Affective Dynamics of Images in the Era of Social Media*, under the leadership of

Vorwort

Im Jahr 2013 erschien der Begriff Social Media erstmals im Duden. Gemeinsam mit dem Web 2.0 steht er für eine Weiterentwicklung des Internets, die den Austausch und die Kommunikation zwischen User*innen vereinfacht und beschleunigt hat. Die digitale Revolution forcierte die Entwicklung neuer, computerbasierter Algorithmen, die es seither ermöglichen, ohne spezielles Expertenwissen selbst Inhalte zu generieren und ins Netz zu stellen. Die Daten sind für alle Bürger*innen der Onlinewelt verfügbar und werden zum Gesprächsstoff anderer, indem sie kommentiert, diskutiert, verlinkt oder geliked werden. Soziale Beziehungen und der Austausch von Gedanken, Meinungen und Gefühlen lassen sich durch die dialogische Struktur des Social Web neu organisieren. Damit ist das Internet zu einer interaktiven Bühne geworden, auf der Bilder zunehmend eine wichtige Rolle spielen.

Dieses Potenzial der sozialen Medien, Menschen an unterschiedlichen Orten zu affizieren und zu verbinden, ist der Ausgangspunkt zahlreicher, aktueller künstlerischer Auseinandersetzungen. Die Ausstellung *Affect Me. Social Media Images in Art* zeigt Arbeiten von neun internationalen Künstler*innen, die sich auf online zirkulierende Bilder mehrheitlich politisch aufgeladener Ereignisse beziehen. Erstmals betrachtet ein Ausstellungsprojekt diese hinsichtlich ihres Affizierungspotenzial. Mit dem Begriff des Affekts, der sich als Leitmotiv durch das gesamte Ausstellungsprojekt zieht, soll diese neue Beziehung zwischen Bildern, den durch sie bezeugten Ereignissen und den Akteur*innen charakterisiert werden. Die Künstler*innen ermöglichen eine Reflexion der neuen Bildphänomene, die in der Ausstellung ganz bewusst nicht direkt mit den Bildpraktiken der User*innen und Aktivist*innen gemeinsam präsentiert werden – auch wenn Künstler*innen heute oft zwischen Kunst und Aktivismus changieren und Grenzen zunehmend verschwimmen.

Künstler*innen wie Thomas Hirschhorn oder Lynn Hershman Leeson greifen auf Bilder extremer Gewalt aus dem Internet und damit auf besonders affizierendes Material zurück und potenzieren dieses in ihren Arbeiten. Demgegenüber verbinden die vom Medium Video ausgehenden Installationen von Lara Baladi und Rabih Mroué Handyfilme aus politischen Protestbewegungen der jüngsten Zeit mit Bildern aus anderen, beispielsweise populärkulturellen, Quellen. Beide Künstler*innen arbeiten die Bildrhetorik und Handlungsmacht der Bilder heraus, die über die sozialen Medien distribuiert werden. Einen enzyklopädischen Ansatz verfolgen Irene Chabr und D.H. Saur, die im Duktus wissenschaftlicher Archive Bildmaterial aus dem Social Web zusammentragen und den mitunter zweifelhaften Informationsgehalt untersuchen. Zu den frühesten Auseinandersetzungen mit dem Affizierungspotenzial der Bilder in den sozialen Medien gehört die *jpeg* Serie von Thomas Ruff. Unter anderem nutzt er im Internet kursierende Bilder der brennenden Twin Towers vom 11. September 2001, die zum Synonym für das Ereignis selbst wurden und zur Bildung von weltweiten Affektgemeinschaften beitrugen. Randa Maroufi schließlich bezieht sich in ihrem

Prof. Tobias Wendl, which is a part of the Collaborative Research Center 1171, *Affective Societies. Dynamics of Social Coexistence in Mobile Worlds* (CRC) at the Freie Universität Berlin. After collaborations with other institutions—Kunsthalle Nürnberg (2015), KINDL – Centre for Contemporary Art Berlin (2017)—, *Affect Me* in KAI 10 brings together competencies from academic research and institutional curatorial practice for the first time. This collaboration has resulted in an exciting exhibition that conceptually originated in the artists' works and echoes the research of the CRC *Affective Societies*. At this point, we would like to thank the two curators, Julia Höner (KAI 10) and Kerstin Schankweiler (FU Berlin). They had the initial idea for this project and conceptualised the exhibition and catalogue together, realising the project in KAI 10 with great commitment.

They were supported above all by Marion Eisele, who has coordinated the whole exhibition in her experienced manner. Aiding her were Julia Schleis, Susanne Kalf-Muhtaroglu and Sabine Allroggen from the KAI 10 team and Linda Huke from the FU Berlin. Our sincere thanks go to all colleagues for their impressive work. We would also like to thank the Deutsche Forschungsgemeinschaft as well as Pro Helvetia, the Goethe-Institut Cairo, and the Rudolf Augstein Stiftung, and the sponsors, CNC-Step and Protiq for their support as well as the lenders Konrad Fischer Galerie, Düsseldorf & Berlin, Sfeir-Semler Gallery, Beirut & Hamburg, Waldburger Wouters, Brussels, and Le Fresnoy for their trust. Our sincere thanks also go to the authors of this catalogue's essays, Ernst van Alphen, Julia Höner, Kerstin Schankweiler and Tobias Wendl, whose inspiring essays shed light on the use of images in art and social media from different perspectives. We further thank Marion Eisele, Linda Huke, Tasja Langenbach, Katja Müller-Helle, Stefanie Stallschus and Verena Straub for their elucidating contributions on the individual artistic positions.

KAI 10 and the CRC *Affective Societies* are very pleased with the fruitful and successful cooperation between exhibition practice and scientific research, which has produced the accomplished exhibition as well as the extensive catalogue designed by Daniel Rother and Krispin Heé.

Monika Schnetkamp (Chairwoman, Arthena Foundation)
Birgitt Röttger-Rössler (Speaker, Collaborative Research Center 1171 *Affective Societies*)

Film auf Selbstinszenierungen von Jugendlichen, die zu einem beliebten Motiv in den sozialen Medien geworden sind. Allen neun Künstler*innen gilt unser erster und größter Dank für ihre inspirierenden Beiträge und ihr Engagement für *Affect Me*.

Die Ausstellung und der vorliegende Katalog sind in enger Kooperation von KAI 10 | Arthena Foundation und dem Projekt *Affektive Dynamiken von Bildern im Zeitalter von Social Media* entstanden, das unter der Leitung von Prof. Dr. Tobias Wendl Teil des Sonderforschungsbereichs 1171 *Affective Societies. Dynamiken des Zusammenlebens in bewegten Welten* (SFB) an der Freien Universität Berlin ist. Nach Kooperationen mit anderen Kunstinstitutionen (2015, Kunsthalle Nürnberg; 2017, KINDL – Zentrum für zeitgenössische Kunst Berlin) führt *Affect Me* erstmalig in KAI 10 Kompetenzen aus akademischer Forschung und institutioneller Ausstellungspraxis zusammen. Dabei ist eine spannende Ausstellung entstanden, die von den künstlerischen Positionen her gedacht ist und durch die aktuellen Fragestellungen des Sonderforschungsbereichs *Affective Societies* inhaltlich flankiert wird. Dafür möchten wir den beiden Kuratorinnen Julia Höner (KAI 10) und Kerstin Schankweiler (FU Berlin) herzlich danken. Sie hatten die initiale Idee zu diesem Projekt und haben die Ausstellung und den vorliegenden Katalog gemeinsam erarbeitet und in KAI 10 mit großem Engagement umgesetzt.

Sie wurden dabei vor allem von Marion Eisele unterstützt, die in routinierter Weise die gesamte Ausstellung koordiniert hat. Zur Seite standen ihnen ebenfalls Julia Schleis, Susanne Kalf-Muhtaroglu, Sabine Allroggen aus dem Team von KAI 10 sowie Linda Huke von der FU Berlin. Allen Mitarbeiterinnen sei für ihren großen Einsatz sehr herzlich gedankt. Der Deutschen Forschungsgemeinschaft sowie den Förderern Pro Helvetia, Goethe-Institut Kairo, Rudolf Augstein Stiftung und den Sponsoren CNC-Step und Protiq danken wir ebenso wie den Leihgebern Konrad Fischer Galerie, Düsseldorf & Berlin, Sfeir-Semler Gallery, Beirut & Hamburg und Walburger Wouters, Brüssel sowie Le Fresnoy. Den Autor*innen der Katalogessays Ernst van Alphen, Julia Höner, Kerstin Schankweiler und Tobias Wendl, die in ihren fundierten Aufsätzen den Umgang mit Bildern in Kunst und sozialen Medien aus unterschiedlichen Perspektiven beleuchten, gilt ebenfalls unser herzlicher Dank. Für die erläuternden Beiträge zu den einzelnen künstlerischen Positionen danken wir ferner Marion Eisele, Linda Huke, Tasja Langenbach, Katja Müller-Helle, Stefanie Stallschus und Verena Straub.

KAI 10 und der SFB *Affective Societies* freuen sich sehr über die fruchtbare und geglückte Kooperation zwischen institutioneller Ausstellungspraxis und kulturwissenschaftlicher Forschung, die in der Ausstellung sowie der umfangreichen, von Daniel Rother und Krispin Heé gestalteten Publikation ihren Ausdruck findet.

Monika Schnetkamp (Vorsitzende Arthena Foundation)
Birgitt Röttger-Rössler (Sprecherin des Sonderforschungsbereichs 1171 *Affective Societies*)

Julia Höner
Kerstin Schankweiler

Affect Me. Social Media Images in Art

Julia Höner
Kerstin Schankweiler

Affect Me. Social Media Images in Art

In the era of Facebook, Instagram, Twitter and Co., the way people deal with images has undergone fundamental changes. Images, circulating in digital networks, have become an essential personal means of expression for a broad public. The interactive component of the social Web creates a new realm based on dialogue, where users can communicate in near real time. Especially when images serve as a vehicle for communication, the frequency of this dialogue tends to accelerate rapidly. In view of their great affective potential, images ingeniously impact the entire gamut of emotions and thus trigger spontaneous responses in their recipients. What others have posted is commented haphazardly or impulsively. This comprises banalities from the users' lives as well as photographic evidence from the global trouble spots of our present times. The significance of these pictures is related to how they are handled, in that they are generated by interactive processes between images and humans, which are, above all, marked by affect-based dynamics. Pictures move users, they are liked in large numbers, they provoke protests, prompt criticism and reckless insults, but are also capable of promoting public debate and a sense of community. In many different ways and cases, they are taken up to be posted or published in new contexts, to be altered with image processing applications or imitated in new takes.

It is especially with regard to contemporary forms of political protest that the democratic promise of the pictures distributed via social media—to offer alternative perspectives on today's political crises—comes to the fore. The rise in ideological propaganda and fake information in social media may have

Im Zeitalter von Facebook, Instagram, Twitter und Co. hat sich der Umgang mit Bildern grundlegend verändert. Bilder, die in digitalen Netzwerken zirkulieren, sind zum wichtigsten persönlichen Ausdrucksmittel einer breiten Öffentlichkeit geworden. Denn die interaktive Komponente des Social Web schafft einen neuen dialogbasierten Raum, in dem die Nutzer*innen annähernd in Echtzeit kommunizieren können. Insbesondere wenn Bilder als Vehikel der Kommunikation genutzt werden, nimmt die Frequenz dieses Dialogs rasant an Fahrt auf. Bilder mit ihrem hohen Affizierungspotenzial spielen geradezu virtuos auf der Klaviatur der Gefühle und lösen spontane Reaktionen bei ihren Adressat*innen aus. Ad hoc und mitunter aus dem Bauch heraus wird kommentiert, was andere posten. Dazu gehören Banalitäten aus dem Leben der User*innen genauso wie Bildbeweise aus den globalen Krisenherden unserer Gegenwart. Die Bedeutung dieser Bilder entsteht durch das Handeln mit ihnen, durch Interaktionsprozesse zwischen Bildern und Menschen, die vor allem durch affektive Dynamiken gekennzeichnet sind. Bilder bewegen die User*innen, werden massenhaft geliked, provozieren Proteste, sind Anlass für Kritik und ungehemmte Pöbelei, befördern öffentliche Debatten und wirken gemeinschaftsbildend. Sie werden vielfach aufgegriffen, in neuen Kontexten gepostet oder publiziert, mit Bildbearbeitungsprogrammen verändert oder mit neuen Aufnahmen nachgeahmt.

Besonders im Hinblick auf zeitgenössische Formen des politischen Protests manifestiert sich das demokratische Versprechen der über die sozialen Medien verbreiteten Bilder, alternative Perspektiven auf die politischen Krisen der Gegenwart zu liefern.

recently damaged the reputation of these channels of knowledge transfer. In the worldwide protest movements of the past years, however, it was particularly the private photo or video, taken with the mobile phone camera and distributed online in the diverse networks, that has advanced to become, perhaps, the most important toolset for shaping an independent opinion.

This is where the exhibition *Affect Me. Social Media Images in Art* comes into play. It presents works from nine international artists that relate to the new image practices in social media and explicitly deal with footage put on the Web in the context of global political debate and civic protest. In their works they reflect on the usage and the semantics of these images, but likewise examine their aesthetic qualities. Some of the works on display virtually draw us into the situations and events of our perpetually changing world, for example by visualizing the Syrian civil war or the mass protests against racism in the USA. In other cases, the artists adopt a more distanced perspective. They focus on the mobilizing capacities of images and reveal how pictures may create a "fait accompli," always navigating on the brittle boundaries between reality and fiction. The exhibition at KAI 10 thus understands the works of the individual artists as not only resulting from global image phenomena on the Internet. It rather intends —flanked by the present publication—to underline and theoretically substantiate the aesthetical fascination that arises from these pictorial sources and inspires the artists to their works.

Why then are artists today working increasingly with fleeting instants captured in snapshots, from anonymous sources, of poor technical quality, whose

Die Zunahme von ideologischer Propaganda und gefälschten Informationen in den sozialen Medien mögen diese als Kanäle der Wissensvermittlung aktuell in Verruf gebracht haben. In den globalen Protestbewegungen der letzten Jahre avancierte jedoch gerade das private, mit der Handykamera aufgenommene und in den Netzwerken online verbreitete Foto oder Video zu dem vielleicht bedeutendsten Instrumentarium einer unabhängigen Meinungsbildung.

Hier setzt die Ausstellung *Affect Me. Social Media Images in Art* an. Sie stellt Arbeiten von neun internationalen künstlerischen Positionen vor, die sich auf die neuen Bildphänomene der sozialen Medien beziehen und explizit Bildmaterial aufgreifen, das im Kontext von globalen politischen Auseinandersetzungen und zivilgesellschaftlichem Protes ins Netz gestellt wurde. Sie reflektieren in ihren Arbeiten die Gebrauchsweisen und die Semantik dieser Bilder, setzen sich aber ebenso mit ihren ästhetischen Qualitäten auseinander. Mitunter lassen sie uns tief eintauchen in die Orte und Ereignisse unserer aktuellen Welt im Umbruch, sie vergegenwärtigen uns etwa den syrischen Bürgerkrieg oder Massenproteste gegen Rassismus in den USA. Ein anderes Mal nehmen die Künstler*innen eine eher distanzierte Perspektive ein. Sie beleuchten das Vermögen der Bilder zu mobilisieren und zeigen auf, wie diese Bilder Tatsachen schaffen und dabei an der porösen Grenze zwischen Realität und Fiktion agieren.
Die Ausstellung in KAI 10 bezieht die Werke der einzelnen Künstler*innen somit nicht nur ursächlich auf globale Bildphänomene im Internet. Sie möchte – flankiert durch die vorliegende Publikation – einen Beitrag dazu leisten, der ästhetischen Faszination,

"visual noise" tends to shroud the motifs rather than unveil occurrences? Because, as one hypothesis of this exhibition proposes, these images circulating online do not only convey incidents but also mediate the underlying relational fabric between people and images, thus providing profound insights into the emotional constitution and excitation dynamics of present-day societies. Two examples derived from the practice of global protest movements visualize the new dynamics of images in the era of social media.

Global Icons of Protest

When in June 2009 a young woman was shot during the protests against the Iranian presidential election results, presumably by a member of an Iranian militia, the cameras of several mobile phones retained the woman's death. The resulting videos were shared virally via Facebook, Twitter and YouTube, receiving millions of clicks and comments. Due to the shocking pictures of "Neda" (her full name

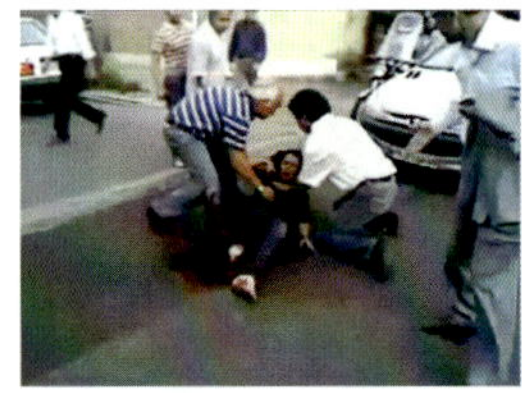

Neda Agha-Soltan, video still

die von diesen Bildquellen ausgeht und die Künstler*-innen zu ihren Arbeiten bewegt, auf den Grund zu gehen.

Warum also arbeiten Künstler*innen heute vermehrt mit flüchtigen Momentaufnahmen aus anonymen Quellen, die von geringer technischer Qualität sind und deren visuelles Rauschen die Motive mitunter mehr verhüllt, als dass es Ereignisse sichtbar macht? Weil, so lautet eine These dieser Ausstellung, diese online zirkulierenden Bilder nicht bloß Ereignisse transportieren, sondern ebenso das relationale Gefüge zwischen Menschen und Bildern, und uns dadurch tiefe Einblicke in die emotionale Konstitution und Erregungsdynamik aktueller Gesellschaften gewähren. Zwei Beispiele aus der Praxis globaler Protestbewegungen veranschaulichen diese neue Dynamik von Bildern im Zeitalter der sozialen Medien.

Globale Ikonen des Protests

Als im Juni 2009 nach den Präsidentschaftswahlen im Iran während Straßenprotesten eine junge Frau erschossen wurde, mutmaßlich von einem Mitglied einer iranischen Miliz, hielten die Kameras mehrerer Mobiltelefone den Tod der Frau fest. Die entstandenen Videos fanden über Facebook, Twitter und YouTube globale Verbreitung, sie wurden millionenfach angeklickt, geteilt und kommentiert. Durch diese schockierenden Bilder erregte der Fall von „Neda“ (mit vollem Namen eigentlich Neda

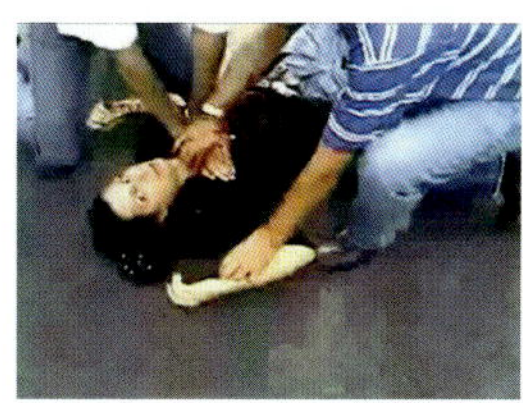

Neda Agha-Soltan, Videostill

was Neda Agha-Soltan), the case aroused attention on an international level. Barack Obama prominently commented on the photos at a press conference as "heartbreaking."[1] #iran-election is viewed as the first political hashtag of international solidarity that was used in countless tweets. "Neda" became a martyr

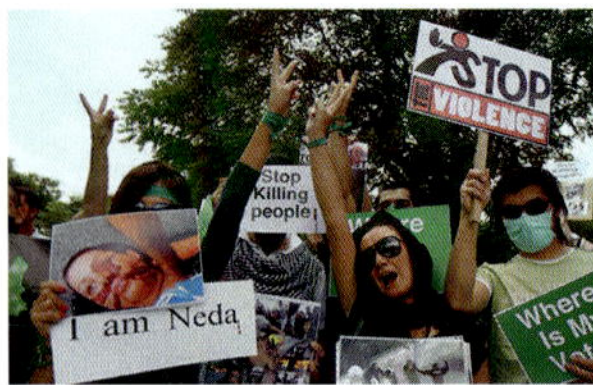

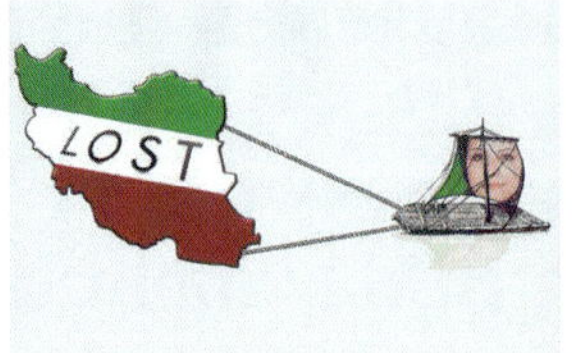

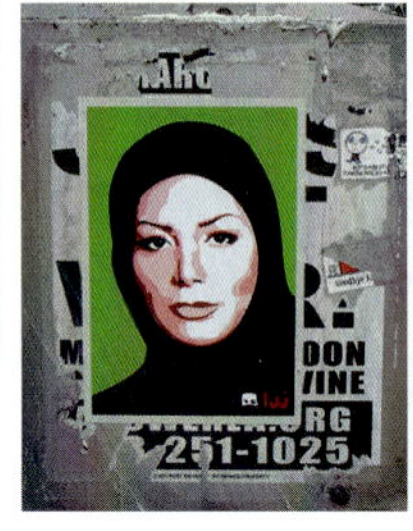

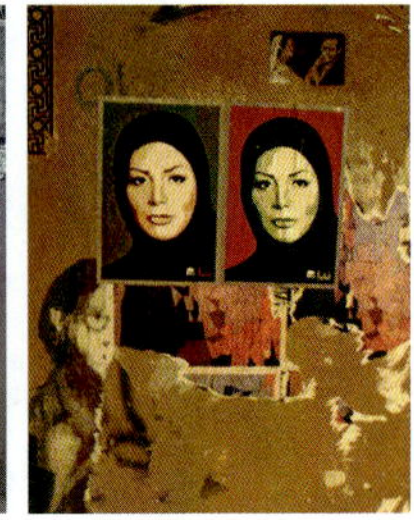

and iconic symbol of protest and resistance of the Iranian opposition, although it was not clear which side the woman was on nor whether she had even participated in the protests or was just coincidently at the scene. "Neda's" case exemplifies the kind of responses such videos can trigger and how they congeal into emotionally charged public opinion (at times quite divergent and contradictory). Equally telling is the fact that we know "Neda's" name but not those of the at least nine others killed during the protests—because there are no comparable images of these victims. The exhibition presents an artwork featuring the image of "Neda": D. H. Saur integrates

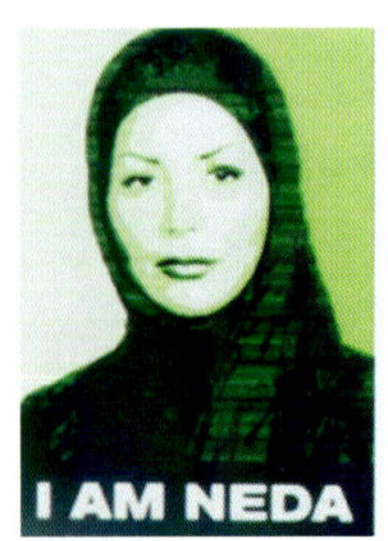

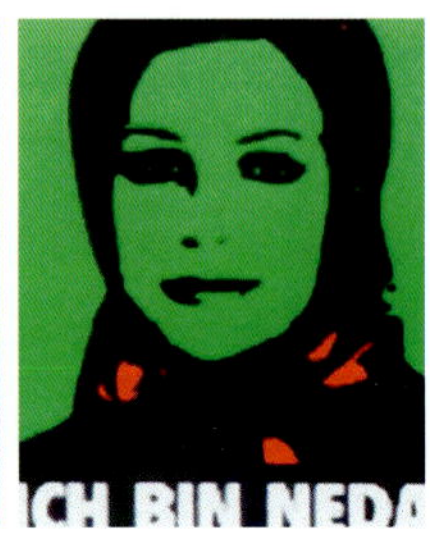

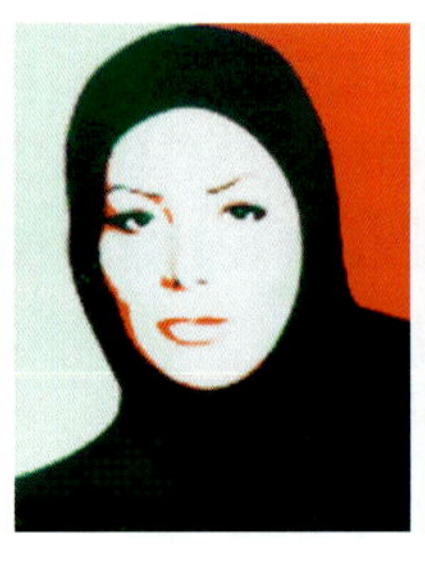

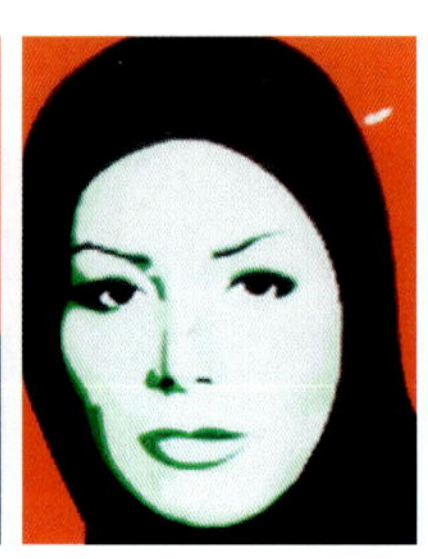

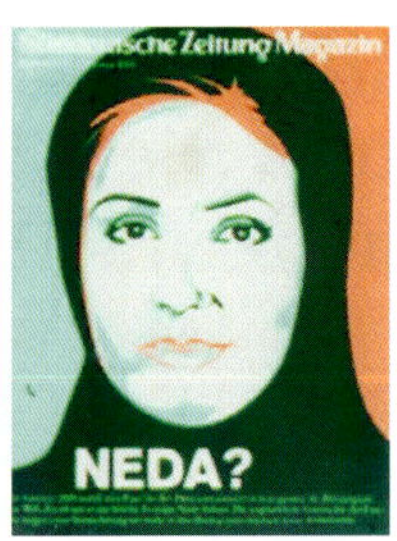

"Neda," appropriations
D. H. Saur, *Hope 2008–2011*, 2011, details

Agha-Soltan) international Aufsehen. Prominent kommentierte Barack Obama die Aufnahmen im Rahmen einer Pressekonferenz als „heartbreaking“[1]. #iranelection gilt als erster politischer Hashtag internationaler Solidarität, der massenhaft in Tweets Verwendung fand. „Neda“ wurde zur Märtyrerin

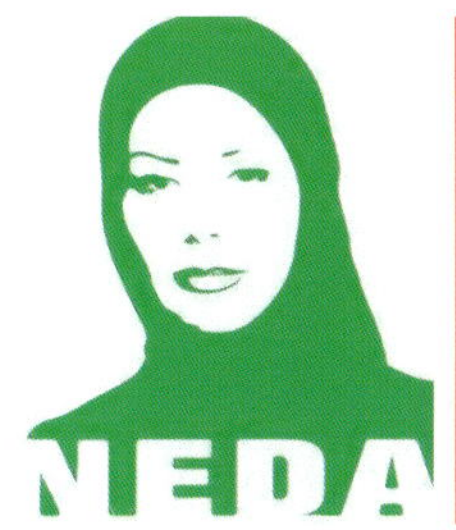

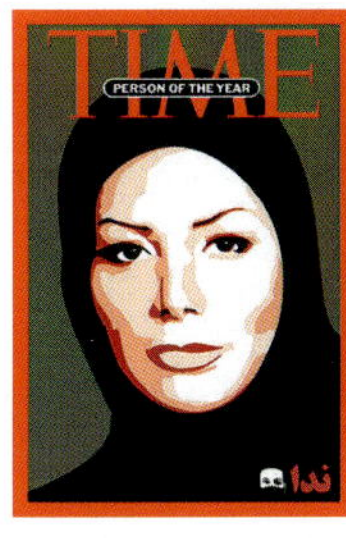

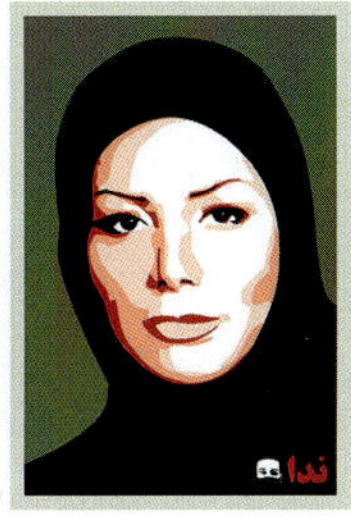

und zur Protestikone des Widerstandes der iranischen Opposition, obwohl weder klar war, auf welcher Seite die Frau stand, noch, ob sie überhaupt an den Protesten teilgenommen hatte oder einfach zufällig am Ort des Geschehens war. Der Fall von „Neda“ zeigt exemplarisch, welche Resonanzen Videos dieser Art hervorrufen können und wie sie in (manchmal höchst unterschiedlichen und widersprüchlichen) emotional grundierten öffentlichen Meinungsbildern gerinnen. Es ist ebenso vielsagend, dass wir „Nedas“ Namen kennen, jedoch keinen der anderen der mindestens neun Getöteten dieser Proteste – weil es von ihnen keine vergleichbaren Bilder gibt. Eine der künstlerischen Arbeiten in der Ausstellung greift das Bild von „Neda“ auf: D. H. Saur integriert es

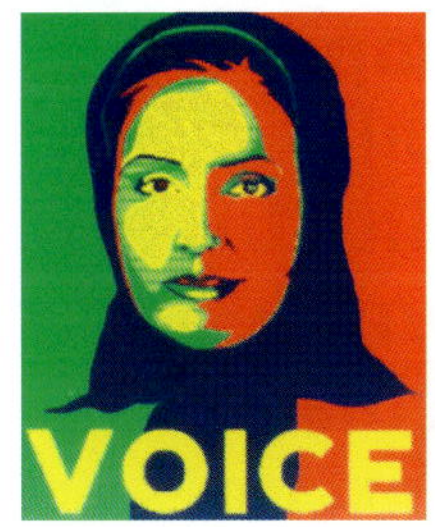

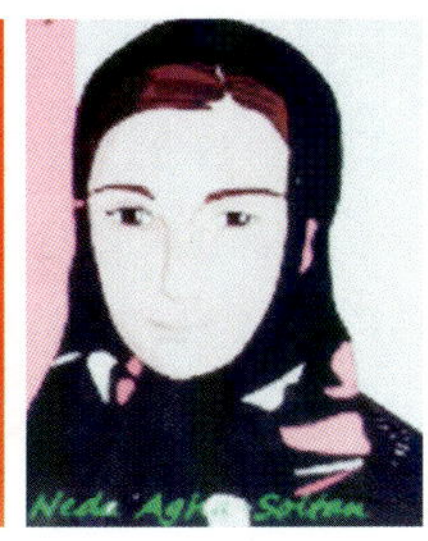

„Neda“, Aneignungen
D. H. Saur, *Hope 2008–2011*, 2011, Details

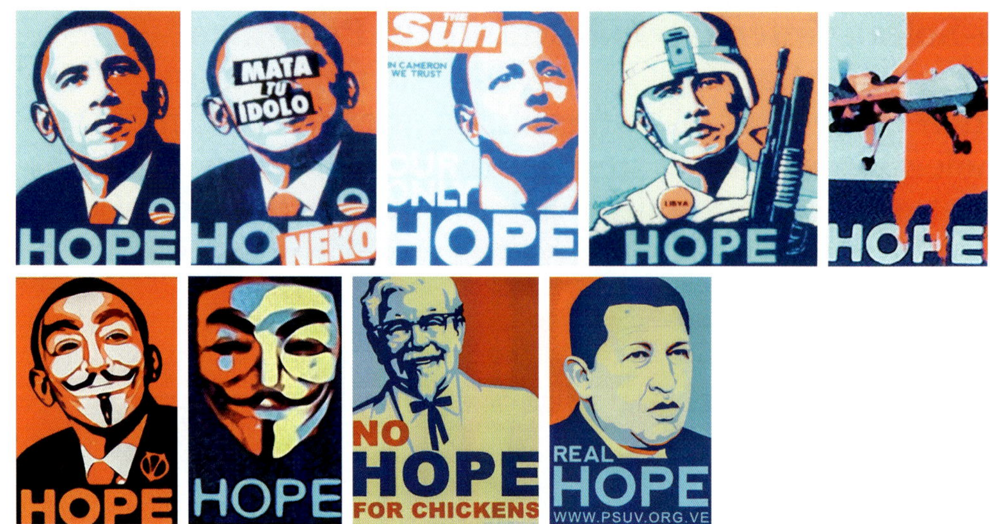

it in one of his collages, where it appears as a meme[2] from the election campaign poster of Barack Obama, titled "Hope."

Exhibited in Düsseldorf for the first time, Lara Baladi's interactive timeline of the Egyptian revolution includes another prominent example of a sad case: that of Khaled Said. The Facebook group "We are all Khaled Said" was founded after the blogger Said was beaten to death by the police in Alexandria in June 2010 and his family had posted a picture of the disfigured corpse on the Web. People empathetically identified with Said and reacted by calling for protests on the Facebook page during the riots that followed in Egypt. He thus became a transnational icon of the so-called Arab Spring.

Both examples illustrate how amateur photos distributed via the social networks assume an important function for the civic protests and political events of today—especially in view of their ability to move people and prompt them to form communities spontaneously. The new image-based social media practices seem to be inseparably linked to the excitation amplitudes of our times. The users feel part of

D. H. Saur, *Hope 2008–2011*, 2011, details

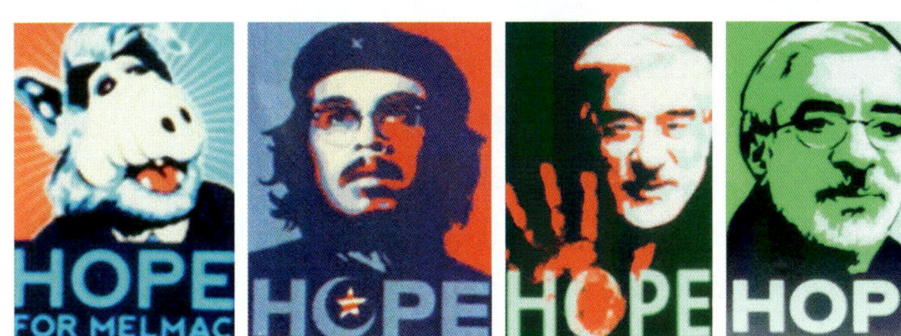

in eine seiner Collagen, als Meme [2] des berühmten Wahlkampf-Plakates „Hope" von Barack Obama.

In Lara Baladis interaktiver Timeline zur Ägyptischen Revolution, die in Düsseldorf erstmals ausgestellt wird, taucht ein weiteres prominentes Beispiel eines traurigen Falls auf: das von Khaled Said. Die Facebook-Gruppe „We are all Khaled Said" wurde gegründet, nachdem der Blogger Said im Juni 2010 von der Polizei in Alexandria zu Tode geprügelt worden war und seine Familie ein Bild der entstellten Leiche im Netz postete. Über die Facebook-Seite wurde zu Protesten aufgerufen und Said wurde nicht nur zur Identifikationsfigur während der folgenden Aufstände in Ägypten, sondern zu einer transnationalen Ikone des sogenannten Arabischen Frühlings.

Beide Beispiele demonstrieren, dass die über soziale Netzwerke in Umlauf gebrachten Amateuraufnahmen eine wichtige Funktion für die zivilgesellschaftlichen Proteste und politischen Ereignisse unserer Tage besitzen – insbesondere durch ihre Fähigkeit, Menschen zu bewegen und spontan Gemeinschaften zu mobilisieren. Die neuen Bildpraktiken in

D. H. Saur, *Hope 2008–2011*, 2011, Details

a (Web) community that is defined not only by common political aims but also through the intensity of one's own excitation, through passionate consent or outrage. Pointedly, one could say: images create affective communities. Especially shared images of victims like Neda Agha-Soltan and Khaled Said bear promise

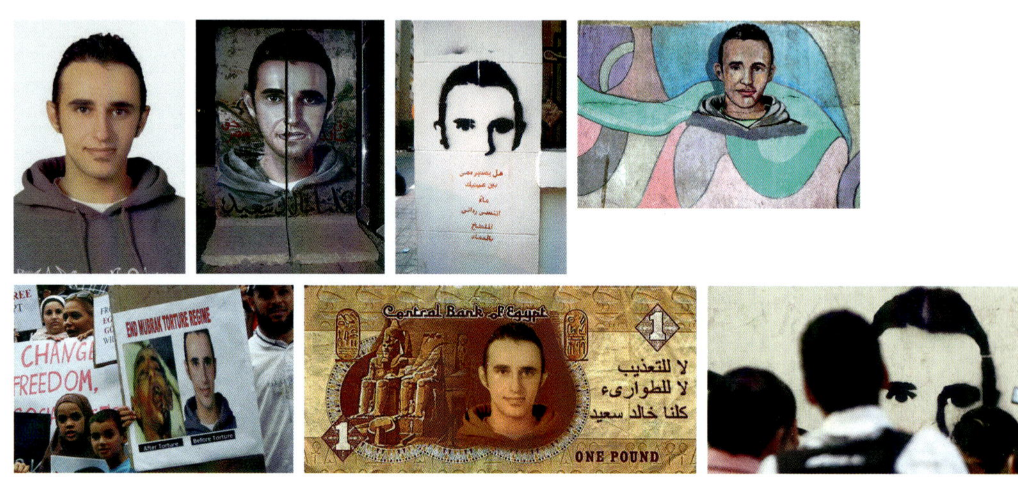

of directly attesting to an infringement on human rights. Even if the users are located far away from the incidents and hardly know the context, they may be strongly affected by the images and respond to them emotionally.

The images distributed in the networks are charged with a promise of verisimilitude, immediacy and objectivity. Lara Baladi has reflected on the pictures of the 2011 uprising on Tahrir Square in Cairo, which were disseminated throughout the world: "In the midst of the emergency, all theories about the subjectivity of photography suddenly became

Khaled Said, appropriations

den sozialen Medien scheinen untrennbar verknüpft mit den Erregungsamplituden unserer Zeit. Die User*innen fühlen sich als Teil einer (Netz-) Gemeinschaft, die nicht nur durch gemeinsame politische Ziele, sondern auch durch die Intensität der eigenen Bewegtheit, durch leidenschaftliche Zustimmung oder Empörung definiert ist. Zugespitzt könnte man sagen: Bilder erzeugen Affektgemeinschaften. Gerade im Netz geteilte Bilder von Opfern wie Neda Agha-Soltan und Khaled Said enthaltendas Ver-

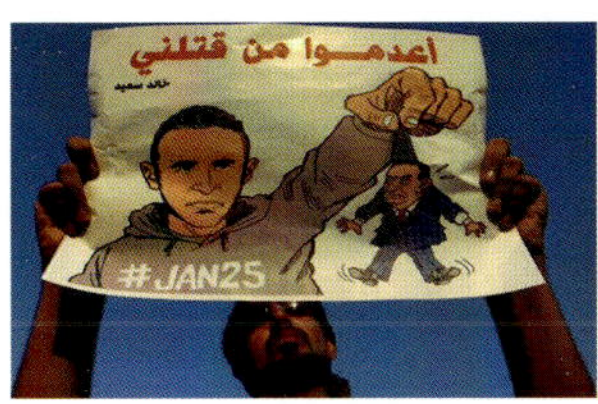

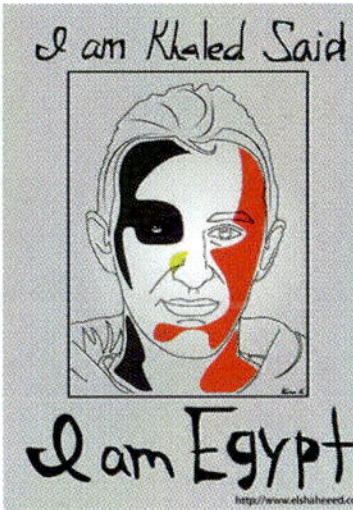

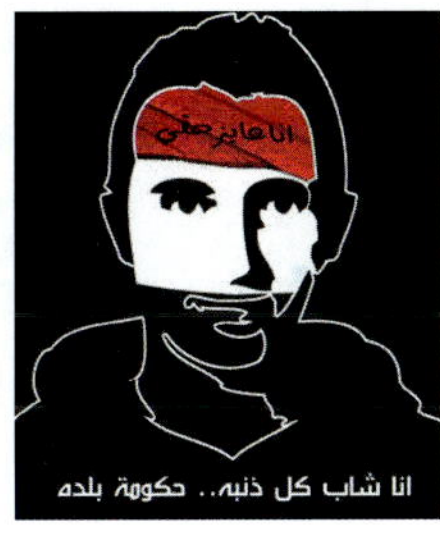
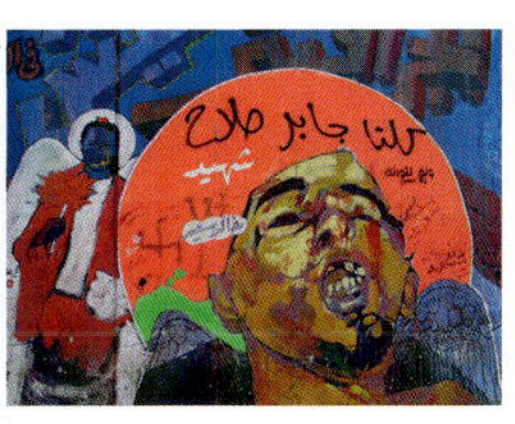
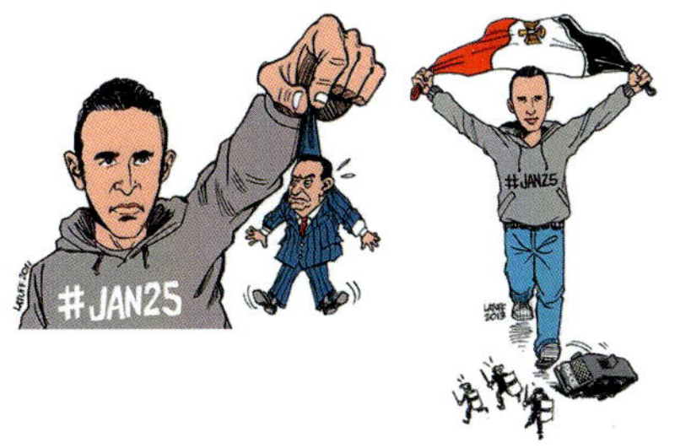

sprechen, die Verletzung von Menschenrechten direkt bezeugen zu können. Auch wenn die User*innen weit entfernt von den Ereignissen sind und den Kontext kaum kennen, werden sie von den Bildern mitunter stark bewegt und reagieren emotional auf sie.

Die in den sozialen Netzwerken kursierenden Bilder sind mit dem Versprechen nach Wirklichkeitsnähe, Unmittelbarkeit und Objektivität aufgeladen. Lara Baladi hat über die weltweit verbreiteten Bilder des Tahrir-Platzes in Kairo 2011 reflektiert: „Auf dem Höhepunkt der Ereignisse wurden alle

Khaled Said, Aneignungen

irrelevant. […] Photography became objective; photography showed the truth—yes, a 'truth' made up of as many truths as there were protesters in the square, but nonetheless one that had urgently to be revealed at this turning point in history."[3] Baladi describes a paradox of these photographs, which, despite all theory-based doubt in terms of their documentary value, bear testimony to given multiple realities and are capable of revealing truth.

Essential for an understanding of such photos as a vehicle for truth and guarantor of objectivity is precisely not a supposedly distanced position of their producers as unconcerned observers or reporters, but the photographers' involvement (also emotionally). They are present at the place of the incident as activists and actors; they feed immediate and subjective impressions into the Web in real-time and thus bear witness to the intensity of the moment and their own excitement. It is, therefore, more a matter of how people "behind the events" think and feel. This form of involvement, combined with the new image practices and the speed at which the pictures are made available, enhances the affectivity of the images. Images have become a kind of "currency" of the affective. Their character is not an exclusively documentary one; instead they have themselves advanced to become instruments of political participation or even actors in the political field.

Theorien zur Subjektivität der Fotografie plötzlich irrelevant. […] Die Fotografie wurde objektiv; Fotografie zeigte die Wahrheit – jawohl, eine ‚Wahrheit' geformt aus ebenso vielen Wahrheiten wie da Protestierende auf dem Platz waren, aber dennoch eine, die dringend an diesem Wendepunkt der Geschichte enthüllt werden musste."[3] Baladi beschreibt hier ein Paradox dieser Fotografien, die trotz allem theoretischen Zweifel an ihrem Dokumentationswert ein Zeugnis für multiple Realitäten ablegen und Wahrheiten ans Licht befördern können.

Entscheidend für ein Verständnis der Fotos als Vehikel der Wahrheit und als Garanten für Objektivität ist nun aber gerade nicht mehr eine vermeintlich distanzierte Position ihrer Produzent*innen als unbeteiligte Beobachter*innen oder Berichterstatter*innen, sondern das (auch emotionale) Involviertsein der Fotograf*innen. Als Aktivist*innen und Akteur*innen sind sie am Ort des Geschehens, sind etwa selbst Demonstrierende in Protesten, speisen unvermittelte, subjektive Eindrücke in Echtzeit ins Netz und bezeugen so die Intensität des Augenblicks sowie ihre eigene Aufregung. Es geht also eher darum, wie die Menschen „hinter den Ereignissen" denken und fühlen. Diese Form der Betroffenheit, in Kombination mit den neuen Bildpraktiken und der Schnelligkeit, mit der Bilder zur Verfügung stehen, steigert die Affektivität der Bilder. Bilder sind zu einer Art „Währung" des Affektiven geworden und haben nicht ausschließlich dokumentarischen Charakter, sondern avancieren selbst zu Instrumenten der politischen Teilhabe oder gar zu Akteuren im Feld des Politischen.

In the Web of Affects

In the common usage of German, the saying "Handeln im Affekt" (to act in affect) is well known. It denotes a vehement reaction in an intensely emotional state that usually occurs spontaneously and without prior reflection. "Acting in the heat of the moment" is tantamount to a sudden irrational act beyond the control of the actor. This does not imply, however, that affect is a purely pre-reflective stirring of emotion, present only in the body of the subject. Essential for the conceptual understanding of affect underlying this exhibition is, in fact, that an emotional act takes place not only "in" bodies, but above all "between" bodies or actors.

"Affect is the opposite of personal: it is social."[4] In the proverbial "acting in the heat of the moment" ("Handeln im Affekt") it is easily overlooked what actually is being reacted to and how the counterpart reacts in turn. So, it is a question of resonance, a relation between bodies. The point of departure for such a notion of "affect" is the potential of bodies to affect and to be affected[5], and such potential is always connected to the historically evolved and culturally charged order of feelings.[6] Another important aspect in this context is that affects are measured primarily in terms of their intensity, and less in their determinacy, directionality or judgement—here we come close to the idea of "acting in the heat of the moment" and its vehemence once more. Affects are rather difficult to grasp or pin down. They are ephemeral entities, occurring in fleeting moments, always experienced in relation to a given situation, and therefore tend to slip through the theoretical grids in which one attempts to

Im Netzwerk der Affekte

Im allgemeinen deutschen Sprachgebrauch kennt man vor allem die Redewendung des „Handelns im Affekt". Damit ist eine heftige Reaktion im Zustand intensiver Gemütsbewegung gemeint, die meist spontan, ohne vorherige Reflexion geschieht. Im Affekt zu handeln kommt einer Kurzschlussreaktion gleich, die sich der Kontrolle des Handelnden entzieht. Das bedeutet jedoch nicht, dass Affekt eine rein vorreflexive Gefühlsregung ist, die nur im Körper des Subjekts zu verorten wäre. Ausschlaggebend für das Affektverständnis, das dem Konzept dieser Ausstellung zugrunde liegt, ist vielmehr, dass ein Affektgeschehen nicht nur „in" Körpern, sondern vor allem „zwischen" Körpern oder Akteur*innen zu verorten ist.

„Affect is the opposite of personal: it is social."[4] Beim sprichwörtlichen „Handeln im Affekt" gerät leicht aus dem Blick, worauf eigentlich reagiert wird und wie das Gegenüber wiederum reagiert. Es geht also um eine Resonanz, um eine Relation zwischen Körpern. Ausgangspunkt für einen solchen Begriff des Affekts ist das Potenzial von Körpern zu affizieren und affiziert zu werden[5], wobei dieses Potenzial immer auf historisch gewachsene und kulturell geprägte Ordnungen des Fühlens bezogen ist.[6] Wichtig für das Verständnis ist auch, dass Affekte sich vor allem in ihrer Intensität bemessen, weniger in ihrer Bestimmtheit, Gerichtetheit oder Wertung – hier kommen wir der Idee des „Handelns im Affekt" und seiner Heftigkeit wieder nah. Affekte sind schwer zu fassende, ephemere Gebilde, weil sie rein situationsbezogen erfahrbar sind, in flüchtigen Momenten passieren und daher leicht

define them. The term emotion, on the other hand, describes categories with relatively clear contours: emotions like anger, hate, joy, love, etc. are culturally coded and sedimented concepts that express subjective feelings. Affects, as intensities and potentials, are integrated into, but not limited to such emotional experiences. They are extremely dynamic in nature and play a role in relationships developing between actors in the first place.[7] These actors are quite diverse—they do not necessarily have to be humans, but likewise can be images or other things. Even if it is hard to imagine how images can be affected, social media and the new image practices demonstrate precisely this: the numbers of likes and retweets linked to the images or the comments and emojis reveal how images are an integral part of social relationships, activities and networks that are influenced by affects and emotions.

With the term affect, which runs through the exhibition project as a leitmotif, a relationship between images, the events witnessed by them and the human actors shall thus be examined and characterized—a relationship which has intensified in the context of the social networks. The imperative *Affect Me* in the title of our show is to be understood as reciprocal: a call for affecting people and images, interrelated in a dynamic connection.

A Prologue to Social Media Images

Media icons have attracted the interest of contemporary artists all along. This is also examined from a historical perspective by Tobias Wendl in his catalogue contribution. Yet, with the attack on the

durch die theoretischen Raster hindurch gleiten, mit denen man sie zu definieren sucht. Der Begriff der Emotion bezeichnet demgegenüber Kategorien mit relativ klaren Konturen. Emotionen wie Wut, Hass, Freude, Liebe etc. sind kulturell kodierte und sedimentierte Konzepte, die subjektives Empfinden ausdrücken. Affekte sind – als Intensitäten und Potenziale – in dieses Gefühlsgeschehen eingebunden, aber nicht darauf zu reduzieren. Sie sind äußerst dynamisch und tragen dazu bei, dass zwischen Akteur*innen überhaupt eine Beziehung entsteht.[7] Diese Akteur*innen sind vielgestaltig – sie müssen nicht menschlich sein, sondern können ebenso Bilder oder andere Dinge sein. Auch wenn es schwer vorstellbar ist, wie Bilder affiziert werden können, so machen die sozialen Medien mit ihren neuen Bildpraktiken genau dies sichtbar: Die mit den Bildern verknüpften Zahlen ihrer Likes und Retweets oder die Kommentare und Emojis veranschaulichen, wie Bilder in soziale Beziehungen, Handlungen und Netzwerke eingebunden sind, die von Affekten und Emotionen geprägt sind.

Mit dem Begriff des Affekts, der sich als Leitmotiv durch das Ausstellungsprojekt zieht, soll also eine Beziehung zwischen Bildern, den durch sie bezeugten Ereignissen und den menschlichen Akteur*innen in den Blick genommen und charakterisiert werden, die sich im Kontext der sozialen Netzwerke intensiviert hat. Der Imperativ unseres Ausstellungstitels *Affect Me* ist wechselseitig zu verstehen: als Aufforderung zur Affizierung von Menschen wie von Bildern, die in einem dynamischen Verhältnis zueinander stehen.

World Trade Center in New York on September 11, 2001, a new form of pictorial iconicity developed. Here, for the first time countless amateur photos of the event were taken (usually by New York tourists equipped with standard cameras), to then appear on online-news pages and be labelled with notes like "amateur newsies," "instant reporters" or "personal journalists."[8] Such images circulating on the Web provided the source material for the *jpeg* series (2004–2007) by the photographer Thomas Ruff. His work *jpeg ny11* (2006) acts as an introduction to our exhibition. Even if the images that Ruff refers to were not yet "social media images" in the narrower sense[9] they nevertheless paved the way for a new form of image-based witnessing, in which affects play a crucial role.

9/11, as a global media event, has reversed the logics of witnessing: it is no longer the single, unique incident that takes the center stage, this specific moment in space and time that is witnessed on site. The process of witnessing itself becomes an event. And this media event of witnessing is no longer unique, but repeatable. Paul Frosh and Amit Pinchevski have referred to this as the "repeatable singularity of 9/11."[10] This perspective opens up a realm for countless reiterations, for appropriations and further developments—so characteristic for our current social media culture.

The remixing of images in social media networks coincides with a shift: from the "discrete icon" to the "generic icon," to use a distinction by David Perlmutter from the field of media studies. The U.S.-American communication and media scholar uses the term "discrete icon" to describe a unique icon. "Generic icon" refers to an iconic image typology which,

Ein Prolog zu den Social Media Bildern

Medienikonen ziehen von jeher das Interesse zeitgenössischer Künstler*innen auf sich. Dies legt auch Tobias Wendl in seinem Beitrag in historischer Perspektive dar. Doch mit dem Anschlag auf das World Trade Center in New York am 11. September 2001 wurde eine neue Form von bildlicher Ikonizität geprägt. Hier gab es erstmals massenhaft Aufnahmen der Ereignisse von Amateur*innen (meist standardmäßig mit Kameras ausgestattete Tourist*innen in New York), die auf Online-Nachrichtenseiten auftauchten und mit Stichworten wie „amateur newsies", „instant reporters" oder „personal journalists" beschrieben wurden.[8] Diese im Internet kursierenden Bilder sind das Ausgangsmaterial für die Serie *jpeg* (2004–2007) des Fotografen Thomas Ruff. Seine Arbeit *jpeg ny11* (2006) fungiert als Einstieg zu unserer Ausstellung, denn die Bilder, auf die sich Ruff bezieht, waren noch keine Social Media Bilder im engeren Sinne[9], bereiteten aber gleichwohl eine neue Form von Bildzeugenschaft vor, bei der Affekte eine wesentliche Rolle spielen.

9/11 hat als globales Medienevent die Logik von Zeugenschaft umgekehrt: Im Vordergrund steht nicht mehr das singuläre, einzigartige Ereignis, dieser spezifische Augenblick in Raum und Zeit, der vor Ort bezeugt wird. Zeugenschaft wird selbst zum Ereignis. Und dieses mediale Event des Bezeugens ist eben nicht mehr einmalig, sondern wiederholbar. Paul Frosh und Amit Pinchevski haben das die „wiederholbare Singularität von 9/11"[10] genannt. Dies eröffnet einen Raum für unzählige Wiederholungen, aber auch für Aneignungen und Weiterentwicklungen, wie sie so typisch für

the Internet and also reverts to uncensored imagery from social media. The work deals with this shift from "the" one representative icon to a mass of structurally similar photographs, which the artist employs to counter the "tendency to iconism"[13] with all its manipulative power.

While in 2008 Elke Grittmann and Ilona Ammann had noted that it was no longer art that created visual icons, but that instead "journalism was 'the' decisive institution,"[14] today this statement needs to be reconsidered: the visual icons of our times are long being created on the Web, in the scope of social media. It is precisely those images with a particularly strong capacity of affecting and of being affected that become iconic. They move and are moved, when they are shared in vast numbers and thus go "viral."

Transfer of Social Media Images into Art

Then again, it is the artists that allow us to cast a glance into the "woods on stage," as it were, to look behind the iconic imagery—revealing not only the complex information networks that these images are embedded in but also how they guide or influence the way of thinking, feeling and acting, even that of larger communities. One could attest a certain autonomous dynamic to these images circulating on the Web, considering their tendency to go viral, to spread infinitely and thus mingle with us, the people and actors. Their quality of stepping out of the line of purpose-oriented action scripts and provoking unpredictable responses at the same time reflects the fascinating and irritating clout the images

unsere aktuelle Social Media-Kultur geworden sind.

Mit dem Remix der Bilder in den sozialen Medien findet eine Verschiebung statt: vom „discrete icon“ zum „generic icon“, um eine medienwissenschaftliche Unterscheidung von David Perlmutter aufzugreifen. Der US-amerikanische Medien- und Kommunikationswissenschaftler bezeichnet mit „discrete icon“ eine einzigartige Ikone, und mit „generic icon“ einen ikonischen Bildtypus, der zwar auf das gleiche Motiv rekurriert, bei dem aber Akteur*innen, Orte oder Situationen wechseln können.[11] Hier handelt es sich also eher um ein Genre, das einen hohen Wiedererkennungswert besitzt. Stanley Cavell hat im Hinblick auf Filme und ihre Zugehörigkeit zu einem Genre geschrieben: „they *are what they are* in view of one another“[12]. Es geht also um die Relationen, die Bilder untereinander ausbilden. So behandelt auch Thomas Hirschhorns bildgewaltige Skulptur *Subjecter (Katastrophé)* von 2010, die den schier grenzenlosen Bildpool des Internets nutzt und dabei auch auf unzensiertes Material aus den sozialen Medien zurückgreift, diese Fokusverschiebung von „der“ einen, repräsentativen Ikone zur Masse von strukturell ähnlichen Fotografien, die er der „Tendenz zur Ikonisierung“[13] mit all ihrer manipulativen Wirkmacht entgegensetzt.

Haben Elke Grittmann und Ilona Ammann im Jahr 2008 noch festgehalten, dass es nicht mehr die Kunst sei, die Bildikonen hervorbringe, sondern „der Journalismus ‚die‘ entscheidende Institution“[14] sei, so muss man dies heute revidieren: Die Bildikonen unserer Tage werden längst im Netz, in den sozialen Medien geprägt. Ikonisch werden nämlich jene Bilder, die besonders stark affizieren und

possess, a capacity the artists address. This is the case even if their works deal critically with processes of iconisation, if they are sceptical towards the affective potential and attempt to diminish it. The show presents a full panorama of different artistic approaches to the evidently affective, often violent images found on social media that range from affirmation all the way to critical analysis and yet will often link both poles.

A whole string of artistic positions examines precisely these "generic icons," those pictorial ideas that reproduce themselves in social media. Irene Chabr and D. H. Saur analytically research the economies of images and affects. While Saur employs a cartographic method and by this means emphasises the systematics and complexity underlying Twitter and Facebook communication, Chabr focusses on a kind of reenactment of specific gestures, transforming originally political image formulas into a template for random content. Lynn Hershman Leeson takes reference to mobile phone videos of police violence, which in the USA have led to the current Black Lives Matter movement, but which have also globally reached a sorry climax, advancing to become a genre in itself.

Art dealing with image phenomena from social networks thus not only sensitises us for specific media practices that have developed along with the use of social media. Sometimes it even unveils tangible political realities, which otherwise presumably would not be brought to light. The complex film projects by Forensic Architecture serve to illustrate such realities: in their works, the group uses photos and videos from various sources in order to reveal and visualise responsibilities related to violence and destruction in

affiziert werden. Sie bewegen und werden bewegt, wenn sie massenhaft geteilt und dadurch ‚viral' werden.

Transfer der Social Media Bilder in die Kunst

Die Künstler*innen lassen uns gleichsam in den „Bühnenraum" hinter die ikonischen Bildmotive blicken und zeigen nicht nur die komplexen Informationsnetzwerke auf, in die diese Bilder eingebettet sind, sondern auch wie sie das Denken, Fühlen und Handeln, auch größerer Gemeinschaften, steuern. Man könnte diesen im Web zirkulierenden Bildern, gerade in ihrer Tendenz, sich viral zu verhalten und grenzenlos zu verbreiten, eine gewisse autonome Dynamik attestieren, mit der sie sich unter uns Handelnde mischen. In ihrer Eigenschaft, aus zweckgebundenen Handlungsskripten auszuscheren und unkalkulierbare Resonanzen hervorzurufen, spiegelt sich die zugleich faszinierende und verstörende Schlagkraft der Bilder, zu der sich die Künstler*innen positionieren. Dies ist auch dann der Fall, wenn sich ihre Arbeiten kritisch mit Ikonisierungsprozessen auseinandersetzen, dem Affizierungspotenzial skeptisch gegenüberstehen und versuchen, es zurückzunehmen. Die Ausstellung präsentiert ein ganzes Panorama unterschiedlicher künstlerischer Strategien im Umgang mit den affizierenden, oftmals gewaltvollen Social Media Bildern, die sich in einem Spektrum von Affirmation bis hin zu kritischer Analyse bewegen und meist beide Pole verbinden.

Eine ganze Reihe der künstlerischen Positionen untersuchen eben jene „generischen Ikonen", die

the scope of geopolitical conflicts.

Another spectrum being differentiated in the works of Forensic Architecture is that between objectivation and fictionalisation. This equally goes to the core of the issues that we are exploring in this exhibition. In which way do the new pictorial practices applied in social media alter the status of the photographic or video image as such? Is the image a guarantor for originality and truth? Can it be objective or only radically subjective? Is it, above all, a nodal point in an affective relationality and dynamic that overwhelms us?

These queries are manifested very distinctly in Rabih Mroué's video installation *The Pixelated Revolution* (2012), in which Mroué refers to a shocking genre of videos: images of insurgents filming their own death—the moment when they are hit by the bullets of snipers. Simultaneously, Mroué interweaves these disturbing mobile phone pictures with sequences from feature films and thus stages a reenactment of the (alleged) incident. In other takes, the artist himself appears in front of the camera and poses precisely those image-theoretical questions mentioned above, examining the validity and objectivity of images in view of the visual source material used.

For Lara Baladi, these questions also play a role. Employing an approach similar to that of Mroué, in her video installation *Alone, Together, … In Media Res* (2012), she deliberately blends material of a more documentary nature—like mobile phone videos from the Egyptian revolution and other videos circulating on YouTube—with sequences from motion pictures and animation films. Lara Baladi exposes what we call reality as a fragile, polycentric construction. While Baladi's work clearly addresses real politi-

sich fortpflanzenden Bildideen in den sozialen Medien. Irene Chabr und D.H. Saur gehen den Bild- und Affektökonomien analytisch auf den Grund. Während Saur kartografisch vorgeht und damit zugleich die Systematik wie auch die Unübersichtlichkeit der Twitter- und Facebook-Kommunikation hervorhebt, geht es Chabr um das Reenactment von spezifischen Gesten, mit denen ursprünglich politische Bildformeln zu einem Template für beliebige Inhalte werden. Lynn Hershman Leeson bezieht sich auf Handyvideos von Polizeigewalt, die in den USA zu der aktuellen Black Lives Matter-Bewegung geführt haben, die aber nicht nur dort, sondern rund um den Globus eine traurige Konjunktur haben und zu einem eigenen Genre avanciert sind.

Die Kunst, die sich auf Bildphänomene aus dem Social Web bezieht, sensibilisiert uns also nicht nur für spezifische mediale Praktiken, wie sie mit dem Gebrauch der sozialen Medien einhergehen. Mitunter deckt sie auch handfeste politische Realitäten auf, die ohne ihr Zutun kaum an die Öffentlichkeit kommen würden. Dies veranschaulichen die komplexen filmischen Projekte der Gruppe Forensic Architecture. In ihren Arbeiten nutzt die Gruppe Fotos und Videos aus unterschiedlichen Quellen, um in geopolitischen Konflikten die Verantwortlichkeiten für Gewalt und Zerstörung kenntlich zu machen.

Ein weiteres Spektrum, das die Arbeiten von Forensic Architecture ausdifferenzieren, ist das zwischen Objektivierung und Fiktionalisierung. Dies trifft ebenfalls den Kern der Fragestellungen, die uns in der Ausstellung umtreiben: Wie verändern die neuen Bildpraktiken in den sozialen Medien den Status des fotografischen oder videografischen Bildes schlechthin? Ist es Garant für Echtheit und Wahrhaftigkeit?

cal events in Egypt, Randa Maroufi uses exclusively fictional narratives to investigate the societal resonances to pictorial practices emerging in social media.

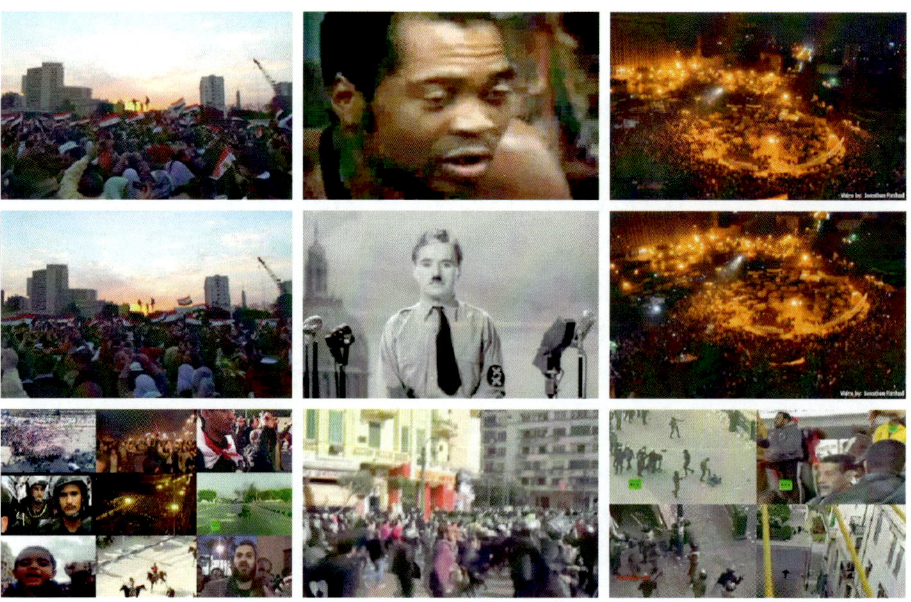

Lara Baladi, *Alone, Together, … In Media Res,* 2012, video stills

Kann es noch objektiv sein oder nur noch radikal subjektiv? Ist es vor allem ein Knotenpunkt einer affektiven Relationalität und Dynamik, die uns überwältigt?

Besonders eindringlich manifestieren sich diese Fragestellungen in Rabih Mroués Videoinstallation *The Pixelated Revolution* (2012). Mroué bezieht sich darin auf ein schockierendes Videogenre: Aufnahmen von Aufständischen, die ihren eigenen Tod filmen – jenen Moment, in dem sie selbst von den Kugeln der Scharfschützen getroffen werden. Gleichzeitig verwebt Mroué diese bestürzenden Handybilder mit Spielfilmsequenzen und inszeniert ein Reenactment des (vermeintlichen) Geschehens. In anderen Einstellungen tritt der Künstler persönlich vor die Kamera und richtet eben jene, weiter oben formulierten bildtheoretischen Fragen nach der Beweiskraft und dem objektiven Gehalt von Bildern an das visuelle Ausgangsmaterial.

Diese Fragestellungen spielen auch für Lara Baladi eine Rolle. Ähnlich wie Mroué verwebt sie in ihrer Videoinstallation *Alone, Together, … In Media Res*

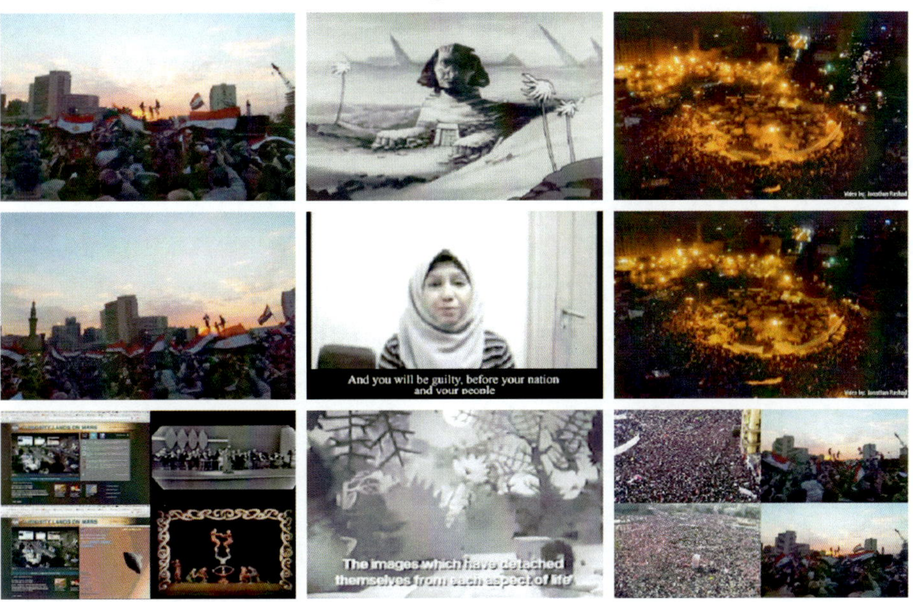

Lara Baladi, *Alone, Together, … In Media Res*, 2012, Videostills

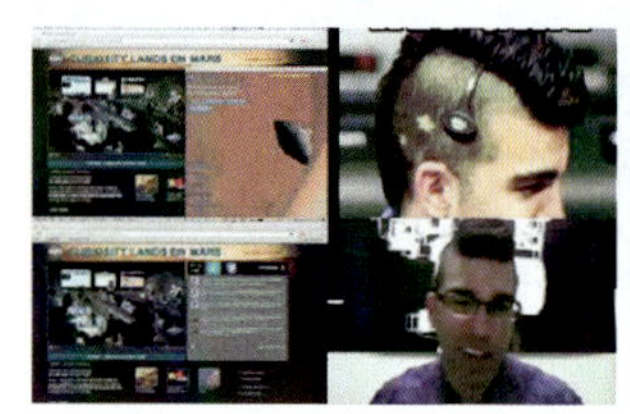

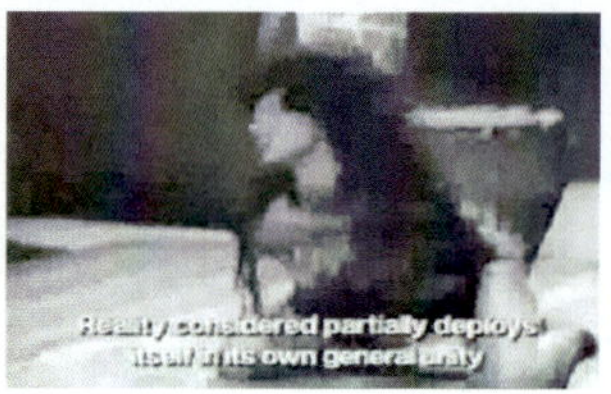

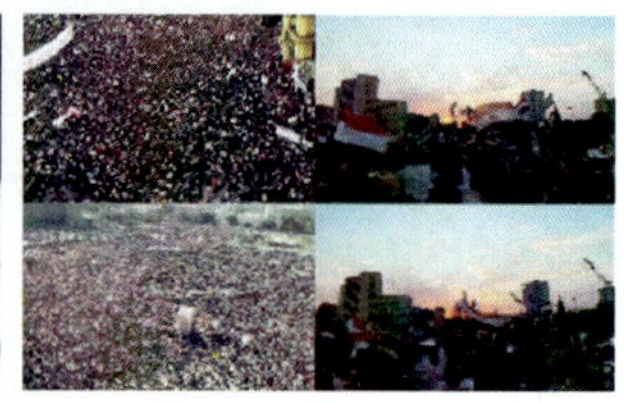

Her film *Le Park* (2015) is concerned with the culture of self-representation among Moroccan youth that finds expression in the social networks. The source material—selfies of adolescents posing in expensive brand-name clothes or reenacting scenes of violence—is no longer visible. It is reframed, dissected, and accompanied by radio reports commenting on the youth's representation of violence in social media. Her focus is on the perception of visual culture and its real impacts, which include the criminalisation of the youth in the public or cases of arrest.

Moving Images and Images that Move

Randa Maroufi's works based on the visual brilliance of classical feature films are rather the exception in this show. Most of the other artists' works feature an intentionally "low key" aesthetics. This formal quality results from the technical characteristics of the digital images being used for a large part of the artworks. Especially the pixel has emerged as an aesthetically formative aspect, which, however, plays an equally vital role with regard to content, and can be found to run like a thread throughout the exhibition. We encounter it not only on the visual level, it is also directly thematised in the works, for example in the *jpeg* series of Thomas Ruff or in Rabih Mroués *The Pixelated Revolution*.

"Pixel" is a term from the field of digital imaging,

Lara Baladi, *Alone, Together, … In Media Res,* 2012, video stills

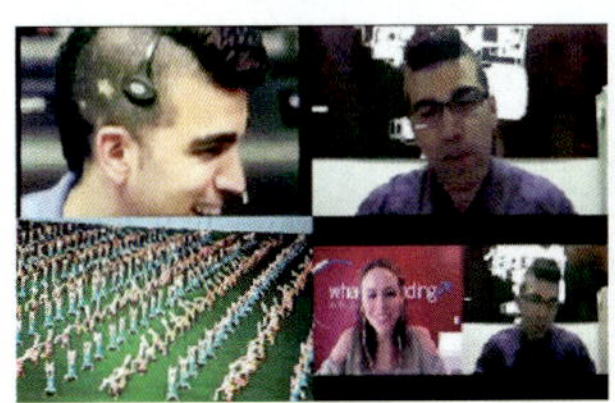
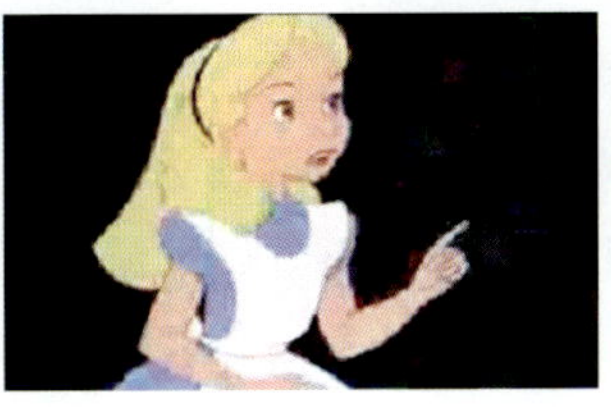
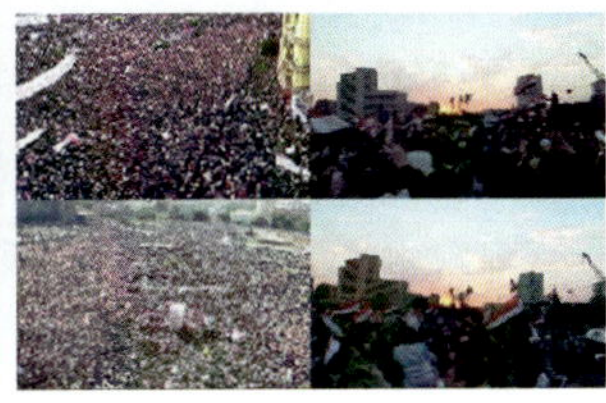

(2012) eher dokumentarisch zu bewertendes Bildmaterial – etwa Handyvideos aus der Ägyptischen Revolution und anderen auf YouTube kursierenden Videos – ganz bewusst mit Sequenzen aus Spiel- und Zeichentrickfilmen. Das, was wir Wirklichkeit nennen, entlarvt Lara Baladi in ihren Arbeiten als eine labile, polyzentrische Konstruktion. Während Baladis Arbeit deutlich auf die realen politischen Ereignisse in Ägypten zielt, nutzt Randa Maroufi ausschließlich fiktionale Narrative, um den gesellschaftlichen Resonanzen der Bildpraktiken in den sozialen Medien nachzuspüren. Ihr Film *Le Park* (2015) bezieht sich auf die Kultur der Selbstdarstellung unter marokkanischen Jugendlichen, die ihren Ausdruck in den sozialen Medien findet. Das Ausgangsmaterial – etwa Selfies der Jugendlichen in teuren Markenkleidern oder beim Nachstellen von Gewaltszenen – tritt hier nicht mehr sichtbar in den Vordergrund. Es wird re-inszeniert, dabei auch seziert, und von Radiobeiträgen untermalt, die die Gewaltdarstellung von Jugendlichen in den sozialen Medien kommentieren. Ihr Schwerpunkt liegt damit auf der Rezeption der Bildkultur und ihren realen Auswirkungen, zu denen etwa die Kriminalisierung der Jugendlichen in der Öffentlichkeit oder Festnahmen zählen.

Lara Baladi, *Alone, Together, … In Media Res*, 2012, Videostills

which denotes a physical point or single picture element of a raster image, to which a colour value is assigned, rendering the image machine-readable. But pixelation also designates a formal characteristic, an aesthetic component that goes hand in hand with blurring and "image artefacts." A pixel image always remains a mere sample of the original, an approximation to reality, because the information density of a pixel is limited on the practical level.

The photos and videos from mobile phone cameras, sometimes taken in life-threatening situations, are usually blurred, pixelated, dilapidated and distorted. It is this impression of testifying authenticity that has contributed to their massive reproduction in the media. One could argue that this is paradoxical, but it is also consistent, in the sense that the pictures reflect both the conditions under which they were created and the uncertainty and doubts regarding their substance. Hito Steyerl described this phenomenon as the "Unschärferelation"[15] (uncertainty principle) of documentary photography, demonstrating little more than its own excitation. Not only the images from the social networks mediate this sense of excitement of the digital era along with the implosion of meaning—to revisit a phrase from the essay by Ernst van Alphen, examining the affective relationships of humans and images in the context of art but also in connection with other contemporary image phenomena.

Especially in the heterogeneous coexistence of visual material from various sources portrayed by the artists—a combination of documentary narratives with strategies of fictionalisation, pixelated snapshots of real life with artificially generated pictorial worlds—a significant trend in contemporary culture

Bewegte und bewegende Bilder

Während Randa Maroufis Arbeiten sich der Bildbrillanz klassischer Spielfilme bedienen, besitzen die meisten Werke der anderen Künstler*innen eine bewusst schlichte low key-Ästhetik. Diese formale Eigenschaft ist auf die technischen Voraussetzungen der den künstlerischen Arbeiten oftmals zugrunde liegenden Internetbilder zurückzuführen. Insbesondere das Pixel kristallisiert sich als gleichzeitig formgebender aber auch inhaltlich relevanter Aspekt heraus, der sich wie ein roter Faden durch die Ausstellung zieht. Nicht nur visuell tritt es uns in den Arbeiten gegenüber, es wird auch direkt thematisiert, etwa in der *jpeg*-Serie von Thomas Ruff oder in Rabih Mroués *The Pixelated Revolution*.

Pixel ist ein Begriff aus der digitalen Bildtechnik, der einen Bildpunkt oder ein einzelnes Bildelement bezeichnet, dem in einer Rastergrafik ein Farbwert zugeordnet ist, um das Bild maschinell lesbar zu machen. Pixelierung bezeichnet jedoch auch ein formales Charakteristikum, eine ästhetische Komponente, die mit Unschärfe und „Bildfehlern" einhergeht. Ein Pixelbild ist immer nur eine Annäherung an die Wirklichkeit, weil die Informationsdichte eines Pixels praktisch begrenzt ist.

Die Bilder und Videos der Handykameras, die in teils lebensbedrohlichen Situationen entstehen, sind meist unscharf, verpixelt und verwackelt und werden gerade deshalb als Zeugnis von Authentizität medial reproduziert. Man könnte sagen, das ist paradox, es ist aber auch konsequent, denn in der Form der Bilder schlagen sich ihre Entstehungsbedingungen ebenso nieder, wie die Ungewissheit und

becomes apparent. Images seem to create among themselves a kind of echo chamber, a sphere where they can mutually reinforce each other. If one challenges these visual works with the classical hermeneutical questions, such as their relation to outer reality or their mimetic function, one easily reaches a state of deadlock. It is not so much the question here of a presumed reality that images represent. It is about their affective potential.[16] Rather than "showing" intense moments, what counts is the "production" of intensity. These images not only display different notions of movement—in the triple sense of: time-based changes, emotional excitement of the involved actors and political movements—they move you.

1 Video of the press conference on 23.6.2009: https://www.youtube.com/watch?v=7ReD–ieDERY (last access 6.9.2017).
2 In the context of social media a meme is a viral phenomenon, often a humourously altered image supplemented with text that spreads quickly around the Web in various iterations. See Limor Shifman, *Memes in Digital Culture*, Cambridge 2014.
3 Lara Baladi, *When Seeing Is Belonging: The Photography of Tahrir*, in: *Cairo. Open City. New Testimonies from an Ongoing Revolution*, exhib. cat., Leipzig 2013, pp. 68–73, here p. 70.
4 Ernst van Alphen, *Explosions of Information, Implosions of Meaning, and the Release of Affects*, in: Patricia Speyer, Mary Margaret Steedly (eds.), *Images That Move*, Santa Fe 2013, pp. 219–236, here p. 223.
5 This understanding of the affective potential of bodies can be culture-historically traced back at least to Spinoza in the 17th century and it also reappears in the writings of Gilles Deleuze.
6 Raymond Williams called this "structures of feeling". Cf. Raymond Williams, *Marxism and Literature*, London, New York 1977, pp. 128–135.
7 See Jan Slaby, *Relational Affect*, Working Paper SFB 1171 Affective Societies 02/16, 2016, Static URL: http://edocs.fu-berlin.de/docs/receive/FUDOCS_series_000000000562 and *Affective Societies – A Glossary. Register of Central Working Concepts*, Working Paper SFB 1171 Affective

der Zweifel am Inhalt. Hito Steyerl nennt dieses Phänomen die „Unschärferelation“[15] dokumentarischer Fotografie, die kaum etwas zeige außer ihrer eigenen Aufregung. Nicht nur die Bilder aus den sozialen Netzwerken transportieren diese Erregtheit des digitalen Zeitalters und die Implosion von Bedeutung – um eine Formulierung aus dem Essay von Ernst van Alphen aufzugreifen, der den affektiven Relationen von Menschen und Bildern im Kontext der Kunst, aber auch hinsichtlich anderer zeitgenössischer Bildphänomene nachgeht. Gerade in dem heterogenen Nebeneinander von visuellem Material aus unterschiedlichen Quellen durch die Künstler*innen – der Verbindung dokumentarischer Narrative mit Strategien der Fiktionalisierung, pixeligen Momentaufnahmen aus dem Leben mit künstlich generierten Bildwelten – manifestiert sich eine wesentliche Tendenz der zeitgenössischen visuellen Kultur: dass Bilder nämlich untereinander eine Art Echokammer erzeugen und sich darin gegenseitig verstärken. Richtet man an diese Bildwerke klassisch hermeneutische Fragestellungen, etwa hinsichtlich ihres Bezugs zur äußeren Wirklichkeit und ihrer mimetischen Funktion, so gerät man leicht in eine Sackgasse. Es geht weniger um die Frage nach einer vermeintlichen Realität, welche die Bilder repräsentieren, sondern um deren Affizierungspotenzial.[16] Wichtiger als das „Zeigen“ intensiver Momente wird das „Produzieren“ von Intensität. Die Bilder „zeigen“ nicht nur Bewegungen – im dreifachen Sinne von zeitbasierten Veränderungen, Gemütserregungen der Akteur*innen und politischen Bewegungen – sie bewegen.

1 Video der Pressekonferenz vom 23.06.2009: https://www.youtube.com/watch?v=7ReD-ieDERY (letzter Zugriff 06.09.2017).

Societies 01/16, 2016, Static URL: http://edocs.fu-berlin.de/docs/receive/FUDOCS_series_000000000562.

8 Stuart Allan, *Citizen Witnessing. Revisioning Journalism in Times of Crisis. Key Concepts in Journalism*, Cambridge, Malden, MA 2013, p. VI.

9 The rapid rise of Facebook & Co. began only in the decade that followed.

10 Paul Frosh, Amit Pinchevski, *Introduction. Why Media Witnessing? Why Now?*, in: idem (eds.), *Media Witnessing: Testimony in the Age of Mass Communication*, Basingstoke et. al. 2009, pp. 1–19, here p. 9.

11 David Perlmutter, *Hypericons. Famous News Images in the Internet-Digital-Satellite Age*, in: Paul Messaris, Lee Humphreys (eds.), *Digital Media. Transformations in Human Communication*, New York et al. 2006, pp. 51–64, here p. 54.

12 Stanley Cavell, *Pursuits of Happiness. The Hollywood Comedy of Remarriage*, Cambridge 1997, p. 29.

13 Thomas Hirschhorn, *Warum ist es wichtig – heute – Bilder zerstörter Menschenkörper zu zeigen und anzuschauen?*, 2012, in: *What's next?*, No. 065, http://whtsnxt.net/065 (last access 28.8.2017).

14 Elke Grittmann, Ilona Ammann, *Ikonen der Kriegs- und Krisenfotografie*, in: idem and Irene Neverla (eds.), *Global, lokal, digital – Fotojournalismus heute*, Cologne 2008, pp. 296–325, here p. 298.

15 Hito Steyerl, *Die dokumentarische Unschärferelation. Was ist Dokumentarismus?*, in: idem, *Die Farbe der Wahrheit. Dokumentarismen im Kunstfeld*, Wien 2008, pp. 7–16.

16 Mieke Bal suggests that affect has replaced the "primacy of representation". Mieke Bal, *Affekt als kulturelle Kraft*, in: Antje Krause-Wahl, Heike Oehlschlägel, Serjoscha Wiemer (eds.), *Affekte. Analysen ästhetisch-medialer Prozesse*, Bielefeld 2006, pp. 7–19, here p. 7.

2 Als Meme bezeichnet man im Kontext der sozialen Medien ein virales Phänomen, häufig ein humoristisch verändertes, mit Text versehenes Bild, das in der Folge immer wieder aufgegriffen wird. Siehe auch Limor Shifman, *Memes in Digital Culture*, Cambridge 2014.

3 Lara Baladi, *Wenn sehen heißt dazuzugehören: Die Bilder vom Tahrir-Platz*, in: *Kairo – Offene Stadt. Neue Bilder einer andauernden Revolution*, Ausst.-Kat., Leipzig 2013, S. 74–80, hier S. 77.

4 Ernst van Alphen, *Explosions of Information, Implosions of Meaning, and the Release of Affects*, in: Patricia Speyer, Mary Margaret Steedly (Hg.), *Images That Move*, Santa Fe 2013, S. 219–236, hier S. 223.

5 Dieses Verständnis des Affizierungspotenzials von Körpern lässt sich kulturgeschichtlich mindestens bis zu Spinoza im 17. Jahrhundert zurückverfolgen und taucht etwa auch in den Schriften Gilles Deleuzes auf.

6 Raymond Williams hat das „structures of feeling" genannt. Raymond Williams, *Marxism and Literature*, London, New York 1977, S. 128–135.

7 Siehe auch Jan Slaby, *Relational Affect*, Working Paper SFB 1171 Affective Societies 02/16, 2016, Static URL: http://edocs.fu-berlin.de/docs/receive/FUDOCS_series_000000000562 und *Affective Societies – A Glossary. Register of Central Working Concepts*, Working Paper SFB 1171 Affective Societies 01/16, 2016, Static URL: http://edocs.fu-berlin.de/docs/receive/FUDOCS_series_000000000562.

8 Stuart Allan, *Citizen Witnessing. Revisioning Journalism in Times of Crisis. Key Concepts in Journalism*, Cambridge, Malden, MA 2013, S. vi.

9 Der rasante Aufstieg von Facebook & Co. begann erst in der folgenden Dekade.

10 Im Original: „the repeatable singularity of 9/11", Paul Frosh, Amit Pinchevski, *Introduction. Why Media Witnessing? Why Now?*, in: dies. (Hg.), *Media Witnessing: Testimony in the Age of Mass Communication*, Basingstoke u.a. 2009, S. 1–19, hier S. 9.

11 David Perlmutter, *Hypericons. Famous News Images in the Internet-Digital-Satellite Age*, in: Paul Messaris, Lee Humphreys (Hg.): *Digital Media. Transformations in Human Communication*, New York u.a. 2006, S. 51–64, hier S. 54.

12 Stanley Cavell, *Pursuits of Happiness. The Hollywood Comedy of Remarriage*, Cambridge 1997, S. 29.

13 Thomas Hirschhorn, *Warum ist es wichtig – heute – Bilder zerstörter Menschenkörper zu zeigen und anzuschauen?*, 2012, in: *What's next?*, Nr. 065, http://whtsnxt.net/065 (letzter Zugriff 28.08.2017).

14 Elke Grittmann, Ilona Ammann, *Ikonen der Kriegs- und Krisenfotografie*, in: dies. und Irene Neverla (Hg.), *Global, lokal, digital – Fotojournalismus heute*, Köln 2008, S. 296–325, hier S. 298.

15 Hito Steyerl, *Die dokumentarische Unschärferelation. Was ist Dokumentarismus?*, in: dies., *Die Farbe der Wahrheit. Dokumentarismen im Kunstfeld*, Wien 2008, S. 7–16.

16 Mieke Bal legt nahe, dass der Affekt das „Primat der Repräsentation" abgelöst hat. Mieke Bal, *Affekt als kulturelle Kraft*, in: Antje Krause-Wahl, Heike Oehlschlägel, Serjoscha Wiemer (Hg.), *Affekte, Analysen ästhetisch-medialer Prozesse*, Bielefeld, 2006, S. 7–19, hier S. 7.

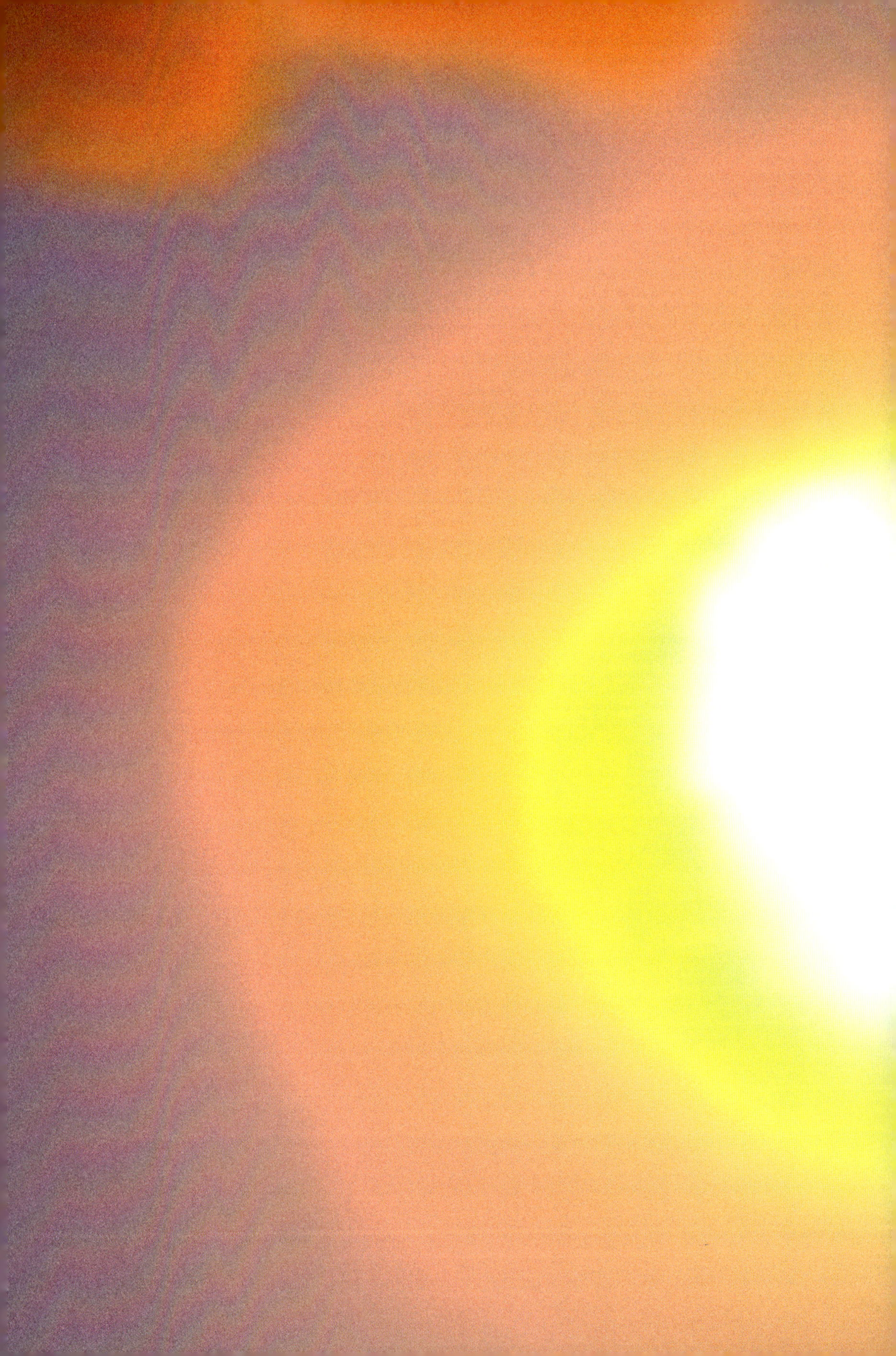

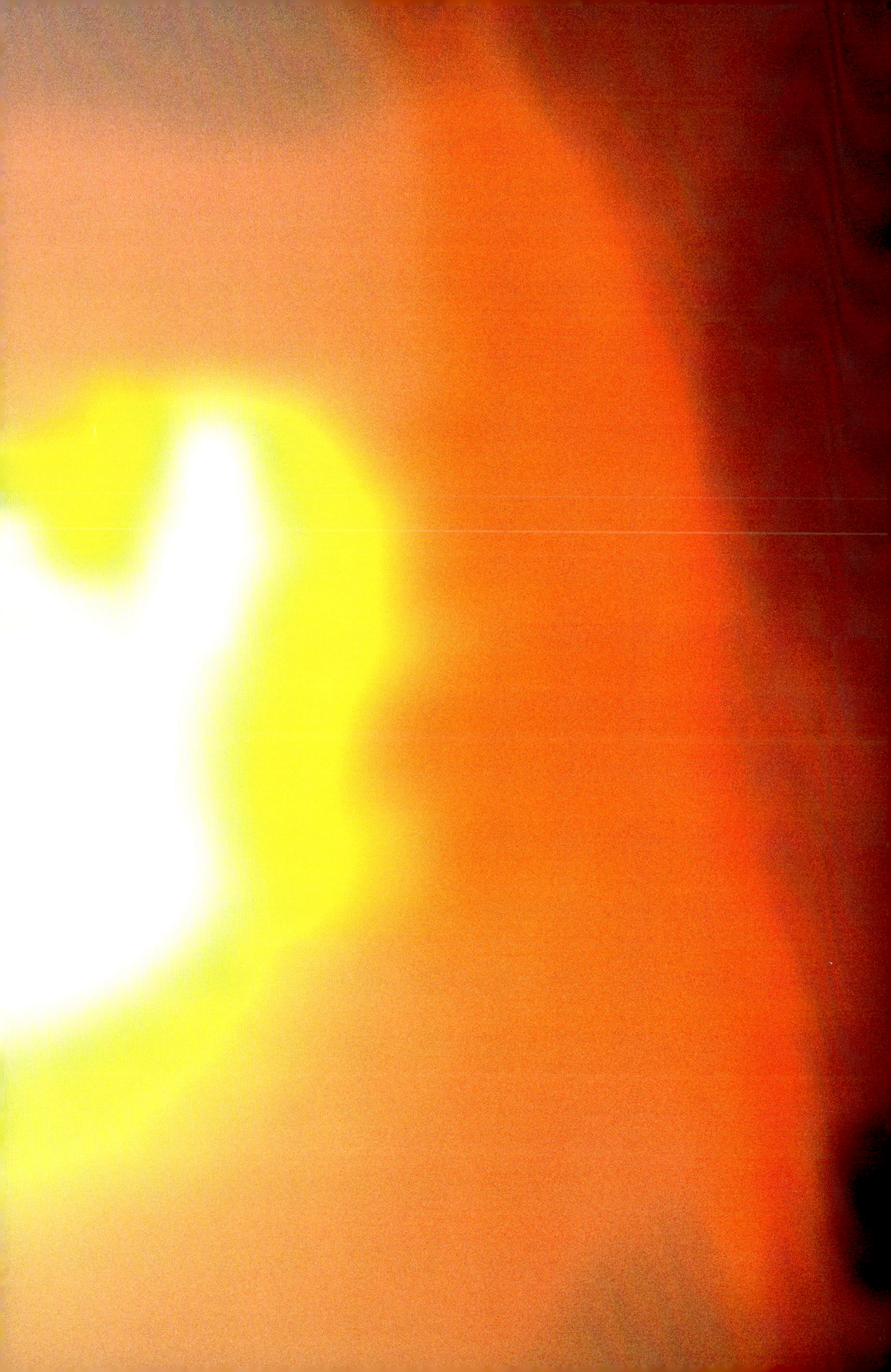

Tobias Wendl

The Return of Images: Appropriations of Iconic Photographs in Selected Artists' Projects from 1945 to 2005[1]

Tobias Wendl

Die Wiederkehr der Bilder: Zur Aneignung fotografischer Bildikonen in ausgewählten Künstlerprojekten zwischen 1945 und 2005[1]

Images provide ample opportunities for binding affects and exploiting them for political ends, to declare them as representations, to charge them (to "like" and "share"), to inflate and iconise them through artistic remediations. Or—in a complementary iconoclastic mode—to vicariously beat them, over-paint them, deface them, protect them from putative insults or take them down from the Internet. The expansion of social media in the first decade of the 21st century has led to a new increase in the affective dynamic of images, principally because the speed with which one can respond to images with more images has drastically improved. Structurally seen, however, the return of images and their appropriation by artists—as I hope to show in selected examples from the second half of the 20th century in this text—is not a novelty per se.

Let us look first at a recent case in point: Alan Kurdi, the three-year-old boy, drowned off the coast of Bodrum on September 2, 2015. A Turkish barman found his lifeless body and laid it on the beach before journalist, Nilüfer Demir, took a series of photos. In the first week, her pictures were "shared" almost three million times on Twitter alone.[2]

Appropriations and remediations of these images followed extremely quickly, for example, in the context of demonstrations against international political failure regarding the so-called refugee crisis. The collectivising slogan, "Notre enfant—our child," was typical. Sand sculptures and graffiti followed. The Finnish sculptor, Pekka Jylhä, reproduced Alan Kurdi's body in plastic and encased it in a vitrine reminiscent of a glass coffin. His work constituted a memorialisation and simultaneously a subtle reflection on previous memorialisations.[3]

The reenactments were also noteworthy. People in similar clothing lay stock-still for twenty minutes with their faces in the sand in the victim pose that had meanwhile become iconic and later posted their photos on social media.[4] The best-known, but—because of its commodification—also heavily criticised reenactment was that by Ai Weiwei in January 2016 on the island of Lesbos, where the artist collected life jackets for his installation projects. It resulted in an aestheticised photo of the artist laying on his stomach on the shingle beach. One has to give Ai Weiwei credit for wanting to draw attention to the ongoing refugee crisis in the winter of 2016, but we cannot dismiss his voracity for the affective potential of the Kurdi photo, which he wanted to instil into his installation. Ai Weiwei's predilection for capitalizing on "affect saturated materials" and his narcissistic self-marketing did not escape one cartoonist!

Such artistic remediations and reenactments of photographic icons have become extremely popular in our daily culture shaped by social media,[5] and artists are quickly falling under the suspicion of wanting to appropriate their affective dynamic for their own work. The impact of artistic appropriations, however, remains at a lower level and subordinate in comparison to the long-established media and culture industries, such as TV and the Internet. This applies particularly to those iconic images—that according to Gerhard Paul—intervene formatively in the historical process itself and significantly shape the memory of the event they reproduce.[6]

Bilder liefern vielfältige Möglichkeiten, Affekte zu binden und mit ihnen Politik zu machen, sie zu Stellvertretern zu erklären, sie aufzuladen (zu „liken" und zu „teilen"), sie durch künstlerische Remediationen und Reenactments zu überhöhen und zu ikonisieren. Oder aber – im komplementären ikonoklastischen Modus – sie stellvertretend zu schlagen, sie zu übermalen, zu schänden, sie gegen vermeintliche Beleidigungen zu schützen oder sie aus dem Netz zu löschen. Durch die Verbreitung der Social Media in der ersten Dekade des 21. Jahrhunderts hat sich die Affektdynamik von Bildern nochmals gesteigert – vor allem, weil die Geschwindigkeit, in der mit Bildern auf Bilder geantwortet wird, sich drastisch erhöht hat. Doch ist die Wiederkehr der Bilder bzw. ihre Aneignung durch Künstler*innen – wie ich in meinem Beitrag an ausgewählten Beispielen aus der zweiten Hälfte des 20. Jahrhunderts zeigen möchte – strukturell gesehen kein wirkliches Novum.

Betrachten wir dazu zunächst ein rezentes Fallbeispiel: Alan Kurdi, den am 2. September 2015 vor der Küste bei Bodrum ertrunkenen dreijährigen Jungen. Ein türkischer Barmann hatte seinen leblosen Körper geborgen und am Strand abgelegt, bevor die Journalistin Nilüfer Demir eine Reihe von Fotos machte. Allein auf Twitter wurden ihre Bilder in der ersten Woche knapp drei Millionen Mal „geteilt".[2]

Aufgriffe und Remediationen dieser Bilder folgten blitzschnell – etwa im Rahmen von Demonstrationen gegen das internationale Politikversagen angesichts der sogenannten Flüchtlingskrise. Typisch war die Kollektivierungsformel: „Notre enfant – our child". Sandskulpturen und Graffitis folgten. Der finnische Bildhauer Pekka Jylhä hat den Körper Alan Kurdis aus Kunststoff nachgebildet und mit einem an einen gläsernen Sarg erinnernden Glassturz versehen. Seine Arbeit betreibt eine Memorialisierung, leistet aber zugleich eine subtile Reflexion vorgängiger Memorialisierungen.[3]

Bemerkenswert waren auch die Reenactments. Personen, die in ähnlicher Kleidung in Gruppen mit dem Gesicht im Sand über zwanzig Minuten lang regungslos die inzwischen ikonische Opfer-Pose einnahmen und später Fotos über die Social Media posteten.[4] Am bekanntesten – wegen seiner kommerziellen Vermarktung aber auch heftig kritisiert – wurde das Reenactment von Ai Weiwei im Januar 2016 auf der Insel Lesbos, wo der Künstler Schwimmwesten für seine Installationsprojekte einsammelte. Es resultierte in einem ästhetisierten Schwarzweiß-Foto des bäuchlings auf dem Kieselstrand liegenden Künstlers. Man muss Ai Weiwei zugutehalten, dass er damit die Aufmerksamkeit auf die auch im Winter 2016 noch anhaltende Geflüchtetenkrise lenken wollte. Doch ist der Vorwurf, er habe durch dieses Reenactment vom Affektpotenzial des Kurdi-Fotos profitieren und dieses auf seine Installationen übertragen wollen, nicht ganz von der Hand zu weisen. Einem Cartoonisten sind Ai Weiweis Vorliebe für die Aneignung „affekthaltiger Materialien" und seine narzisstische Selbstvermarktung nicht entgangen!

Solche künstlerischen Remediationen und Reenactments fotografischer Bildikonen sind in unserer, von den Social Media geprägten Alltagskultur

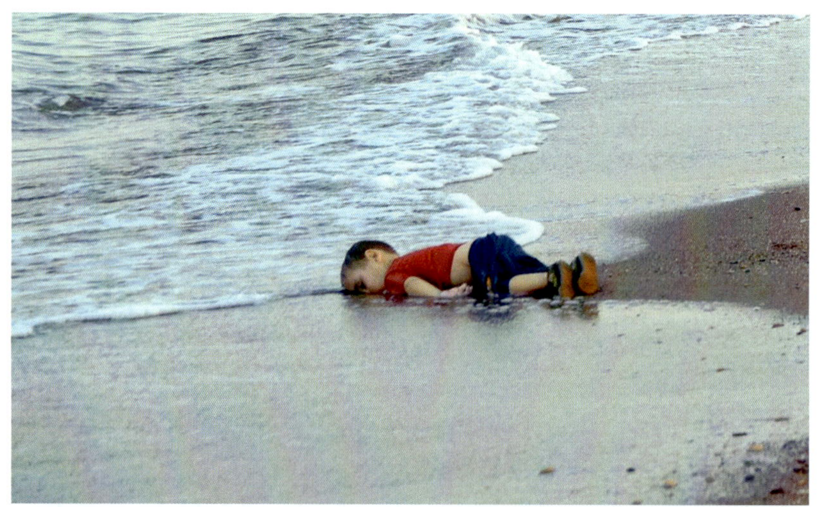

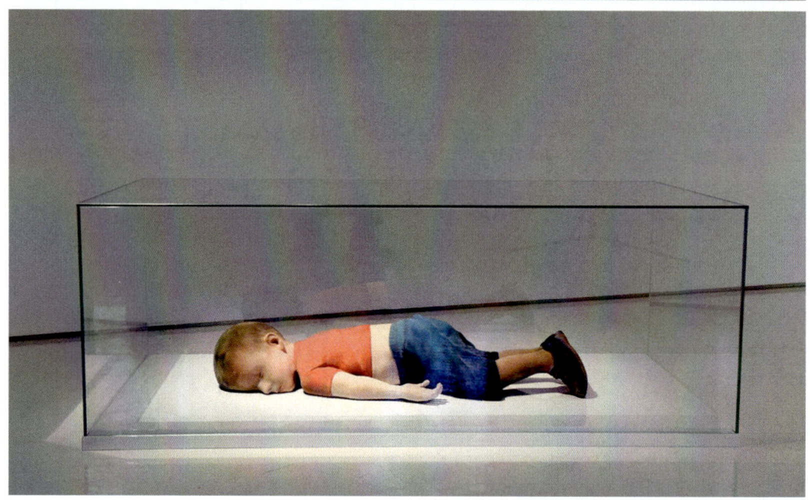

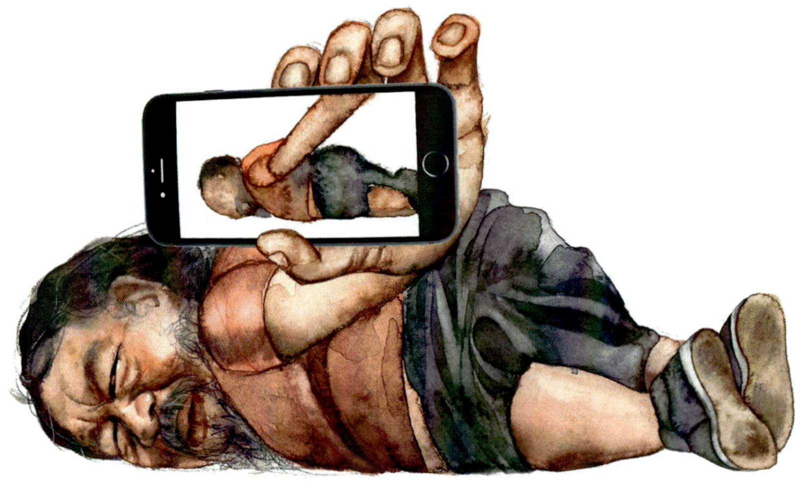

Nilüfer Demir, Photograph of Alan Kurdi, 2015
Pekka Jylhä, *Until the sea shall free him*, 2016
Carlos Rodríguez Casado, Cartoon with Ai Weiwei, 2016

inzwischen überaus populär,[5] und die Künstler*innen geraten rasch in den Verdacht, sich die Affektdynamiken der Bilder aneignen zu wollen. Doch bleibt die Reichweite der künstlerischen Verwertungen immer eher zweitrangig und nachgeordnet im Vergleich zur seit langem etablierten und um Aufmerksamkeit buhlenden Medien- und Kulturindustrie, die die Verwertungsketten von Bildern im Print-, TV- und Internetbereich reguliert und steuert. Und das gilt besonders für die Verwertung jener ikonischen Bilder, von denen Gerhard Paul schreibt, dass sie gestaltend in den historischen Prozess selbst eingreifen und die Erinnerung an die Ereignisse, die sie abbilden, wesentlich mitprägen.[6] Betrachtet man die Aneignung fotografischer Bildikonen im Rahmen zeitgenössischer Kunstpraktiken seit dem Ende des Zweiten Weltkriegs, so erkennt man immer wieder Perioden, in denen solche Aufgriffe eine besondere Konjunktur erfuhren.

I. Der Atompilz

Die Nachkriegszeit begann mit den Bildern der Bomben von Hiroshima und Nagasaki. Dabei sorgte die US-amerikanische Bildzensur dafür, dass zunächst nur Aufnahmen aus der Vogelperspektive veröffentlicht wurden. Der Bombenabwurf wurde so von Anfang an ästhetisiert, und es etablierte sich eine Ikonografie des Atompilzes als Abstraktion der Bombardierung, die die humanitären Folgen für die Zivilbevölkerung gezielt verschleierte.[7] Während japanische Künstler*innen wie Iri und Toshi Maruki in ihren *Hiroshima-Tafeln* das Leid und die Not der Überlebenden und die Zerstörungen der Städte durchaus drastisch in Szene setzten,[8] waren die Reaktionen westlicher Künstler*innen deutlich weniger empathisch und zeigten sich oftmals sogar beeindruckt vom geradezu biblischen Ausmaß der atomaren Zerstörungskraft. Auf dem Gemälde *Drei Sphinxen von Bikini* von Salvador Dalí, das 1947 im Nachgang zu den Atomtests auf dem Bikini-Atoll entstand, erkennen wir den von Dalí als Chimäre gefassten Atompilz, der nun bereits deutlich ästhetisiert, sowohl als Hinterkopf wie auch als Baumkrone erscheint. Die Ikonisierung des Atompilzes, der in den ersten Jahren des Kalten Kriegs zu einer dominanten Bildchiffre für die militärische Überlegenheit der USA avancierte, wurde von Künstler*innen wie Weaver Hawkins (*Atomic Power*, 1947) einerseits fortgeschrieben, andererseits aber auch kritisch kommentiert, wie etwa in der Fotomontage *Apoteoza* (1947) von Mieczysław Berman.

Durch die euphorische Fotoberichterstattung von den Atomversuchen auf dem Bikini-Atoll entwickelte sich in der Populärkultur der USA bald ein regelrechtes „atomares Fieber“, das man später auch als „atomic culture“ bezeichnete. In Animationsfilmen tauchten Personifizierungen der Atomkraft auf – etwa in Walt Disneys *Our Friend the Atom* (1957), in dem der Rauchwolke ein muskulöser Flaschengeist entsteigt.[9] Die flüchtige Gestalt der atomaren Staubwolke hatte sich als „symbol of strength [...] for freedom loving people“[10] in der kollektiven Imagination festgesetzt und wurde bald im Sinne eines entpolitisierten Superlativs auch als Werbechiffre für

If one revisits the appropriation of photographic icons in contemporary art practices since the end of the World War II, one can identify certain periods in which such remediations particularly boomed.

I. The Mushroom Cloud

The post-war period began with images of the bombing of Hiroshima and Nagasaki. Image censorship in the USA limited published pictures to aerial view photos only. The bombing was thus aestheticised from the beginning, and the iconography of the mushroom cloud established itself as an abstraction of the bombing, deliberately veiling the humanitarian consequences for the civil population.[7] Whereas Japanese artists such as Iri and Toshi Maruki drew attention to the suffering and plight of the survivors and the destruction of the cities in their *Hiroshima Panels*,[8] the reactions of Western artists were markedly less empathic and they often even appeared to be impressed by the almost biblical scale of atomic destructive power. In the oil painting *Three Sphinxes of Bikini* by Salvador Dalí, made in 1947 after the atomic tests on the Bikini Atoll, we recognise the mushroom cloud portrayed as a chimaera, now clearly aestheticised and appearing as the back of a head or a tree top. The iconisation of the mushroom cloud, which progressed to become a dominant pictorial cypher for the military superiority of the USA during the beginnings of the Cold War, was on the one hand continued by artists such as Weaver Hawkins; on the other, critically commented on, for example, in the photo montage, *Apoteoza* (1947) by Mieczysław Berman.

An unmitigated "atomic fever", later known as "atomic culture", developed in the popular culture of the USA as a result of the euphoric photographic coverage of the atomic tests on the Bikini Atoll. Personifications of atomic power began to appear in animation films, for example, in Walt Disney's *Our Friend the Atom* (1957) in which a muscular genie arose from the dust cloud.[9] The transient shape of the atomic cloud quickly conquered the collective imagination as a "symbol of strength [...] for freedom loving people"[10] and was also exploited, as a de-politicised superlative, as an adverting cypher for the most varied products. Highly bizarre is the photo of an officer's party, first published in the *Washington Post*, which shows the commanding officer of the Bikini tests, W.H.P. Blandy, together with his wife, cutting a cake decorated as a mushroom cloud and serving it to guests. Shortly after its publication, angry Christians in Washington responded with outrage, as did Soviet newspaper editorials which saw the photo as evidence of the decadence of USA atomists.[11] In 1957 in Las Vegas, a beauty contest elected as its winner the show dancer, Lee Martin, dressed in a bathing suit designed as a mushroom cloud: "Miss Atomic Bomb."[12] While the weapons industry and pop culture uncritically and almost exuberantly celebrated atomic technology,[13] artists in the post-war period struggled in different ways, sometimes critically, sometimes affirmatively, to aesthetically express the effects of the Holocaust and atomic bombings.

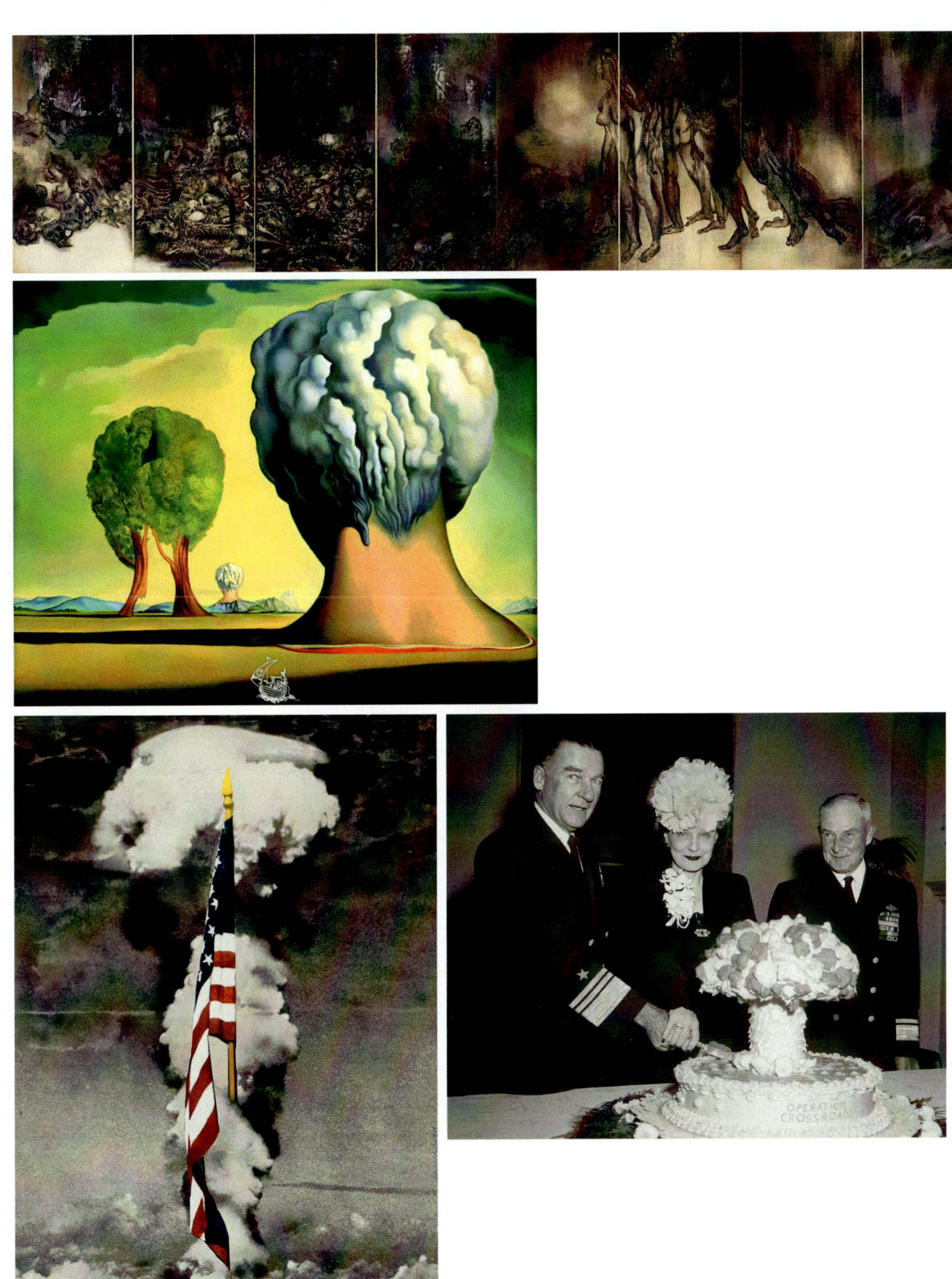

Iri and Toshi Maruki, *Hiroshima Tafeln, Tafel 6: Atomic Desert,* 1952
Salvador Dalí, *Die drei Sphinxen von Bikini*, 1947
Mieczysław Berman, *Apoteoza*, 1947; Atombombentorte, Washington, November 1946

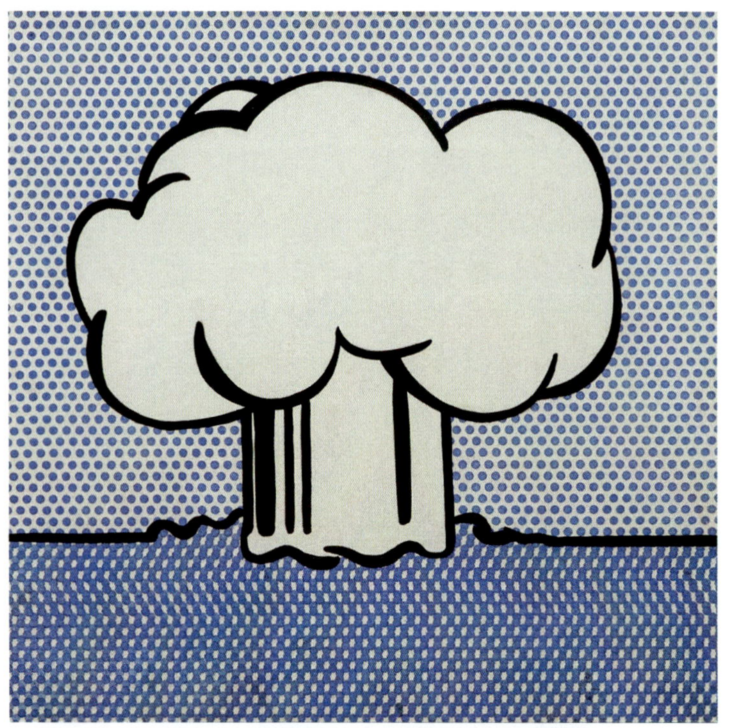

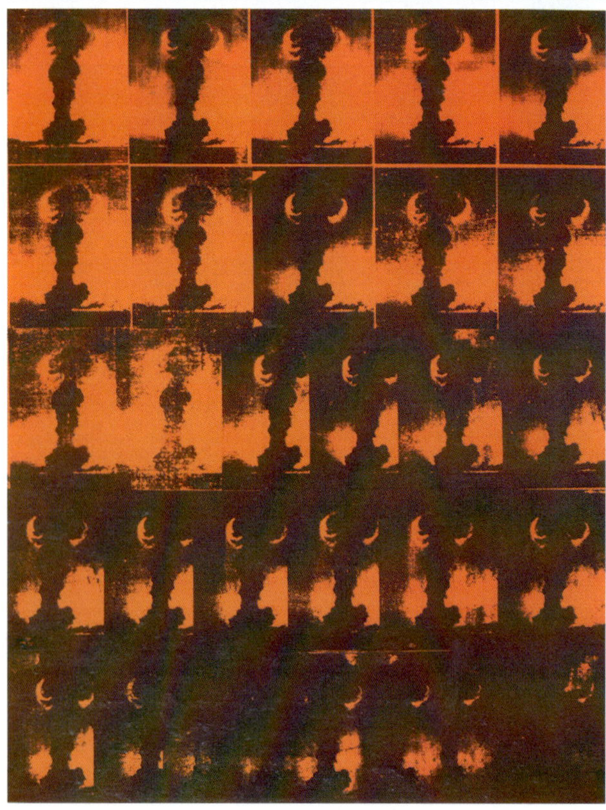

Roy Lichtenstein, *Atom Burst*, 1965
Andy Warhol, *Atomic Bomb*, 1966

die unterschiedlichsten Produkte instrumentalisiert. Höchst skurril ist auch die zuerst in der *Washington Post* publizierte Aufnahme von einer Offiziersfeier, auf der der Oberkommandeur der Bombentests auf Bikini W.H.P. Blandy zusammen mit seiner Gattin eine mit einem Atompilz dekorierte Torte anschnitt und unter den Gästen verteilen ließ. Die Aufnahme sorgte bereits kurz nach ihrem Erscheinen für Empörung, bei aufgebrachten Christen in Washington ebenso wie bei sowjetischen Zeitungskommentatoren, die das Foto als Beleg für die Dekadenz der US-amerikanischen Atomisten werteten.[11] Ein Schönheitswettbewerb kürte 1957 in Las Vegas die Showtänzerin Lee Martin mit ihrem einem Atompilz nachempfundenen Badeanzug zur „Miss Atomic Bomb“.[12]

Während Rüstungsindustrie und Populärkultur die Atomtechnologie kritiklos und auf geradezu überschwängliche Art feierten,[13] rangen die Künstler*innen der frühen Nachkriegszeit auf unterschiedliche Weise, mal kritischer, mal affirmativer um einen Ausdruck für die Nachwirkungen des Holocaust und der Atombombenabwürfe. Ein solches Nachwirken hat die Kunstgeschichtsschreibung für den Gestus des Dripping bei Jackson Pollock, dessen Gemälde zeitgenössische Kritiker auch gerne als „explosiv“ bezeichneten, ebenso konstatiert wie für die Auflösung des Figürlichen in den Gemälden Willem de Koonings, die Renato Barilli mit einer „atomaren Verpuffung“[14] verglich. Die 1951 in Mailand gegründete Künstlergruppe Arte nucleare forderte ein neues Bildvokabular, um die Explosivität des neuen Atomzeitalters poetisch und künstlerisch zu interpretieren – auch und gerade in Abgrenzung zu Dalí, dessen Atomgemälde sie als zu verhalten und symbolistisch kritisierten.[15] Yves Klein, der Anfang der 1950er Jahre in Japan gelebt hatte und sich ab 1957 Arte nucleare anschloss, erprobte seinerseits auf unterschiedliche Weise mögliche Antworten – am radikalsten in seiner Ausstellung *Le Vide* (Die Leere, 1957), die keinerlei Exponate zeigte und genau dadurch das atomare Vernichtungspotenzial unterstreichen sollte. Gleichwohl war Klein auf eine heute nur mehr schwer nachvollziehbare Art von der Atomtechnologie fasziniert und wandte sich in einem Brief an die Internationale Konferenz zur Erfassung von Atomexplosionen mit dem Vorschlag, zukünftige A- und H-Bomben in dem von ihm patentierten *International Klein Blue* (IKB) kolorieren zu dürfen, so dass deren Explosionen und Fallout fortan mit einer wiedererkennbaren Färbung versehen seien.[16] Als die oberirdischen Atomwaffentests im Jahre 1964 eingestellt wurden, verblasste allmählich auch das Bild des Atompilzes. Und in späteren Künstlerarbeiten wurde denn auch entsprechend die massenmediale Reproduktion des Bildes in den Blick gerückt. Das ist besonders deutlich in Roy Lichtensteins *Atom Burst* von 1965 und Andy Warhols *Atom Bomb* von 1966. Beide Künstler thematisieren im Geist der Popart die Kommodifizierung von Konsumgütern wie von Bildern als zentrale Chiffren der modernen Konsumgesellschaft. Bei Lichtenstein geschieht dies durch Rasterung und kräftige Umrisslinien, die den Atompilz beinahe zu einem Comic-Motiv banalisieren. Bei Warhol ist es die serielle Reihung der Pilze, deren Farbgebung das Bild zunehmend dunkler macht und das Motiv dadurch gleichsam zum Verschwinden bringt.

Art-historical writings identified such imprints in the dripping gestures of Jackson Pollock, whose paintings contemporary critics liked to designate "explosive." Renato Barilli likewise stated that the dissolution of the figure in Willem de Kooning's paintings could be compared to an "atomic explosion."[14] The artists group, Arte nucleare, founded in Milan in 1951, called for a new pictorial vocabulary to poetically and artistically interpret the explosiveness of the new atomic times—and also to distance themselves from Dalí, criticising the retention of and symbolism in his atomic paintings.[15] Yves Klein, who lived in Japan at the beginning of the 1950s and was affiliated with Arte nucleare from 1957, tried out possible answers in different ways—the most radical was his exhibition, *Le Vide* (The Void, 1957), that was empty of exhibits in an attempt to underline the destructive potential of atomic power. Nevertheless, Klein was also fascinated by nuclear technology in a way scarcely comprehensible today, and addressed a letter to the International Conference on Peaceful Uses of Atomic Energy suggesting to colour future a- and h-bombs with his patented *International Klein Blue* (IKB) so that their explosions and fallout would from now on be given a recognisable colour.[16]

When the above ground nuclear weapons tests ceased in 1964, the image of the mushroom cloud also slowly faded away. In later artworks, mass media reproductions of the image accordingly came into focus. Particular examples of this are Roy Lichtenstein's *Atom Burst* from 1965 and Andy Warhol's *Atomic Bomb* from 1966. Both artists dealt with the commodification of consumer goods and of images in the spirit of Pop Art, reflecting on the central cyphers of the modern consumer society. Lichtenstein achieved this through his rasterisation and heavy outlines which almost trivialised the mushroom cloud into a comic motif. Warhol placed the clouds in serial rows, gradually darkening the colouring so that the motif disappears.

II. Vietnam: The execution in Saigon (1968) and the Napalm Girl (1972)

The Cold War between the USA and the USSR cropped up in the 1950s in a series of proxy wars including the Vietnam War, which resulted from France's defeat in Indo-China. There are two photographs above all which have burnt themselves as shock images into our collective memory and triggered numerous artistic remediations and reenactments later on. The first is from 1968, as the North Vietnamese army intensified attacks on South Vietnam as part of the Tet Offensive.[17] It shows the execution of the Vietcong fighter, Nguyễn Văn Lém, who was suspected of a terrorist attack and subsequently killed with a shot to the head by the then police chief, Nguyễn Ngọc Loan, in the presence of AP photographer, Eddie Adams, and an NBC cameraman.[18] Adam's photograph shows the agitated police chief with rolled-up sleeves. The muscle tension in his right arm is clearly

II. Vietnam: Die Exekution von Saigon (1968) und das Napalm-Girl (1972)

Bereits in den 1950er Jahren bricht sich der Kalte Krieg zwischen den USA und der UdSSR in einer Reihe von Stellvertreterkriegen Bahn, zu denen auch der aus der Niederlage Frankreichs in Indochina erwachsende Vietnamkrieg gehört. Es sind vor allem zwei Fotografien, die sich als Schockbilder in unser kollektives Gedächtnis eingebrannt haben und zahlreiche Remediationen erfuhren. Die erste entstand 1968, als die nordvietnamesische Armee im Rahmen ihrer Tet-Offensive[17] die Angriffe gegen Südvietnam intensivierte. Es zeigt die Erschießung des Vietcong-Kämpfers Nguyễn Văn Lém, dem ein terroristischer Anschlag unterstellt wurde und der daraufhin in Anwesenheit des AP-Fotografen Eddie Adams und eines NBC-Kameramanns vom damaligen Polizeichef Nguyễn Ngọc Loan durch einen gezielten Kopfschuss getötet wurde.[18] Adams' Aufnahme zeigt den erregten Polizeichef mit hochgekrempelten Ärmeln. Die Muskelspannung seines rechten Unterarms ist deutlich erkennbar; der Abzug der Pistole ist durchgedrückt. Der ausgestreckte Arm lenkt den Blick auf das in genau diesem Moment erschossene Opfer, dessen Hände mit Handschellen auf den Rücken gebunden sind.

Das Ziehen des Pistolenabzugs und das Drücken des Kameraauslösers geschahen im selben Moment. Doch wie Susan Sontag bemerkt, weist das Foto trotz seines offenkundig dokumentarischen Charakters einen hohen Grad an Inszeniertheit auf. Loan inszenierte diese Hinrichtung auf offener Straße für die hinter ihm stehenden Journalisten.[19] Die Publikation der Foto- und Filmaufnahmen führte zu einer Verschärfung der Anti-Vietnam-Proteste in den USA und Europa. Unter dem direkten Eindruck von Adams' Fotografie fertigte Wolf Vostell 1968 seine Siebdruckcollage mit dem Titel *Miss America*, in der er einen Ausschnitt der Fotografie mit dem Bild eines Fotomodells kombinierte. Einige Stellen ihres Körpers sind mit roter Farbe übermalt. Der Farbklecks über ihren Augen wirkt wie eine Augenbinde. Das von Vostell zur *Miss America* geadelte Püppchen fungiert hier als Allegorie, stellvertretend für eine Gesellschaft, die die Menschenwürde aus den Augen verloren hat. Auf einer weiteren Ebene thematisiert Vostell dabei auch den Warencharakter und die Kommodifizierung von Bildern aus der Nachrichtenbranche ebenso wie aus der Unterhaltung. Beide Bildmotive sind Teil einer sich globalisierenden visuellen Ökonomie, zwei Extreme, die sich aber wie die zwei Seiten einer Medaille ergänzen.

Resonanzen von Adams' Fotografie finden sich ebenso im Film, beispielsweise bei Woody Allen. Er platziert das Foto im Hintergrund einer Szene seines Films *Stardust Memories* (1980), in dem der von ihm selbst gespielte Protagonist sich weigert, angesichts einer von immer größerem Kriegsleid gezeichneten Welt weiterhin unterhaltsame Filme zu drehen.

Obwohl das von Nick Út 1972 fotografierte, vor einem Napalmangriff flüchtende Mädchen Kim Phúc unbestreitbar zu den bedeutendsten Antikriegs-Bildern der Geschichte gehört, triggerte das Foto erst mit

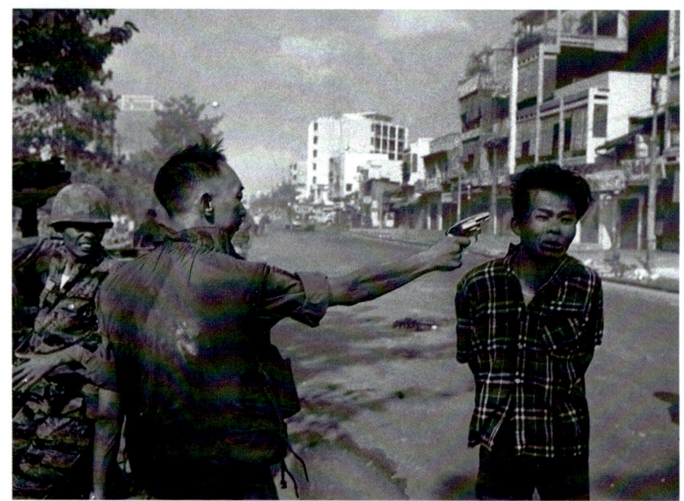

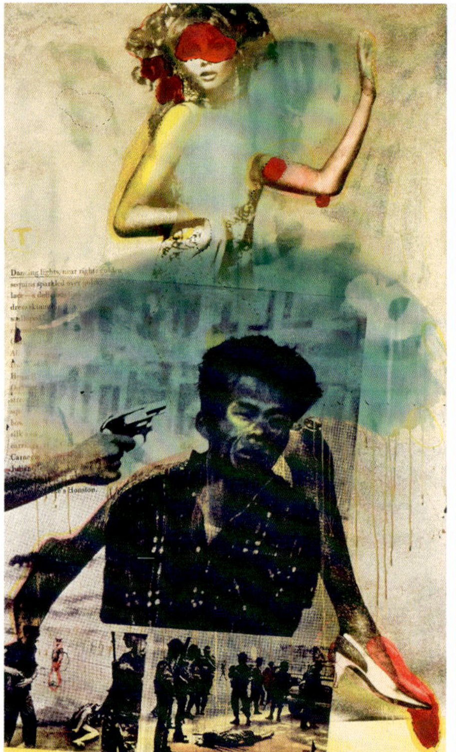

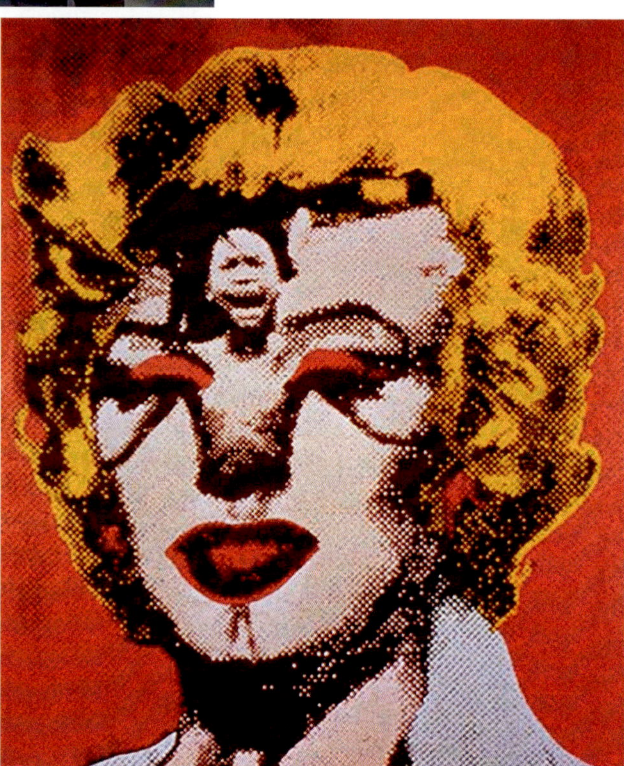

Eddie Adams, Photograph of Nguyễn Văn Lém, 1 February, 1968
Wolf Vostell, *Miss America*, 1968
Jerry Kearns, *Madonna and Child*, 1987

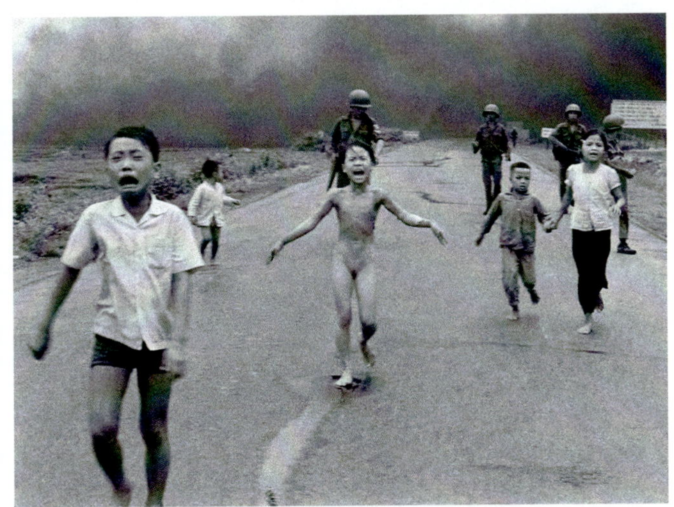

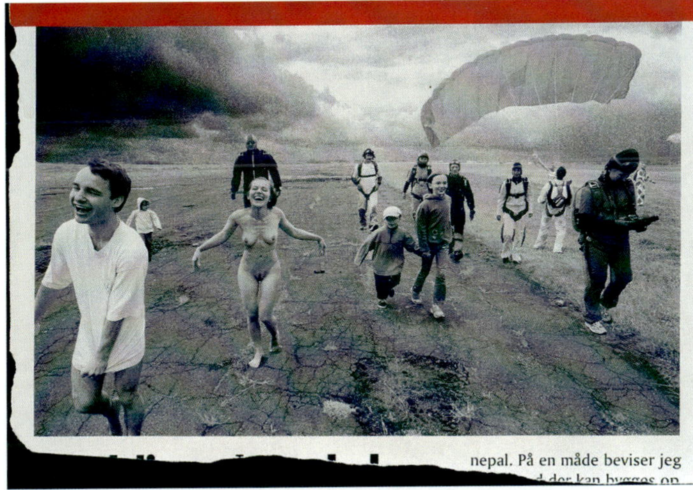

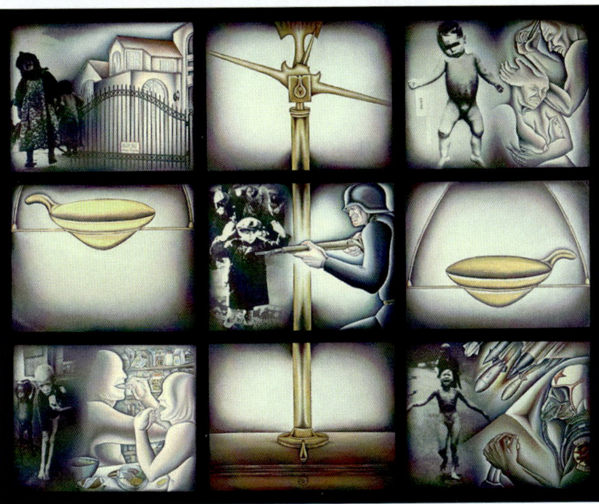

Nick Út, *The Terror of War*, 8. Juni 1972
Zbigniew Libera, *Nepal, from the Positives series*, 2003
Judy Chicago & Donald Woodman, *Im/Balance of Power, Holocaust Project,* 1991

visible; the trigger is cocked. His outstretched arm directs attention to the victim, shot exactly in this instant, his hands cuffed behind his back.

The pulling of the trigger and the click of the camera shutter happened in the same instant. However, as Susan Sontag remarks, the photo exhibits a high degree of staging in spite of its evidently documentary character. Loan staged this execution on the street for the journalists standing behind him.[19] The publication of the photo and the film led to an increase in anti-Vietnam protests in the USA and Europe. As a direct reaction to Adam's photograph, Wolf Vostell made his silkscreen print, titled *Miss America* (1968), which combined a detail of the photo and an image of a photographic model. Parts of her body are overpainted in red. The colour splotch on her eyes looks like a blindfold. The model-doll, ennobled by Vostell, functions as an allegory, a substitute for a society that has lost sight of humanity. On a further level, Vostell's theme is the commodity character and commodification of images from the news and entertainment branches. Both pictorial motifs are part of a globalising visual economy; two extremes which appear as flip sides of the same coin.

Reactions to Adam's photograph also appeared in films, for example, Woody Allen's movie *Stardust Memories* (1980). Allen places the photo in the background of one of the scenes in which he plays the protagonist who refuses to make entertainment films in a world increasingly marked by the sufferings of war. Although the 1972 photograph by Nick Út of a girl, Kim Phúc, running from a napalm attack unarguably belongs to the most important anti-war images in history, there was a comparably long period of latency before it triggered artistic media remediations. The photo was only rediscovered as a historical image in the 1980s. The soaring napalm clouds in the background unmistakably provide the reason for the children's flight towards the photographer. The affective constellation—shock, horror and pain—immediately readable from the children's mimic and gestures, is frozen in time. The trimming of the photo at the right edge increases its pleading character, which could, with the now central placing of the naked Phúc, hardly be stronger. Moreover, images of children as victims are extremely harrowing, since children are always innocent and in need of protection.

Judy Chicago placed Phúc on one of her *Holocaust Project* tables (1985–92); the table assembled images of other child victims such as the boy from the Warsaw ghetto and children from the war in Biafra. Chicago juxtaposed the black and white silhouette of the vulnerable Phúc in need of protection with a uniformed soldier and a huge, coloured rain of bombs bursting in from the right side of the image.[20] References to and other uses of the motif can be found in *Madonna and Child* (1987) by Jerry Kearns, *Memory Rendering of Tram Bang* (1989) by Vik Muniz, in the photo series, *This Bloodless War* (1997) by Manit Sriwanichpoom and and in Banksy's grafitti, *Can't beat the feeling* (2005).

In comparison to the Saigon reenactment of Yasumasa in which the artist played all the protagonists himself, Zbigniew Libera's photographic works are even more confusing. At first, we believe we recognise the iconic

einer vergleichsweise längeren Latenzzeit künstlerische Remediationen. Tatsächlich wurde das Bild erst in den 1980er Jahren gleichsam als Historienbild wieder ausgegraben. Die im Bildhintergrund aufsteigenden Napalm-Wolken verweisen unmissverständlich auf den Grund der Flucht der auf den Fotografen zulaufenden Kinder; in ihrem Gesichtsausdruck und den Gebärden ist das Schrecken, Entsetzen und Schmerz signalisierende affektive Geschehen still gestellt und eingefroren. Durch den Beschnitt des Bildes am rechten Rand wurde der Appellcharakter der Aufnahme zusätzlich gesteigert und könnte durch die nunmehr im Zentrum platzierte unbekleidete Phúc kaum stärker sein. Zudem sind Bilder von Kindern als Opfern immer in höchstem Maße erschütternd, da Kinder grundsätzlich unschuldig und schutzbedürftig sind.

Judy Chicago präsentiert Phúc auf einer der Tafeln ihres *Holocaust Project* (1985–92); die Tafel versammelt auch andere Kinderopfer wie den Jungen aus dem Warschauer Ghetto oder Kinder aus dem Biafra-Krieg. Chicago kontrastiert die verletzliche und schutzbedürftige Schwarzweiß-Silhouette Phúcs mit einem martialisch gekleideten Soldaten und einem massiven farbigen Bombenhagel, der vom rechten Bildrand hereinplatzt.[20] Verweise und weitere Aufgriffe des Motivs finden sich in der Arbeit *Madonna and Child* (1987) von Jerry Kearns, *Memory Rendering of Tram Bang* (1989) von Vik Muniz, bei Manit Sriwanichpoom (in der Fotoserie *This Bloodless War* von 1997) und in Banksys Graffiti *Can't beat the feeling* (2005).

Im Vergleich mit dem fotografischen Reenactment der Exekution von Saigon, in dem der Künstler Yasumasa alle Beteiligten selbst darstellt, sind die Fotoarbeiten Zbigniew Liberas noch irritierender. Auf seinem Bild *Nepal* (2003) glauben wir zunächst das ikonische Pressefoto von Út wiederzuerkennen. Doch Libera zieht hier alle Register, um unser Bildgedächtnis zu verstören. Keine der im Bild erkennbaren Personen versprüht Angst oder Schrecken. An Stelle von Phúc läuft uns eine junge europäische Frau entgegen, und auch die Personen im Hintergrund sind keine US-amerikanischen Soldaten, sondern ausgelassene Touristen, die – so scheint es zumindest – mit einem Kiteboard-Schirm von einem Strandausflug zurückkommen. Wie Inke Arns gezeigt hat, wurzelt die Verstörung, die von dieser und anderen inszenierten Fotografien Liberas ausgeht, darin, dass wir auf ihnen eine geradezu unheimliche Rückkehr an den Ort eines historischen Traumas erleben. Doch „was auf den ersten Blick schrecklich bekannt erscheint, zerfällt im nächsten Moment in einzelne – positive – Elemente“[21].

III. Soweto 1976: Sam Nzimas Fotografie des sterbenden Hector Pieterson

Betrachten wir noch eine letzte Bildikone – diesmal aus dem Jahr 1976 in Südafrika. Ausgangspunkt der Schüleraufstände bzw. „Soweto Uprisings“ war die geplante Einführung von Afrikaans als verbindlicher

press photo by Út in his image, *Nepal* (2003). Libera, however, uses every means to destroy our visual memory. Not one of the people recognisable in the image is expressing angst or shock. In the place of Phúc, a young European woman runs towards us, and the people behind are not USA soldiers but boisterous tourists—at least they seem to be—returning from an excursion to the beach with a kiteboard sail. The disturbance in this and other staged photos by Libera is rooted, as Inke Arns has shown, in our experience of an uncanny return to the site of a historical trauma. But, "what appears to be shocking at first glance collapses in the next moment into single—positive—elements."[21]

III. Soweto 1976: Sam Nzima's Photographs of the Dying Hector Pieterson

Let us look at one last iconic image—this time from 1976 in South Africa. The starting point of the schoolchildren's rebellion and the "Soweto uprising" was the planned introduction of Afrikaans as the mandatory official teaching language. The youngsters, who left their schools on the morning of June 16 to go on a protest march to the Orlando Stadium, were stopped on their way by military police barricades and caught up in street fights. Twenty-three people died on the first day of the protest. Among them was 13-year-old Hector Pieterson, who was shot from the front. The famous photograph by Sam Nzima shows the dying Hector in the arms of Mbuyisa Makhubu, accompanied by Hector's sister, Antoinette, walking towards the photographer's car. The photo appeared the next day in the Black daily paper, *The World*, and after that, worldwide.
In the case of Hector Pieterson, many commentators have drawn par-allels to the sacrilisation of death in Christian iconography. The photo was seen as a variation of the Pietà motif in which Mbuyisa Makhubo slipped into the role of the mother grieving the death of her son.[22] We know from Aby Warburg's pathos formula that the processes of iconisation takes place when formalised actions are repeated and passed on. Warburg spoke here of "energy stocks" which can be understood as suspended affect events. These energy stocks can evolve independently of the tangible image medium —indeed over wide-ranging times and spaces; from antiquity, through the Renaissance and up to the political iconography of Modernism.[23] Alongside the death throe, the theme of Laocoön, the Pietà surely is one of the most important "affect stocks" and controls our unconscious reception of images. We know the connection from other images that have gained a similar iconic status, for example, the 1967 photo of the death of the student, Benno Ohnesorg, who was shot during an anti-Shah demonstration in Berlin.
In contrast to the photo of Hector Pieterson, the usual Christian gender iconography is here retained.[24] The facial expressions in both cases, however, are neither devotion nor grief but a cry of outrage, although Antoinette's protective hand gesture unquestionably signals grief. The image was

offizieller Unterrichtssprache. Die Jugendlichen, die am Morgen des 16. Juni von ihren Schulen aus zu einem Sternmarsch zum Orlando-Stadium aufgebrochen waren, wurden auf ihrem Weg dorthin von martialischen Polizei-Barrikaden aufgehalten und in Straßenkämpfe verwickelt. Am ersten Tag der Proteste zählte man bereits 23 Tote. Unter ihnen der 13-jährige Hector Pieterson, der von vorne erschossen wurde. Die berühmte Aufnahme von Sam Nzima zeigt den sterbenden Hector in den Armen von Mbuyisa Makhubo, begleitet von Hectors Schwester Antoinette, die beide auf das Auto des Fotografen zulaufen. Das Bild erschien tags darauf in der schwarzen Tageszeitung *The World* und danach weltweit.

Zahlreiche Kommentatoren haben im Fall von Hector Pieterson auf Parallelen zur Sakralisierung des Todes in der christlichen Ikonografie verwiesen. Das Foto wurde als eine Variation des Pietà-Motivs identifiziert. Hier sei Mbuyisa Makhubu in die Rolle der um ihren toten Sohn trauernden Mutter geschlüpft.[22] Durch Aby Warburgs Konzept der „Pathosformel" wissen wir, dass Ikonisierungsprozesse auch darauf zurückgehen, dass sie bestimmte formelhafte Gebärden aufgreifen und weitertradieren. Warburg sprach hier von „Energiekonserven", die man als stillgestellte Affektgeschehen verstehen kann. Diese vermögen sich unabhängig vom materiellen Bildträgermedium zu entfalten – und zwar über weite Räume und Zeiten hinweg – von der Antike, über die Renaissance bis in die politische Ikonografie der Moderne.[23] Neben dem im Laokoon thematisierten Todeskampf ist die Pietà hier sicherlich eine der bedeutendsten „Affektkonserven" und steuert unsere unbewusste Bildrezeption.

Wir kennen den Zusammenhang auch von anderen Bildern, die einen vergleichbaren ikonischen Status erlangten – etwa dem Foto des 1967 bei einer Anti-Schah-Demonstration in Berlin erschossenen Studenten Benno Ohnesorg. Im Gegensatz zum Hector Pieterson-Foto ist hier der aus der christlichen Ikonografie geläufige Geschlechterdualismus noch erhalten.[24] Doch ist der Gesichtsausdruck in beiden Fällen weder Andacht noch Trauer, sondern ein Aufschrei der Empörung, wobei die abwehrende Handgeste von Antoinette in Nzimas Aufnahme durchaus Schmerz und Trauer signalisiert. Das in Südafrika sofort zensierte Foto löste international eine Welle der Solidarisierung mit der Anti-Apartheid-Bewegung aus. Als Märtyrerbild avancierte es aber auch in Südafrika selbst zur wichtigsten Ikone im Kampf gegen die Rassensegregation und erfuhr auch später zahlreiche künstlerische Remediationen.

Im Rahmen der Ausstellung *Faultlines* (1996) – zum 20. Jahrestag der Soweto-Aufstände – fertigte Kevin Brand ein Mosaik aus schwarzen, weißen und grauen Klebebandstreifen am Castle of Good Hope in Kapstadt an. Durch seine Rasterung unterstrich es die massenmediale Vermitteltheit (aber auch die Porosität der Erinnerung). Neben künstlerischen Mediationen erfuhr das Foto – ähnlich wie die Bilder von Nguyễn Văn Lém, Kim Phúc oder Alan Kurdi – auch Reenactments. Der 16. Juni 1976 gilt inzwischen als Wendepunkt der südafrikanischen Geschichte und wurde zum Andenken an die Schüleraufstände zu einem Nationalfeiertag erhoben. Neben offiziellen Reden und Kranzniederlegungen am Hector Pieterson Memorial

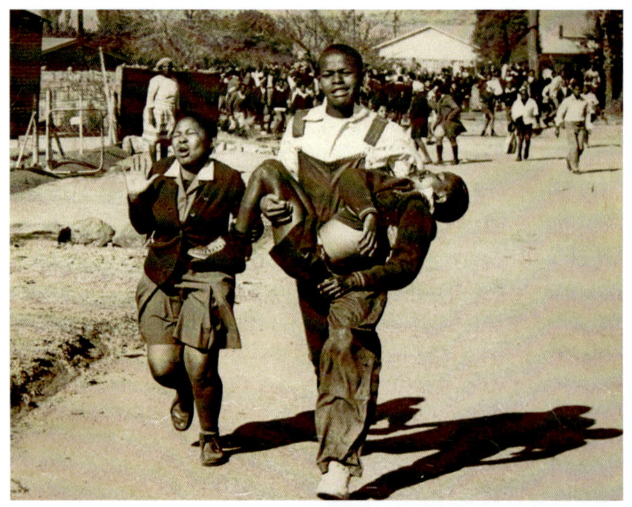

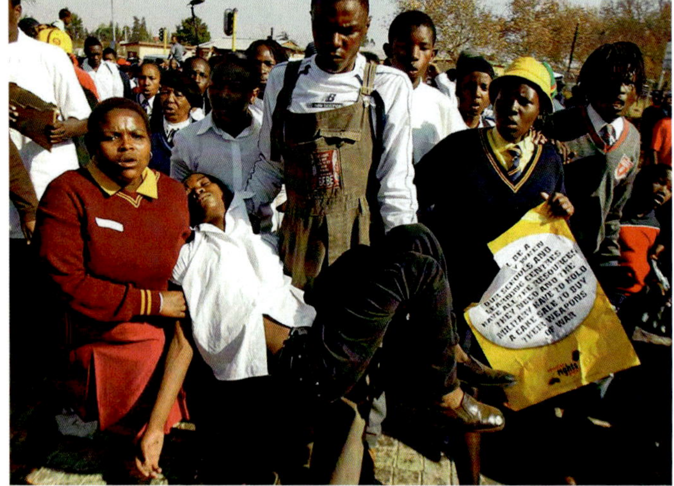

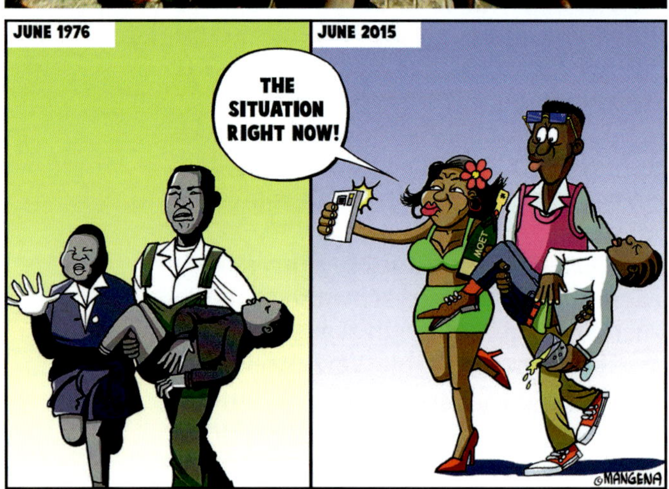

Sam Nzima, Photograph of Hector Pieterson, 1976
Str, *Safrica Reenactment*, 2003
Mangena, Cartoon with Hector Pieterson, 2015

werden hier die Schülerdemonstrationen von 1976 nachgestellt und die ikonische Fotografie gleichsam „re-animiert".[25] Solche im Rahmen von Heritage-Tourismus und Living History-Initiativen inzwischen überaus populären Reenactments versuchen Gegenwart und Geschichte kurzzuschließen: um Geschichtsbilder emotional und somatisch zu erleben. Allerdings wird von den Zeitzeugen der Aufstände inzwischen häufig eine Verflachung beklagt. Vor allem der Generation der „Born Frees" (der nach 1994 Geborenen) wird vorgeworfen, den Anlass zum „Partying" zu missbrauchen. In der rechten Spalte des Cartoons, der ein solches Party-Reenactment thematisiert, ist die abgespreizte rechte Hand von Antoinette, die man fast als ein Barthessches „Punctum" lesen könnte, bezeichnenderweise mutiert zu einer ein Smartphone haltenden Selfie-Hand – dem ultimativen Symbol einer neuen „globalen Spaßkultur".

Entlang von Bildern – ich hoffe, das haben die vorgestellten Fallbeispiele deutlich gemacht – artikulieren sich die unterschiedlichsten Affektdynamiken; mal langsamer – mal schneller, mal stärker lokalisiert – mal über Nationalstaatsgrenzen hinweg – immer aber in Abhängigkeit von den jeweils verfügbaren Medien der Kommunikation. Während Affekte in ihrer Modalität vor allem als Intensitäten zirkulieren, tragen Bilder entscheidend zu ihrer Konkretion und Konsolidierung bei. Ihre Handlungsmacht beziehungsweise ihre Rolle als Aktanten entfaltet sich dabei im Kontext der Akteursnetzwerke, in die sie eingebunden werden. Diese Aktantenrolle der Bilder lässt sich mit Alfred Gell dahingehend präzisieren, dass Bilder ebenso wie die sie hervorbringenden menschlichen Akteure im Hinblick auf das Affizierungsgeschehen stets aktivische Aspekte von Subjekten (agency) und von Objekten (patiency) in sich vereinen.[26] Auch die Kunst als Instanz gesellschaftlicher Selbstbeobachtung und Reflexion ist dabei von den jeweilig vorhandenen medialen Voraussetzungen geprägt. Die im vorliegenden Beitrag besprochenen künstlerischen Remediationen und Reenactments aus der zweiten Hälfte des 20. Jahrhunderts zeigen in struktureller Hinsicht durchaus ähnliche Bildphänomene, doch ist im Vergleich zum gegenwärtigen Unmittelbarkeitsversprechen der Social Media die Latenzzeit für die Wiederkehr der Bilder meist noch deutlich verlängert. Das Tempo, mit dem heute fotografische Bildikonen aus der Zeitgeschichte und Populärkultur künstlerisch angeeignet und kommentiert werden und in die Kunstgeschichte Eingang finden, ist ungleich rasanter geworden.

1 Der vorliegende Text ist im Rahmen des Sonderforschungsbereichs 1171 *Affective Societies* entstanden. Für finanzielle Unterstützung danke ich der Deutschen Forschungsgemeinschaft, für Anregungen und Diskussionen Kerstin Schankweiler und Verena Straub.

2 Vgl. Studie von Farida Vis, Olga Goriunova (Hg.), *The Iconic Image on Social Media: A Rapid Research Response to the Death of Aylan Kurdi**, 2015, auf: https://research.gold.ac.uk/14624/1/KURDI%20REPORT.pdf (letzter Zugriff 05.08.2017).

3 Vgl. Donna Roberts, *The Drowned Refugee Aylan Kurdi and Other Horrors on Display at Helsinki Contemporary*, 2016, auf: http://finlandtoday.fi/the-drowned-refugee-aylan-and-other-horrors-on-display-at-helsinki-contemporary/ (letzter Zugriff 05.08.2017).

4 Vgl. Natalie Evans, Richard Wheatstone, *Aylan Kurdi's death recreated by 30 people dressed as Syrian boy on Moroccan beach*, auf: http://www.mirror.co.uk/news/world-news/aylan-kurdis-death-recreated-30-6415214 (letzter Zugriff 05.08.2017).

immediately banned in South Africa but released a worldwide outpouring of solidarity with the anti-apartheid movement. In South Africa, too, it became an image of martyrdom and the most important icon in the fight against racial segregation and eventually triggered many artistic remediations.

For the exhibition, *Faultlines* (1996), on the 20th anniversary of the Soweto uprising, Kevin Brand completed a mosaic from black, white and grey strips of tape on the Castle of Good Hope in Cape Town. Its rasterisation underlined its reproduction in the mass media (and also the porosity of memory). Next to artistic remediations, the photo underwent reenactments in the same vein as those of Nguyễn Văn Lém, Kim Phúc or Alan Kurdi. July 16 became a turning point in the history of South Africa and was elevated to a national day of remembrance in honour of the school uprisings. Official speeches, the laying of wreaths and reenactments of the 1976 school demonstrations—including spontaneous "re-animations" of the iconic photograph—are performed at the Hector Pieterson memorial in Orlando.[25] In the context of heritage tourism and Living History initiatives, such reenactments, nowadays extremely popular, attempt to connect the past and the present: to emotionally and somatically experience the pictures of history. However, eye witnesses to the uprisings frequently complain of trivialisation. The generation of the "Born Frees" (those born after 1994), above all, are accused of misusing the event as an excuse to party. On the right-hand side of the cartoon that illustrates such a party reenactment, Antoinette's stretched out hand, which could almost be read as a Barthes "Punctum," has significantly mutated into a selfie hand holding a smart phone; the ultimate symbol of a new, "global fun culture."

Through images—I hope that the examples above have made this clear—the most varied affect dynamics may be articulated; sometimes slower, sometimes faster, sometimes limited to a particular locality and sometimes crossing national boundaries, but always dependent on the available means of communication. While affects in their modality circulate primarily as intensities, images contribute to their concretisation and consolidation. The agency of images (respectively their role as actants) unfolds in the context of the actor-networks in which they are embedded. One can make this issue more precise with Alfred Gell who has conceived of both entities—human actors and image actants—as combined entities, simultaneously uniting aspects of subjects (agency) as well as of objects (patiency).[26] In addition, art as a means of social self-observation and reflection is equally dependent on the media environment in which it operates. The artistic remediations and reenactments from the second half of the 20th century discussed above show very similar image phenomena—although, in comparison to social media's promise of immediacy, the latency period for the return of the images was usually markedly longer. The speed with which today's photographic icons from contemporary history and popular culture are artistically appropriated, commented on and find their way into art history has massively increased.

1 This text was written within the programme of the Collaborative Research Centre 1171 *Affective Societies*. I would like to thank the German Research Foundation for financial support, and Kerstin Schankweiler and Verena Straub for discussions and suggestions.

5 Siehe dazu auch das neu entstandene Bildphänomen der Selfie-Proteste: Kerstin Schankweiler, *Selfie-Proteste. Affektzeugenschaften und Bildökonomien in den Social Media*, Working Paper SFB 1171 Affective Societies, Berlin 2016, Static URL: http://edocs.fu-berlin.de/docs/receive/FUDOCS_series_000000000562
6 Gerhard Paul, *Bilder, die Geschichte schrieben. Medienikonen des 20. u. beginnenden 21. Jahrhunderts. Einleitung*, in: Gerhard Paul (Hg.), *Bilder, die Geschichte schrieben. 1900 bis heute*, Göttingen 2011, S. 7–16, hier S. 7.
7 Daniel Bürkner, *Fotografie und atomare Katastrophe. Die visuelle Repräsentation der Ereignisse von Hiroshima/Nagasaki und Tschernobyl*, Dissertation Humboldt-Universität zu Berlin 2014, auf: https://edoc.hu-berlin.de/handle/18452/17851, S. 81–88.
8 Vgl. die *Hiroshima-Tafeln* von Iri und Toshi Maruki 1950–52. Yasufumi Nakamori, *Die Stadt durch die Fotografie imaginieren: Japan zwischen 1945 und 1968*, in: Okwui Enwezor u.a. (Hg.), *Postwar 1945–65. Kunst zwischen Pazifik und Atlantik*, München 2016, S. 134–139.
9 Regie: Hamilton Luske, Autor: Milt Banta, auf: https://www.youtube.com/watch?v=QRzl1wHc43I (letzter Zugriff 05.08.2017).
10 Spencer R. Weart, *Nuclear fear. A History of Images*, Cambridge MA 1988, S. 403.
11 Vgl. Bill Geerhart, *The Atomic Cake Controversy of 1946*, 2010, auf: http://conelrad.blogspot.de/2010/09/atomic-cake-controversy-of-1946.html (letzter Zugriff 05.08.2017).
12 Ebd.
13 Vgl. A. Costandina Titus, *The Mushroom Cloud as Kitsch*, in: Scott C. Zeman, Michael A. Amundson (Hg.), *Atomic Culture: How We Learned to Stop Worrying and Love the Bomb*, Boulder 2004, S. 101–123.
14 Zit. n. Stephen Petersen, *Formen lösen sich auf: Malerei im Schatten der Atombombe*, in: Okwui Enwezor u.a. (Hg.), *Postwar 1945–65. Kunst zwischen Pazifik und Atlantik*, München 2016, S. 141–145, hier S. 141.
15 Ebd., S. 143.
16 Ebd., S. 144.
17 Benannt nach dem vietnamesischen Neujahrsfest Tet, an dem die Großangriffe begannen.
18 Vgl. auch die deutsche TV-Adaption des NBC-Filmmaterials durch den Sender Phoenix, auf: https://www.youtube.com/watch?v=7iQ7LTsaZyY (letzter Zugriff 05.08.2017).
19 Susan Sontag, *Das Leiden anderer betrachten*, Frankfurt a.M. 2005, S. 71f.
20 Siehe http://www.judychicago.com/gallery/holocaust-project/hp-artwork/ (letzter Zugriff 05.08.2017).
21 Inke Arns, *History Will Repeat itself. Strategien des Reenactment in der zeitgenössische (Medien-)Kunst und Performance*. online, auf: http://www.inkearns.de/files/2011/01/2007_HWRI-Arns-Kat_dt.pdf (letzter Zugriff 05.08.2017).
22 John Peffer, *Art and the End of Apartheid*, Minneapolis 2009, S. 55f.
23 Der Begriff „Energiekonserve“ wird in Warburgs Notizbuch *Grundbegriffe II* (1929) elaboriert, S. 21. Zitiert nach Ernst H. Gombrich, *Aby Warburg – eine intellektuelle Biographie*, Frankfurt a.M. 1981, S. 245. Vgl. auch Aby Warburg, *Der Tod des Orpheus. Bilder zu dem Vortrag über Dürer und die Italienische Antike*, (1905), neu herausgegeben von Dieter Wuttke, Peter Schmidt, *Aby Warburg und die Ikonologie*, Wiesbaden 1993.
24 Vgl. Christoph Hamann, *Pieta 1967, Jürgen Henschels Fotografie des toten Benno Ohnesorg. Das kanonische Bild*, in: Praxis Geschichte 20 (2007), S. 56–57.
25 Ruth Kerkham Simbao, *The Thirtieth Anniversary of the Soweto Uprisings: Reading the Shadow in Sam Nzima's Iconic Photograph of Hector Pieterson*, in: *African Arts*, Vol. 40, No. 2 (2007), S. 52–69.
26 Vgl. Alfred Gell, *Art and Agency. An Anthropological Theory*, Oxford 1998.

2 Cf. study by Farida Vis, Olga Goriunova (eds.), *The Iconic Image on Social Media: A Rapid Research Response to the Death of Aylan Kurdi**, 2015, on: https://research.gold.ac.uk/14624/1/KURDI%20REPORT.pdf (last access 5.8.2017).

3 Cf. Donna Roberts, *The Drowned Refugee Aylan Kurdi and Other Horrors on Display at Helsinki Contemporary*, 2016, on: http://finlandtoday.fi/the-drowned-refugee-aylan-and-other-horrors-on-display-at-helsinki-contemporary/ (last access 5.8.2017).

4 Cf. Natalie Evans, Richard Wheatstone, *Aylan Kurdi's death recreated by 30 people dressed as Syrian boy on Moroccan beach,* on: http://www.mirror.co.uk/news/world-news/aylan-kurdis-death-recreated-30-6415214, (last access 5.8.2017).

5 See also the new image phenomenon of the selfie-protest: Kerstin Schankweiler, *Selfie-Proteste. Affektzeugenschaften und Bildökonomien in den Social Media*, Working Paper SFB 1171 Affective Societies, Berlin 2016, Static URL: http://edocs.fu-berlin.de/docs/receive/FUDOCS_series_000000000562.

6 Gerhard Paul, *Bilder, die Geschichte schrieben. Medienikonen des 20. u. beginnenden 21. Jahrhunderts. Einleitung*, in: Gerhard Paul (ed.), *Bilder, die Geschichte schrieben. 1900 bis heute*, Göttingen 2011, pp. 7–16, here p. 7.

7 Daniel Bürkner, *Fotografie und atomare Katastrophe. Die visuelle Repräsentation der Ereignisse von Hiroshima/Nagasaki und Tschernobyl*, Dissertation Humboldt University, Berlin 2014, on: https://edoc.hu-berlin.de/handle/18452/17851 (last acces 5.8.2017) pp. 81–88.

8 Cf. *The Hiroshima Panels* by Iri and Toshi Maruki 1950–52. Yasufumi Nakamori, *Die Stadt durch die Fotografie imaginieren: Japan zwischen 1945 und 1968*, in: Okwui Enwezor a.o. (eds.), *Postwar 1945–65. Kunst zwischen Pazifik und Atlantik*, Munich 2016, pp. 134–139.

9 Director: Hamilton Luske, author: Milt Banta, on: https://www.youtube.com/watch?v=QRzl1wHc43I (last access 5.8.2017).

10 Spencer R. Weart, *Nuclear Fear. A History of Images*, Cambridge MA 1988, p. 403.

11 Cf. Bill Geerhart, *The Atomic Cake Controversy of 1946*, 2010, on: http://conelrad.blogspot.de/2010/09/atomic-cake-controversy-of-1946.html (last access 5.8.2017).

12 Ibid.

13 Cf. A. Costandina Titus, *The Mushroom Cloud as Kitsch*, in: Scott C. Zeman, Michael A. Amundson (eds.), *Atomic Culture: How We Learned to Stop Worrying and Love the Bomb*, Boulder 2004, pp. 101–123.

14 Quote after Stephen Petersen, *Formen lösen sich auf: Malerei im Schatten der Atombombe*, in: Okwui Enwezor 2016 (note 8), 141–145, here p. 141.

15 Ibid., p.143.

16 Ibid.

17 Called after the Vietnamese New Year's festival, Tet, when the major offensive began.

18 Cf. also the German TV adaptation of the NBC film material by the broadcaster, Phoenix, on: https://www.youtube.com watch?v=7iQ7LTsaZyY (last access 5.8.2017).

19 Susan Sontag, *Regarding the Pain of Others*, New York 2003, p. 48.

20 See http://www.judychicago.com/gallery/holocaust-project/hp-artwork/ (last access 5.8.2017).

21 Inke Arns, *History Will Repeat Itself. Strategies of Re-enactment in Contemporary (Media) Art and Performance*, Berlin 2007, online: http://www.inkearns.de/files/2011/01/2007_HWRI-Arns-Kat_dt.pdf (last access 5.8.2017).

22 John Peffer, *Art and the End of Apartheid*, Minneapolis 2009, pp. 55f.

23 The term "energy stock" (Energiekonserve) was elaborated in Warburg's notebook *Grundbegriffe II* (1929), p. 21. Quoted after Ernst H. Gombrich, *Aby Warburg – eine intellektuelle Biographie*, Frankfurt a.M. 1981, p. 245. Cf. also Aby Warburg, *Der Tod des Orpheus. Bilder zu dem Vortrag über Dürer und die Italienische Antike*, (1905), newly edited by Dieter Wuttke, Peter Schmidt, *Aby Warburg und die Ikonologie*, Wiesbaden 1993.

24 Cf. Christoph Hamann, *Pieta 1967, Jürgen Henschels Fotografie des toten Benno Ohnesorg. Das kanonische Bild*, in: *Praxis Geschichte* 20 (2007), pp. 56–57.

25 Ruth Kerkham Simbao, *The Thirtieth Anniversary of the Soweto Uprisings: Reading the Shadow in Sam Nzima's Iconic Photograph of Hector Pieterson*, in: *African Arts*, Vol. 40, No. 2 (2007), pp. 52–69.

26 Cf. Alfred Gell, *Art and Agency. An Anthropological Theory*, Oxford 1998.

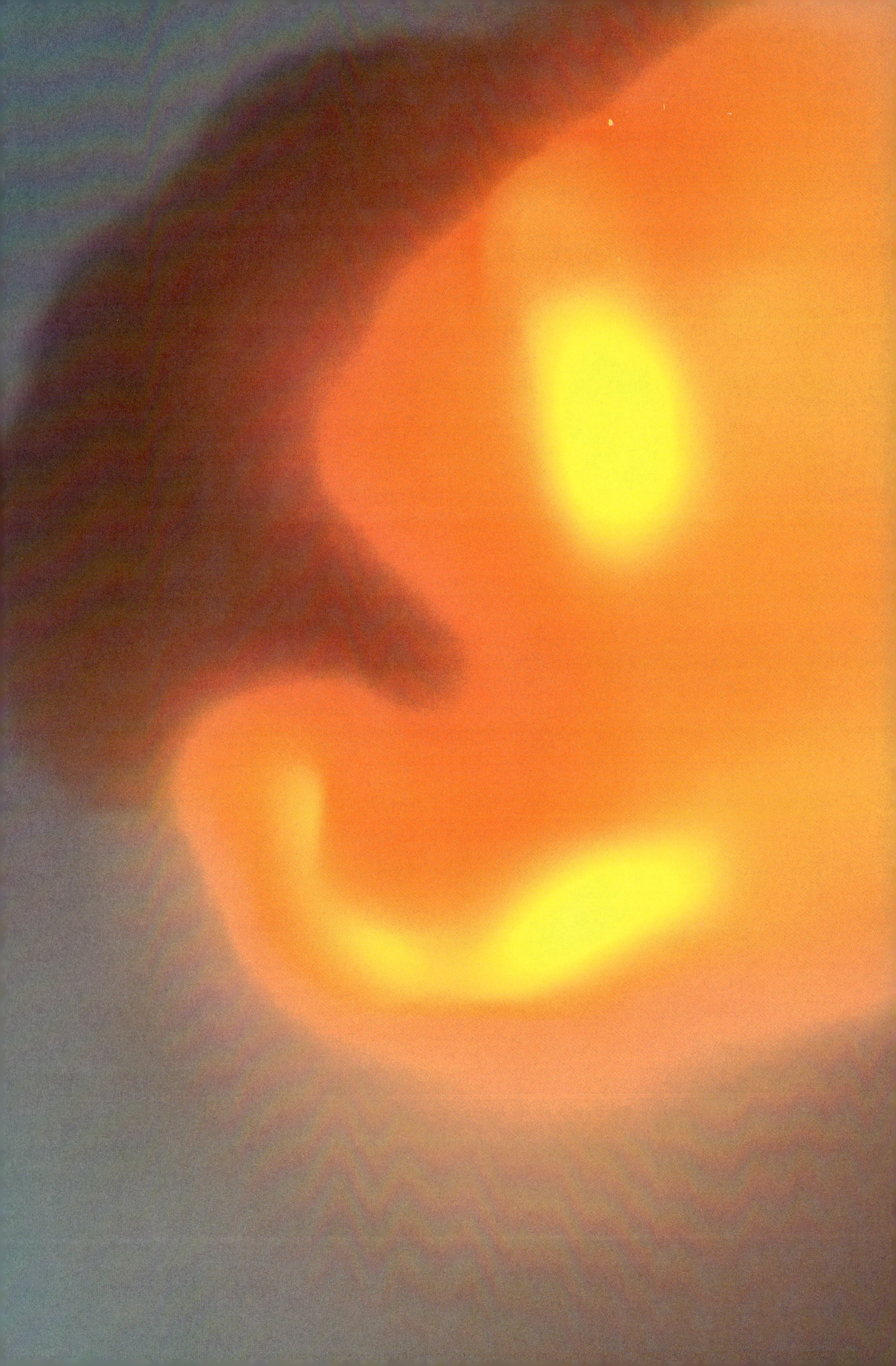

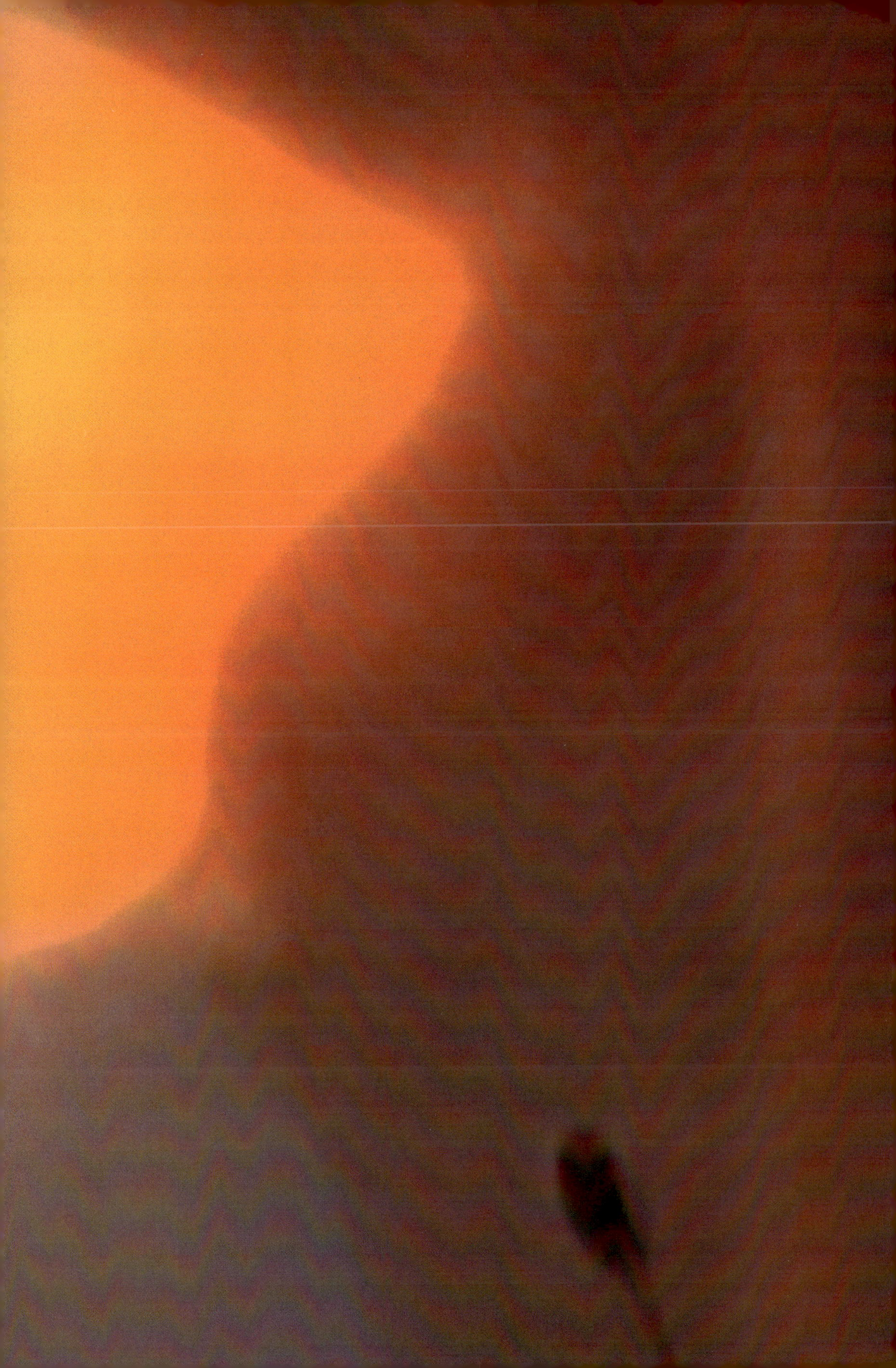

Ernst van Alphen

"Poor Images" and the Affect of Exhibitionism

Ernst van Alphen

„Poor Images" und der Affekt des Exhibitionismus

In the last ten years a turn to affect has taken place. The work of French philosopher Gilles Deleuze and American psychologist Silvan Tomkins are the sources of inspiration for an understanding of how texts and images work beyond—or before, or below—signification. In many respects, this has been a paradigmatic revolution because with structuralism and post-structuralism all attention was focused on the production of meaning by texts and images. But already 40 years ago, Susan Sontag, in her programmatic essay *Against Interpretation*, pleaded passionately for more serious attention to the affective operations of art and literature. She declared that the prevalent idea that a work of art is its content, or that a work of art says something, is "today mainly a hindrance, a nuisance, a subtle or not so subtle philistinism."[1] According to Sontag, the transformation of texts or works of art into meanings is a revenge of the intellect upon art. "To interpret is to impoverish, to deplete the world—in order to set up a shadow world of 'meanings'."[2] To counter this tendency she pleads for a more immediate experience of the object or text itself. What is important now is to recover our senses. We must learn to see more, to hear more, to feel more. And she ends her essay with the famous words that "in place of a hermeneutics of art we need an erotics of art."[3]

For Sontag, hermeneutics is not bad in itself, but it has become a harmful, or better yet powerless, mode of reading at this particular historical moment:

> Interpretation takes the sensory experience of the work of art for granted, and proceeds from there. This cannot be taken for granted, now. Think of the sheer multiplication of works of art available to every one of us, superadded to the conflicting tastes and odours and sights of the urban environment that bombard our senses. Ours is a culture based on excess, on overproduction; this results in a steady loss of sharpness in our sensory experience. All the conditions of modern life—its material plenitude, its sheer crowdedness—conjoin to dull our sensory faculties.[4]

Sontag's advocacy for an erotic, affective approach to art is historically motivated: the conditions of modern life of the 1960s were dulling the sensory faculties and thus requiring more attention for affect. But the 1960s are not the same as the beginning of the 21st century. What these different periods have in common is radical changes in how subjects relate to their social environment. But whereas its explosion of commodity culture defines the 1960s, an increasing explosion of information, especially through social media and the Internet, characterises the 1990s and after. In both periods the subject is exposed to abundance, an abundance that is ultimately sensorial and brings with it an increased sensitivity for affects.

When Sontag claims that commodity culture has dulled our senses, she seems to suggest that affects no longer play a role in that kind of culture. However, what she means is that affects play a more important role than ever, but we are no longer able to deal with them.[5] Our culture excels in

In den letzten zehn Jahren hat eine Wende zum Affekt stattgefunden. Die Arbeit des französischen Philosophen Gilles Deleuze und des amerikanischen Psychologen Silvan Tomkins sind die Inspiration für ein Verständnis der Funktionsweise von Texten und Bildern jenseits von Signifikation – oder auch vor oder unterhalb von ihr. In vielerlei Hinsicht ist dies eine paradigmatische Revolution, denn im Strukturalismus und im Poststrukturalismus konzentrierte sich alle Aufmerksamkeit auf die Produktion von Bedeutung durch Texte und Bilder. Doch bereits vor vierzig Jahren plädierte Susan Sontag in ihrem programmatischen Essay *Gegen Interpretation* leidenschaftlich für eine ernsthafte Auseinandersetzung mit den affektiven Verfahren von Kunst und Literatur. Sie behauptet dort, die vorherrschende Vorstellung, ein Kunstwerk sei sein Inhalt, oder es sage etwas aus, sei heute „in erster Linie ein Hindernis, eine Last, eine subtile oder auch weniger subtile Philisterei".[1] Sontag zufolge ist das Überführen von Texten oder Kunstwerken in Bedeutungen eine Rache des Intellekts an der Kunst. „Interpretieren heißt die Welt arm und leer machen – um eine Schattenwelt der ‚Bedeutungen' zu errichten."[2] Um dieser Tendenz entgegenzuwirken, plädiert sie für eine direktere Erfahrung des Objekts oder Textes selbst. Jetzt sei es wichtig, unsere Sinne wiederzuentdecken. Wir müssten lernen, mehr zu sehen, mehr zu hören, mehr zu fühlen. Sie beendet ihren Essay mit den berühmten Worten: „Statt einer Hermeneutik der Kunst brauchen wir eine Erotik der Kunst."[3]

Für Sontag ist Hermeneutik nicht an sich schlecht, aber sie ist ein schädlicher oder besser gesagt kraftloser Modus des Lesens in diesem speziellen historischen Moment geworden.

> Die Interpretation setzt ein sinnliches Erlebnis des Kunstwerks als selbstverständlich und basiert darauf. Aber dieses sinnliche Erlebnis lässt sich heute nicht mehr ohne weiteres voraussetzen. Man denke allein daran, dass jedem von uns heute ein Vielfaches an Kunstwerken zugänglich ist, dazu die zahllosen widersprüchlichen Geschmacks- und Geruchsempfindungen und die optischen Eindrücke der Stadtschaft, die unsere Sinne bombardieren. Unsere Kultur beruht auf dem Übermaß, der Überproduktion: das Ergebnis ist ein stetig fortschreitender Rückgang der Schärfe unserer sinnlichen Erfahrung. Sämtliche Bedingungen des modernen Lebens – sein materieller Überfluss, seine Überladenheit – bewirken eine Abstumpfung unserer sensorischen Fähigkeiten.[4]

Sontags Eintreten für eine erotische, affektive Herangehensweise ist historisch motiviert. Es sind die modernen Lebensbedingungen in den 1960er Jahren, die die sensorischen Fähigkeiten abstumpfen lassen und dem Affekt mehr Aufmerksamkeit verschaffen. Die 1960er Jahre unterscheiden sich stark vom Beginn des 21. Jahrhunderts. Was diese unterschiedlichen Epochen jedoch gemeinsam haben, sind die radikalen Veränderungen hinsichtlich dessen, wie Subjekte sich auf ihre gesellschaftliche Umgebung beziehen. Während eine Explosion der Warenkultur die 1960er Jahre

signification and interpretation, and as a result we have a blind spot for affects, how they work and what they do. The real problem is not the dulling of our senses, but that we no longer know how to recognise affects and how to process them. The reason for this increased insensitivity for affects is not only cultural, but also theoretical. As Brian Massumi has argued, our cultural-theoretical-political vocabulary offers few possibilities for dealing with affect. Our entire vocabulary has been derived from theories of signification. These theories and approaches "are incomplete if they operate only on the semantic or semiotic level, however that level is defined (linguistically, logically, narratologically, ideologically, or all of these in combination) as a Symbolic. What they lose, precisely, is the expression *event*—in favour of structure."[6]

Different as they are, Sontag's and Massumi's pleas for more attention to transmissions of affect, both imply that there should be *less* attention to signification and interpretation. Theoretically, because our vocabulary has already done that excessively and abundantly. Historically, because the explosion of information since the 1990s has brought with it an implosion of meaning. As a result, human subjects seem to act less and less upon meanings, insights or knowledge, and unreflectively more and more upon affects. The recent phenomenon of the success of populist political parties demonstrates this convincingly. One of the reasons for this implosion of meaning is the increasing role of social media. The significance of texts and images disseminated through social media is usually of little importance. They are disseminated not because of what they mean, but with regard to how they work performatively and affectively.

In the exhibition *Affect Me*, artists relate with their works in one way or another to the implosion of meaning through social media and the affects transmitted by the formal and temporal characteristics of social media. I will distinguish the following kinds of formal and temporal conditions of the implosion of meaning and the release of affect in social media: contextless images and the implosion of meaning, affect transmitted by poor images, and affect transmitted by exhibitionism. I will reflect on the formal and temporal structures of social media and how they shape affects. This may suggest that I believe in a medium specificity of social media that is formal. However, that is not the case.[7] Although social media, like all other media, have some formal conditions, their specificity is mainly determined by specific practices of users deploying these media. The addictive use of social media by large groups of people is highly specific. The practices of these groups is what I will focus on in order to better understand the formal and temporal conditions of affective transmission by social media. I suggest that also the artists in this exhibition reflect on, and work with, dominant practices in the use of social media. It is through the works of only some of these artists that I will address the affectivity of social media.

definiert, ist die Zeit ab den 1990er Jahren von einer Explosion an Informationen geprägt, insbesondere durch soziale Medien und das Internet. In beiden Epochen ist das Subjekt einem Überfluss ausgesetzt; dieser ist letztendlich sensorisch und bringt eine höhere Empfindlichkeit für Affekte mit sich.

Wenn Sontag behauptet, die Warenkultur habe unsere Sinne abstumpfen lassen, scheint sie anzudeuten, dass Affekte keine Rolle mehr in dieser Art Kultur spielten. Was sie jedoch meint, ist, dass Affekte eine wichtigere Rolle als je zuvor spielen, wir aber nicht mehr mit ihnen umgehen können.[5] Unsere Kultur leistet Hervorragendes auf den Gebieten von Signifikation und Interpretation, in Folge dessen haben wir einen blinden Fleck, wenn es um Affekte und ihre Wirkungsweise geht. Das eigentliche Problem ist nicht das Abstumpfen unserer Sinne, sondern vielmehr, dass wir nicht mehr wissen, wie man Affekte erkennt und sie verarbeitet. Diese wachsende Unempfindlichkeit für Affekte hat nicht nur kulturelle, sondern auch theoretische Gründe. Wie Brian Massumi argumentiert, bietet unser kulturtheoretisches und -politisches Vokabular wenige Möglichkeiten, um mit Affekten umzugehen. Unser gesamtes Vokabular leitet sich von Theorien der Signifikation ab. Diese Theorien und Herangehensweisen sind „unvollständig, wenn sie nur auf der semantischen oder semiotischen Ebene operieren, wie immer diese Ebene auch als ein Symbolisches definiert sein mag (linguistisch, logisch, narratologisch, ideologisch oder alles zusammen). Was sie eben genau verlieren, ist der Ausdruck *Ereignis* – zugunsten von Struktur."[6]

So unterschiedlich sie auch sein mögen, Sontags und Massumis Appelle, den Übertragungen von Affekten mehr Aufmerksamkeit zu widmen, implizieren beide, dass Signifikation und Interpretation *weniger* Aufmerksamkeit zuteil werden sollte. Theoretisch gesehen, weil unser Vokabular ihnen ohnehin schon exzessiv und reichlich Aufmerksamkeit gewidmet hat. Historisch, weil die Explosion von Information seit den 1990er Jahren eine Implosion von Bedeutung mit sich gebracht hat. Infolgedessen scheinen menschliche Subjekte immer weniger nach Bedeutungen, Einsichten und Wissen zu handeln, sondern unreflektiert immer mehr nach Affekten. Das relativ neue Phänomen des Erfolgs populistischer politischer Parteien zeugt davon. Einer der Gründe für diese Implosion der Bedeutung ist die wachsende Rolle der sozialen Medien. Die inhaltliche Aussage von Texten und Bildern, die über soziale Medien verbreitet werden, ist meistens nicht von großer Wichtigkeit. Sie werden nicht wegen ihrer Bedeutung verbreitet, sondern wegen der Art, wie sie performativ und affektiv funktionieren.

In der Ausstellung *Affect Me* beziehen sich Künstler*innen mit ihren Arbeiten auf die eine oder andere Art auf die Implosion von Bedeutung durch die sozialen Medien und die Affekte, die mit den formalen und zeitlichen Eigenschaften der sozialen Medien zusammenhängen. Ich werde folgende formale und zeitliche Bedingungen der Implosion von Bedeutung und der Freisetzung von Affekten in den sozialen Medien unterscheiden: kontextlose Bilder und die Implosion von Bedeutung, von „armen Bildern" ausgelöster Affekt und von Exhibitionismus ausgelöster Affekt. Ich werde die formalen und zeitlichen Strukturen der sozialen Medien reflektieren

Images without Context

The explosion of information since the 1990s through digital media has had as its effect the implosion of meaning with the release of affects as a result. This happened and happens most of all through the dissemination of images. Although modern media like film and television and new media like the Internet and cell phones are not exclusively visual, it is their visual character that usually dominates our senses.

The intimate relation between the implosion of meaning and the release of affects is demonstrated by the recent "post-truth" regime in populist politics, especially, but not exclusively, in the US. This regime accommodates flagrant lies and contradictions in order to produce its own truth as affect. In 2016 the Oxford Dictionaries declared "post-truth" as word of the year. The editors define it as "relating to or denoting circumstances in which objective facts are less influential in shaping public opinion than appeals to emotion and personal belief." They explain that the concept gained ground against the backdrop of "the rise of social media as a news source" in combination with a "growing distrust of facts offered up by the establishment."[8]

How can the rise of social media as a news source have this effect on politics? "Post-truth" politics does not rely on meaningful truths and positions but on strong affects. Traditionally affects have played an important role in politics; they were mobilised in debating important political issues. As Chantal Mouffe has argued, with the rise of "consensus democracy after the Cold War, political thinkers welcomed a so-called post-political world, in which passions would have no place in a politics dominated by reason."[9] Maria Boletsi explains: "Consensus democracy envisions politics as devoid of substantial antagonisms and dissent, and focuses on a rational treatment of political questions without a mobilisation of affects."[10] Before consensus democracy became standard, affects were mobilised as "shocks to thought," to meaningful and political positioning. With consensus democracy affect is displaced; it no longer enables and supports meaningful politics. Affects are now used as means of trivializing political discourse. "Post-truths" replace meaningful truths, and affects undermine politics instead of supporting them. Social media function as mediators and distribution channels of such "post-truths" and of affects trivialising meaningful politics.

Images and messages spread by social media and the Web usually miss contexts that provide meaning and background to what these images show and tell. Thomas Hirschhorn's installation *Subjecter (Katastrophé)* (2010)

und untersuchen, wie diese Affekte prägen. Daraus ließe sich ableiten, dass ich von einer formalen Medienspezifität sozialer Medien ausgehe. Dies ist allerdings nicht der Fall.[7] Obgleich soziale Medien – wie alle Medien – einige formale Bedingungen haben, wird ihre Spezifizität vor allem durch spezifische Praktiken der Nutzer*innen dieser Medien geprägt. Das Suchtpotenzial sozialer Medien für große Gruppen von Menschen trifft in hohem Maße nur auf diese User*innen zu. Ich werde mich auf die Praktiken dieser Gruppen konzentrieren, um die formalen und zeitlichen Konditionen von affektiver Übertragung durch soziale Medien besser zu verstehen. Meiner Meinung nach reflektieren auch die Künstler*innen dieser Ausstellung über die vorherrschenden Praktiken der Nutzung sozialer Medien und arbeiten sich an ihnen ab. Anhand der Werke einiger dieser Künstler*innen werde ich die Affektivität sozialer Medien beleuchten.

Bilder ohne Kontext

Die Explosion von Information seit den 1990er Jahren durch die digitalen Medien hatte eine Implosion von Bedeutung mit der Freisetzung von Affekten zur Folge. Dies geschah und geschieht vor allem durch die Verbreitung von Bildern. Obwohl moderne Medien wie Film und Fernsehen und Neue Medien wie das Internet und Mobiltelefone nicht exklusiv visuell sind, beherrscht doch vor allem ihre Visualität unsere Sinne.

Die enge Verbindung zwischen der Implosion von Bedeutung und der Freisetzung von Affekten zeigt sich in dem neuerdings auftretenden „postfaktischen" Regime in der populistischen Politik, insbesondere, aber keineswegs ausschließlich, in den USA. Dieses Regime setzt offenkundige Lügen und Widersprüche ein, um seine eigene Wahrheit als Affekt zu produzieren. Oxford Dictionaries erklärte 2016 *post-truth* zum Wort des Jahres. Die Redaktion des Verlages definiert den Begriff folgendermaßen: „[Post-truth] bezieht sich auf oder bezeichnet Umstände, in denen objektive Tatsachen weniger einflussreich für die Bildung der öffentlichen Meinung sind als Appelle an Emotion und persönliche Überzeugungen." Weiterhin wird dort erklärt, das Konzept habe vor dem Hintergrund „des Aufstiegs der sozialen Medien als Nachrichtenquelle" in Kombination mit einem „steigenden Misstrauen gegen vom Establishment angebotenen Tatsachen" an Boden gewonnen.[8]

Wie kann der Aufstieg der sozialen Medien als Nachrichtenquelle diesen Effekt auf die Politik haben? Postfaktische Politik stützt sich nicht auf bedeutsame Wahrheiten oder Positionen, sondern auf starke Affekte. Traditionell spielen Affekte eine wichtige Rolle in der Politik; sie wurden stets in den Debatten wichtiger politischer Fragen mobilisiert. Wie Chantal Mouffe argumentiert, begrüßten mit dem Aufstieg der „Konsensdemokratie nach dem Kalten Krieg politische Denker eine sogenannte post-politische Welt, in der Leidenschaften keinen Platz in einer von Vernunft beherrschten Politik haben sollten"[9]. Maria Boletsi erklärt: „Konsensdemokratie stellt sich Politik ohne Antagonismen und Dissens vor und konzentriert sich

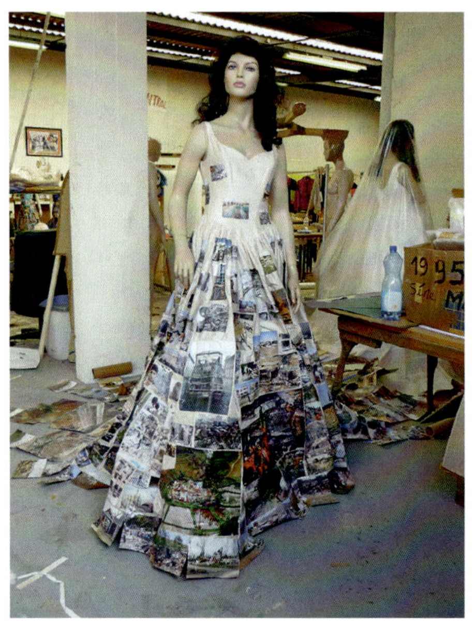

addresses this lack. Photographs of human drama in the face of war and natural disasters are scattered on the skirt and train of a white wedding dress. The photographs are the kind of images disseminated widely via social

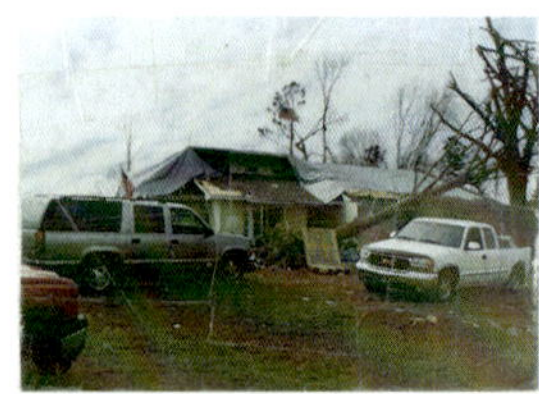

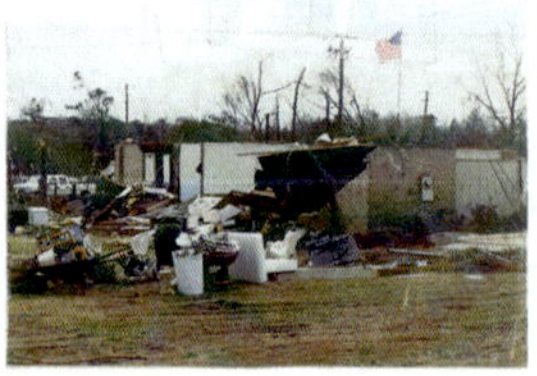

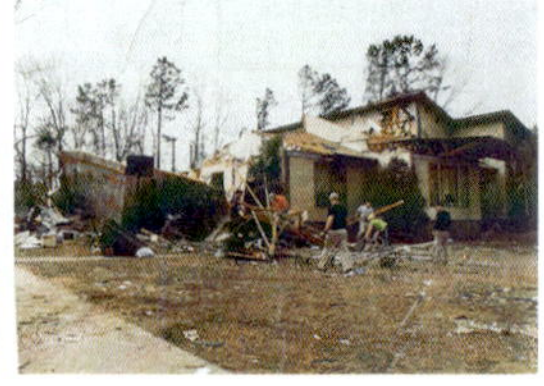

media to share an impression of an event. People in war zones or victims of natural disasters try to get the attention of the rest of the world by sharing such images. But access to the event is only provided by means of the shared image, not by contexts and background information. Because

Thomas Hirschhorn, *Subjecter (Katastrophé)*, 2010, studio view

Thomas Hirschhorn, *Subjecter (Katastrophé)*, 2010, details

auf eine rationale Behandlung politischer Fragen ohne eine Mobilisierung von Affekten."[10] Bevor die Konsensdemokratie zum Standard wurde, wurden Affekte als „Schocks für das Denken" eingesetzt, für ein bedeutsames politisches Positionieren. Mit der Konsensdemokratie wird der Affekt verdrängt; er ermöglicht und stützt keine aussagekräftige Politik mehr; Affekte werden nun als Mittel zur Trivialisierung des politischen Diskurses eingesetzt. Das „Postfaktische" ersetzt bedeutsame Wahrheiten und Affekte untergraben die Politik, statt sie zu stützen. Die sozialen Medien fungieren als Vermittler und Verbreitungskanäle dieses Postfaktischen und der Affekte, die bedeutsame Politik trivialisieren.

In sozialen Medien und im Netz verbreitete Bilder und Botschaften lassen gewöhnlich Kontexte weg, die den Hintergrund beleuchten und eine Bedeutung dessen anbieten würden, was diese Bilder zeigen und erzählen. Thomas Hirschhorns Installation *Subjecter (Katastrophé)* (2010) thematisiert

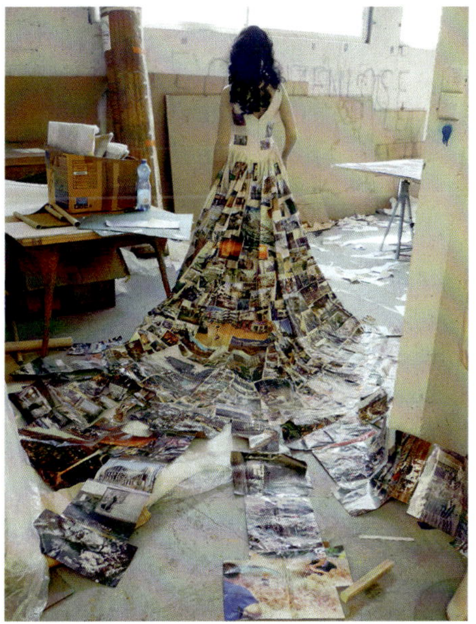

diesen Mangel. Fotografien menschlicher Dramen angesichts von Krieg und Naturkatastrophen sind über den Rock und die Schleppe eines weißen Hochzeitskleids verteilt. Derartige Fotografien werden in großem Stil über

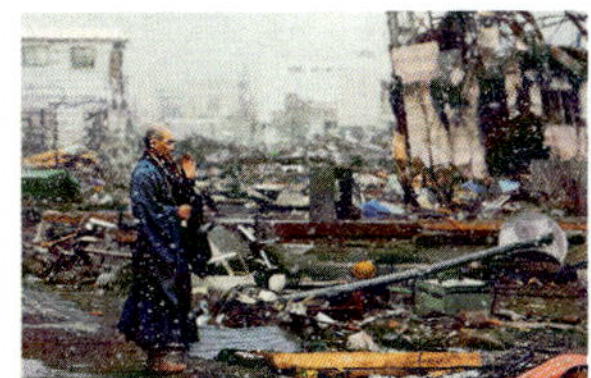

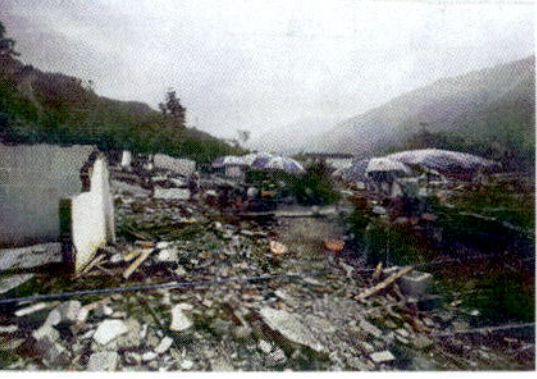

die sozialen Medien verbreitet, um einen Eindruck von einem Ereignis mit anderen zu teilen. Menschen in Kriegsgebieten oder Opfer von Naturkatastrophen versuchen, die Aufmerksamkeit der Welt auf sich zu ziehen, indem sie solche Bilder verbreiten. Aber Zugang zu dem Ereignis wird

Thomas Hirschhorn, *Subjecter (Katastrophé)*, 2010, Atelieransicht

Thomas Hirschhorn, *Subjecter (Katastrophé)*, 2010, Details

the events on the images are of human drama they release strong affects in the viewers. But for the viewers it is difficult to channel or process these affects, for instance into meaningful action, because the events are devoid of context, meaning, substance. The heterogeneous collection of contextless images in Hirschhorn's installation does not enable access to the background of the conflicts and disasters shown in the images. Whereas the affective intensity of the images is strong, their meaning is empty.

The work *Facebook* (2011) by the artist D.H. Saur in this show is based on a similar mechanism of undermined significance and the release of affects. His images of graffiti made during the "Arab Spring" were part of political events directed by people using Facebook, which is why the events are also called the "Facebook Revolution." Presenting these images in relation to each other and comparing them reveals that many of the images have been edited and that their references are ambiguous and cannot be trusted. Here, too, an implosion of meaning takes place, but that does not prevent the images from having an affective charge.

The Affects of "Poor Images"

German photographer Thomas Ruff never mistakes a photographic image for the world it shows. He systematically explores different photographic genres such as portrait photography, architectural photography, landscape photography, and nude photography; different uses of the medium in scientific photography and press photography; the distribution of photographic images in various media; and last but not least the different conditions of the medium in analogue as well as digital form, as negatives, or as photograms (camera-less photography).

Among the many photographic genres Ruff has taken on, nude photography occupies a special place. The stakes of this generic exploration demonstrates a paradigmatic revolution in visual culture, namely the transformation of visuality defined by voyeuristic positions into one determined by exhibitionist positions. In view of the fact that this transformation is more outspoken, and more literally at stake in Ruff's nude photography, I will first pay attention to his exploration of this genre, and then see if and how it applies to his *jpeg* series (2006) that is part of the exhibition.

Ruff was not interested in "contemporary nude photography of the kind currently carried on by fashion photographers, who take supposedly interesting photographs of pretty models in some pleasant ambiance."[11] Implicitly, Ruff seems to take distance from successful photographers like Helmut Newton. He did some research on the Internet and found there a whole marketplace of pornographic images that interested him much more. He was especially interested in exploring the conditions under which such imaginary is perceived.

nur mittels des geteilten Bildes gewährt, nicht durch Kontexte und Hintergründe. Weil es Bilder von menschlichen Dramen sind, lösen sie bei den Betrachter*innen starke Affekte aus. Aber für die Betrachter*innen ist es schwierig, diese Affekte zu kanalisieren oder zu verarbeiten, sie beispielsweise in sinnvolles Handeln zu übersetzen, denn es fehlt an Kontext, Bedeutung, Substanz. Die heterogene Sammlung von kontextlosen Bildern in Hirschhorns Installation ermöglicht keinerlei Zugang zum Hintergrund der in den Bildern gezeigten Konflikte und Katastrophen. Während die affektive Intensität der Bilder hoch ist, ist ihre Bedeutung leer.

Die Arbeit *Facebook* (2011) des Künstlers D. H. Saur in dieser Ausstellung basiert auf einem ähnlichen Mechanismus von untergrabener Bedeutung und der Freisetzung von Affekten. Seine Bilder von Graffitis, die während des sogenannten Arabischen Frühlings entstandenen sind, waren Teil politischer Ereignisse, die von Leuten über Facebook gesteuert wurden, weshalb diese Ereignisse auch als „Facebook-Revolution" bekannt sind. Diese Bilder in Bezug zueinander zu präsentieren und sie miteinander zu vergleichen, offenbart, dass viele von ihnen bearbeitet wurden, ihre Verweise mehrdeutig sind und man ihnen nicht vertrauen kann. Hier findet ebenfalls eine Implosion von Bedeutung statt, aber das nimmt den Bildern nichts von ihrer affektiven Aufladung.

Die Affekte von „Poor images"

Der deutsche Fotograf Thomas Ruff verwechselt ein fotografisches Bild nie mit der Welt, die es zeigt. Systematisch erkundet er unterschiedliche fotografische Genres wie Porträtfotografie, Architekturfotografie, Landschaftsfotografie und Aktfotografie; unterschiedliche Anwendungen des Mediums in Wissenschaftsfotografie und Pressefotografie; die Verbreitung fotografischer Bilder in diversen Medien; und nicht zuletzt die unterschiedlichen Bedingungen des Mediums als analog oder digital, als Negative oder Fotogramme (kameralose Fotografie).

Unter den vielen fotografischen Genres, die Ruff aufgegriffen hat, nimmt die Aktfotografie einen besonderen Raum ein. Was bei dieser generischen Erkundung auf dem Spiel steht, zeugt von einer paradigmatischen Revolution in der Bildkultur, nämlich die Transformation von einer durch voyeuristische Positionen definierten Visualität in eine, die von exhibitionistischen Positionen bestimmt wird. Weil diese Transformation in Ruffs Aktfotografie offensichtlicher ist und es hier wortwörtlich darum geht, werde ich meine Aufmerksamkeit zunächst auf seine Erkundung dieser Gattung richten und dann sehen, ob und wie dies auch auf seine Serie von *jpegs* (2006) zutrifft, die Teil der Ausstellung ist.

Ruff interessierte sich nicht für „die ganze zeitgenössische Aktfotografie, wie sie im Moment von Modefotografen betrieben wird, die hübsche Models in irgendeinem schönen Ambiente vermeintlich interessant nackt abbilden"[11]. Implizit scheint sich Ruff von einem erfolgreichen Fotografen

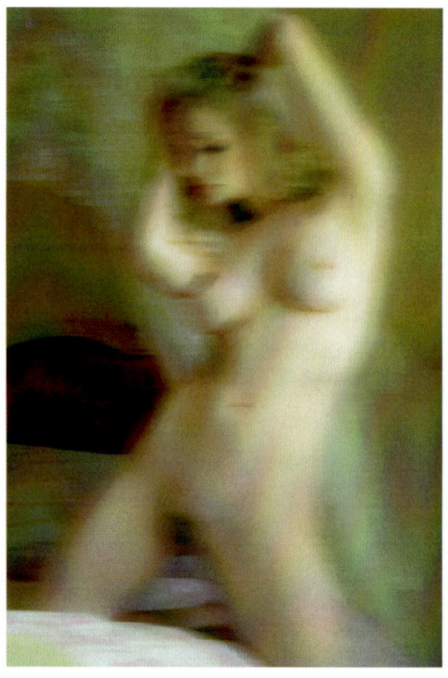

The pornographic images that can be found on the Internet are, to use the words of Hito Steyerl, "poor images."[12] She defines the poor image as follows:

> The poor image is a copy in motion. Its quality is bad, its resolution substandard. As it accelerates, it deteriorates. It is a ghost of an image, a preview, a thumbnail, an errant idea, an itinerant image distributed for free, squeezed through slow digital connections. Compressed, reproduced, ripped, remixed, as well as copied and pasted into other channels of distribution.[13]

Steyerl's description is not only a precise description of pornographic images on the Internet, but also of Ruff's enlargements of them. Both are ghosts of images and poor in all respects. Ruff emphasised the poorness of the images by enlarging them to very large formats of up to 200 x 130 cm. The visible pixels create an overall blurred image. The blurred condition of his images seems to have been required by the "ugly" nature of pornography; however, it installs a specific mode of looking that is highly self-reflective. Conventional pornography in photography and film always relies on two crucial components. First of all, its reality effect. This explains why pornography is always realistic; sexual stimulation by means of modernist or postmodernist texts or images seems to be unconceivable. The other crucial element is the voyeuristic gaze it enables. The viewer is outside of the scene that he looks at, belonging to another world. This voyeuristic positioning provides power and pleasure to the viewer. Both defining elements of pornography seem to be missing in the poor images of Internet pornography, and

Thomas Ruff, *Nudes cs02*, 2011

wie Helmut Newton zu distanzieren. Er recherchierte im Internet und fand dort einen ganzen Markt von pornografischen Bildern, die ihn viel mehr

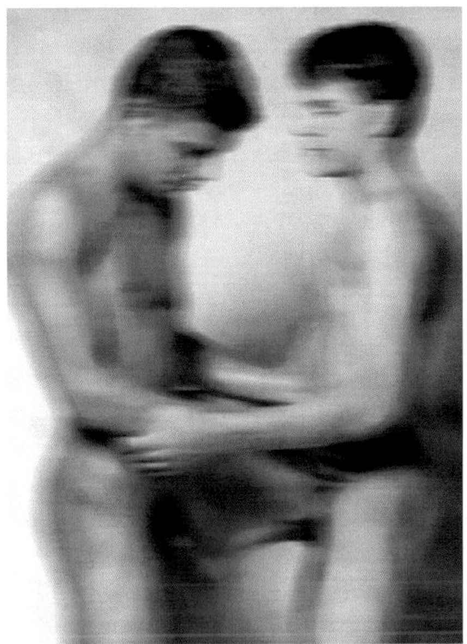

interessierten. Insbesondere interessieren ihn die Bedingungen, unter denen solche Bilder wahrgenommen werden.

Die pornografischen Bilder im Internet sind, um einen Begriff von Hito Steyerl zu verwenden, „poor images".[12] Sie definiert das „arme Bild" folgendermaßen:

> Das arme Bild ist eine Kopie in Bewegung. Es ist grob, seine Auflösung ist unterdurchschnittlich. Während es sich beschleunigt, verschlechtert es sich. Es ist der Geist eines Bildes, eine Vorschau, ein Miniaturbild, eine umherstreifende Idee, ein sich wiederholendes, gratis verbreitetes Bild, durch langsame digitale Verbindungen gepresst. Gestaucht, reproduziert, eingerissen, geremixt und auch kopiert und in andere Verbreitungskanäle eingesetzt.[13]

Dies ist nicht nur eine genaue Beschreibung von pornografischen Bildern im Internet, sondern auch von Ruffs Vergrößerungen von ihnen. Beide sind Geister von Bildern und in jeder Hinsicht „arm". Ruff betont die „Armut" dieser Bilder, indem er sie zu sehr großen Formaten von bis zu 200 x 130 cm vergrößert. Die sichtbaren Pixel schaffen ein insgesamt verschwommenes Bild. Das „hässliche" Wesen der Pornografie scheint den verschwommenen Zustand seiner Bilder zu fordern; allerdings installiert dies einen spezifischen Modus des Sehens, der in hohem Maße selbstreflexiv ist. Konventionelle Pornografie in Fotografie und Film stützt sich immer auf zwei entscheidende Komponenten. Erstens auf ihren Realitätseffekt. Dies erklärt, warum Pornografie immer realistisch ist; sexuelle Stimulierung mittels moderner oder postmoderner Texte oder Bilder ist schwer vorstellbar.

Thomas Ruff, *Nudes vg02*, 2000

even more so in the enhanced poor images of Thomas Ruff. The poor images do not function like windows through which the viewer voyeuristically gazes at sexual action. They are rather opaque screens onto which the viewer can project his fantasy in order to be part of the scene he is watching.

The poverty of the image is, I contend, an important precondition for this transformation of window into screen. I will argue this by the detour of another new media: not photography, but the webcam. Although usually producing moving instead of still images, the webcam excels in producing poor images. Only recent practices in the old "new" medium of photography can be qualified as poor. Internet pornographic still images are a prime example.

The visual medium of the webcam is the small camera, which sends images to a computer connected to the Internet. After this medium was introduced in the mid-1990s, it has become a standard apparatus in many studios, households and bedrooms. I do not want to suggest that this medium has any essential function or specificity. Its medium specificity is only partly defined by its technical features and possibilities. It is also determined by how it is used through historical and cultural practices. New media uses and practices tend to cause changes in the media landscape at large. A new media practice can cause shifts in the functions and practices of other media. For example, the introduction of photography into the media landscape of the mid-19th century has deprived painting of, or perhaps we should say liberated from, some of its functions. The same can be said of the webcam. The webcam has fulfilled some ideals which were earlier pursued with the video camera and longer ago with the film camera. The dream concerning one medium is realised in another, more recent medium. For many webcam users the ambition of a comprehensive representation of the world, spatially as well as temporally is finally fulfilled: "The webcam makes possible the endless, unedited film, the eternal film."[14]

The ways and contexts in which webcams are being used are many. Its first use is extremely simple and is exemplary for most of its later uses. The very first webcam was used in 1993 in the department of computer science at the University of Cambridge for surveilling a coffeepot. In order not to walk in vain to the room where one could get coffee, the so-called "Trojan room", students installed this new apparatus to the pot and connected it to their computers so that they could check from their desk if there was any coffee left. Two years later they connected these images to the World Wide Web and the information was shared with millions of people. The fact that so many people watched these images was not motivated by what the images showed, but by what they promised: a comprehensive representation of the world. Soon after, in 1996, Jennifer Ringley, a student from Pennsylvania, materialised part of the promise by showing on the Web images of her life at home in real time, taken by a camera connected to her computer. Internet users could see everything she was doing: playing with her animals, sleeping, combing her hair, making love with her boyfriend and so on. The stream of images depicted life, it was unedited, and it was in real time. The webcam is used as LifeCam.

Das andere entscheidende Element ist der voyeuristische Blick, den sie ermöglicht. Die Betrachter*innen sind außerhalb der Szene, die sie betrachten, gehören zu einer anderen Welt. Diese voyeuristische Positionierung gibt den Betrachter*innen Macht und bereitet ihnen Lust. Beide definierenden Elemente der Pornografie scheinen in den „armen Bildern" der Internetpornografie zu fehlen, und erst recht in den Bildern von Thomas Ruff mit ihrer verstärkt minderwertigen Auflösung. Die „armen Bilder" funktionieren nicht wie Fenster, durch die der Betrachter voyeuristisch sexuelle Aktivitäten ansieht. Sie sind vielmehr opake Bildschirme, auf die der Betrachter seine Fantasie, Teil der von ihm betrachteten Szene zu sein, projizieren kann.

Die „Armut" der Bilder ist, so denke ich, eine wichtige Voraussetzung für diese Transformation des Fensters in einen Bildschirm. Ich möchte dies anhand eines Umwegs zu einem anderen Medium erklären: nicht zur Fotografie, sondern zur Webcam. Obwohl sie normalerweise bewegte statt unbewegter Bilder produziert, macht die Webcam hervorragende „arme Bilder". Vergleichbar lassen sich nur jüngere Praktiken in dem alten „neuen" Medium der Fotografie als „arm" bezeichnen. Pornografische Internetbilder sind ein herausragendes Beispiel.

Die Webcam ist eine kleine Kamera, die Bilder an einen mit dem Internet verbundenen Computer sendet. Nachdem dieses Medium Mitte der 1990er Jahre eingeführt wurde, ist es zur Standardausstattung vieler Ateliers, Haushalte und Schlafzimmer geworden. Ich meine nicht, dass dieses Medium irgendeine essentielle Funktion oder Spezifität hat. Seine Medienspezifität ist nur teilweise von seinen technischen Eigenschaften und Möglichkeiten definiert. Sie ist ebenfalls davon bestimmt, wie sie durch historische und kulturelle Praktiken eingesetzt wird. Neue Medienanwendungen und Praktiken neigen dazu, in der Medienlandschaft insgesamt Veränderungen auszulösen. Eine neue Medienpraxis kann Veränderungen in den Funktionen und Praktiken anderer Medien verursachen. Die Einführung der Fotografie in die Medienlandschaft Mitte des 19. Jahrhunderts beispielsweise hat der Malerei einige ihrer Funktionen genommen, oder vielleicht sollte man eher sagen, sie von einigen ihrer Funktionen befreit. Dasselbe lässt sich von der Webcam sagen. Die Webcam hat einige Ideale erfüllt, die zuvor von der Videokamera, und davor von der Filmkamera angestrebt wurden. Der Traum des einen Mediums wird in einem anderen, jüngeren Medium umgesetzt. Für viele Webcamnutzer*innen ist das Ziel einer umfassenden Repräsentation der Welt, räumlich wie zeitlich, endlich erreicht: „Die Webcam ermöglicht den endlosen, unredigierten, den ewigen Film."[14]

Die Arten und Kontexte, in denen Webcams eingesetzt werden können, sind vielfältig. Ihre erste Nutzung war extrem einfach und exemplarisch für die meisten späteren Nutzungen. Die allererste Webcam wurde 1993 im Institut für Informatik an der Universität Cambridge zur Überwachung einer Kaffeemaschine eingesetzt. Damit niemand umsonst in den Raum gehen musste, in dem es Kaffee gab – den sogenannten „Trojan room" –, installierten Student*innen diesen neuen Apparat neben der Kaffeemaschine und

But the dream or ideal materialised by the webcam is not new at all. There are several films and videos by artists demonstrating a similar practice. A prime example is Andy Warhol's film *Sleep* (1963). It shows

the poet John Giorno, Warhol's lover at the time, while he is sleeping. He is filmed from a number of different angels and some shots are repeated. Although this film is not really, or not completely in real time, it creates this impression. In that respect, Warhol's *Empire* (1964) is more radical.

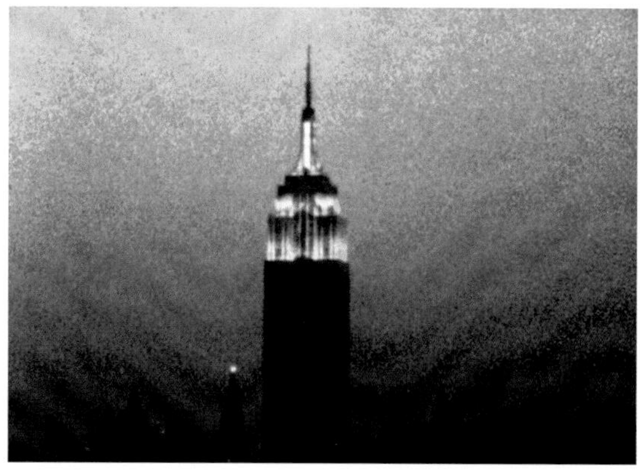

Andy Warhol, *Empire*, 1964, film still

verbanden ihn mit ihren Computern. So konnten sie von ihren Schreibtischen aus nachsehen, ob noch Kaffee da war. Zwei Jahre später stellten sie diese Bilder in das World Wide Web ein, und die Information wurde mit Millionen Menschen geteilt. Dass so viele Menschen diese Bilder betrachteten, war nicht davon motiviert, was die Bilder zeigten, sondern, was sie versprachen: eine umfassende Repräsentation der Welt. Nicht viel später, im Jahr 1996, materialisierte Jennifer Ringley, eine Studentin aus Pennsylvania, einen Teil dieses Versprechens, indem sie Internetbilder ihres Lebens zu Hause in Echtzeit zeigte, die von einer mit ihrem Computer verbundenen Kamera aufgenommen wurden. Internetuser*innen konnten alles sehen, was sie so machte: mit ihren Haustieren spielen, schlafen, sich die Haare kämmen, mit ihrem Freund schlafen und so weiter. Der Bilderstrom war das Leben, unredigiert und in Echtzeit. Die Webcam wurde als Lifecam verwendet.

Aber der Traum oder das Ideal, das von der Webcam materialisiert wurde, war überhaupt nicht neu. Es gibt diverse Filme und Videos von Künstler*innen, in denen eine ähnliche Praxis vorgeführt wird. Ein Musterbeispiel ist Andy Warhols Film *Sleep* (1963). Er zeigt den Dichter John

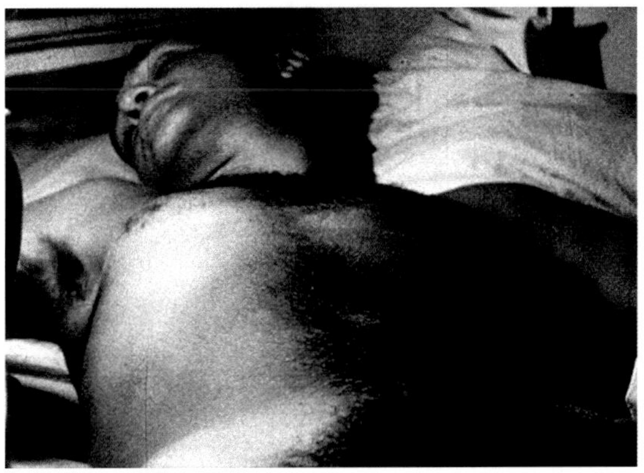

Giorno, Warhols damaligen Liebhaber, schlafend. Er wird aus einer Reihe unterschiedlicher Blickwinkel gefilmt und einige Einstellungen werden wiederholt. Obwohl dieser Film nicht wirklich oder jedenfalls nicht komplett in Echtzeit ist, erweckt er doch den Anschein, als wäre er es. In dieser Hinsicht ist Warhols *Empire* (1964) radikaler. Er besteht aus acht Stunden

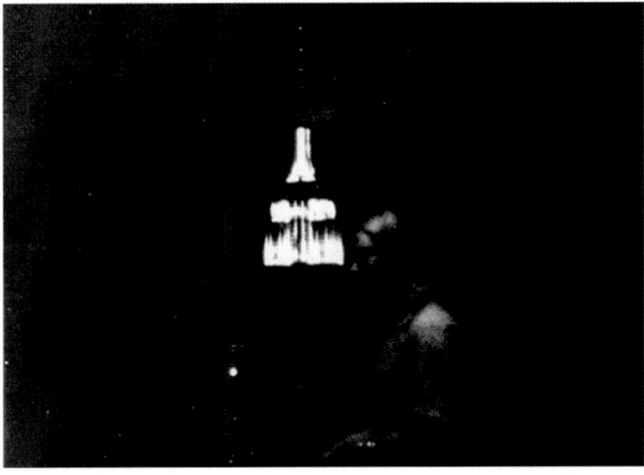

Andy Warhol, *Sleep*, 1963, Filmstill
Andy Warhol, *Empire*, 1964, Filmstill

It consists of eight hours and six minutes of continuous real-time, black-and-white film of the Empire State Building, from early evening until nearly 3 am the next day. In his video installation, *Mapping the Studio* (2002), Bruce Nauman records the nocturnal activity in the artist's studio, showing his cat and an infestation of mice during the summer of 2000. With seven projections and multiple audio tracks of ambient sound, Nauman used this traffic as a way of mapping the leftover parts and work areas of the last several years of other completed, unfinished or discarded projects.

The webcam has given rise to a great variety of practical uses. Webcams are now focused on mountains so that you can see if there is enough snow on the ski run; on young children, so that the parents can see if they are still asleep; on roads, so that drivers know if there are traffic jams; on the person behind a computer, so that the person s/he is chatting with knows what s/he looks like. The latter example demonstrates a fundamental change in visual technologies. The possibility of showing your interlocutor at the chat box what you look like is first of all used by friends and family members in order to enhance the connection and its intimacy. The speaking or writing of words is completed by showing the face behind them. This possibility is being fully exploited in the sex industry. Thanks to the webcam, in addition to just chatting with the woman or man who is supposed to fulfil the client's sexual desires, the girl or boy also shows her/himself, or better his/her face and body while talking with the client. This use of the webcam is so extraordinary because voyeurism, a crucial aspect of more traditional visual technologies, is now overshadowed by its complementary other: exhibitionism. This exhibitionism is not only exploited in the sex industry. Most webcam images shown on the Internet are utterly boring. Showing these images seems to be more important than seeing them. The transformation caused by the webcam is that for the first time there are now more people who want to be looked at than people who want to watch. This is also true for people using social media like Facebook and Instagram.

This change is not only exploited by the sex industry; it also seems to be its demise. There is less and less interest in professionally made porn film with professional porn actors. People who watch porn movies now prefer to watch amateur porn films shown on websites exclusively devoted to these webcam films. The fact that these films are clumsily made and that they usually do not show particularly attractive bodies appears not to be experienced as negative. The point is not *what* viewers are *seeing*, but *that* amateur actors are *showing.* It is the identification with these amateurs showing themselves that makes watching them into an erotic experience, an experience which is affectively more exciting than voyeuristically watching attractive bodies performing sexual acts.[15] This difference is fundamental, because it displaces the nature of our relationship to these images from voyeuristic to exhibitionistic.

The attraction of pornographic and other webcam images is foremost based on its strong reality effect. Their reality effect is, however, stronger and of a different nature than that produced by conventional film and photographic images ("rich images") because, paradoxically, they are unedited

und sechs Minuten kontinuierlichem Schwarzweiß-Film in Echtzeit und zeigt das Empire State Building vom frühen Abend bis kurz vor drei Uhr morgens am nächsten Tag. In seiner Videoinstallation *Mapping the Studio* (2002) zeichnet Bruce Nauman die nächtliche Aktivität seiner Katze während einer Mäuseplage in seinem Atelier im Sommer 2000 auf. Mit sieben Projektionen und vielen Aufnahmen des Raumklangs benutzte Nauman diese Bewegungen, um in seinem Atelier die übriggebliebenen Teile von anderen abgeschlossenen, unfertigen oder verworfenen Projekten der letzten Jahre zu kartieren.

Die Webcam hat zu einer großen Vielfalt praktischer Nutzungen geführt. Webcams zeigen heutzutage Bilder von Bergen, so dass man nachsehen kann, ob auf der Piste genug Schnee liegt; sie nehmen kleine Kinder auf, damit die Eltern sehen, ob sie noch schlafen; sie werden auf Straßen eingesetzt, so dass Fahrer wissen, ob es dort Staus gibt; sie zeigen die Person am Computer, so dass die die Chat-Partner*in sieht, wie man aussieht. Das letzte Beispiel illustriert eine grundsätzliche Veränderung in heutigen Bildtechnologien. Die Möglichkeit, den Gesprächspartner*innen an der Chatbox zu zeigen, wie man aussieht, wird zunächst von Freund*innen und Familienmitgliedern genutzt, um die Verbindung und Nähe zu verstärken. Das Sprechen oder Schreiben von Worten wird komplettiert, indem das Gesicht gezeigt wird, das die Worte spricht. Diese Möglichkeit wird in der Sexindustrie voll ausgenutzt. Dank der Webcam können die Kund*innen nicht nur mit der Frau oder dem Mann, der sexuelles Begehren befriedigen soll, sprechen, sondern die Frau oder der Mann können sich – oder besser gesagt ihr Gesicht und ihren Körper – zeigen, während sie mit den Kund*innen sprechen. Diese Nutzung der Webcam ist so außergewöhnlich, weil Voyeurismus – ein zentraler Aspekt traditioneller visueller Technologien – jetzt von seinem komplementären Anderen überschattet wird: Exhibitionismus. Dieser Exhibitionismus wird nicht nur in der Sexindustrie ausgenutzt. Die meisten Webcambilder im Internet sind vollkommen langweilig. Es scheint wichtiger zu sein, diese Bilder zu zeigen, als sie zu sehen. Die von der Webcam verursachte Transformation ist, dass es nun zum ersten Mal mehr Menschen gibt, die betrachtet werden wollen, als solche, die schauen wollen. Dies trifft ebenso auf Menschen zu, die soziale Medien wie Facebook oder Instagram nutzen.

Diese Veränderung wird von der Sexindustrie nicht nur genutzt; sie scheint auch deren Niedergang zu bedeuten. Es gibt immer weniger Interesse an professionell produzierten Pornofilmen mit professionellen Pornodarsteller*innen. Menschen, die Pornofilme anschauen, bevorzugen nun, sich Amateurpornofilme auf Webseiten anzusehen, die ausschließlich solchen Webcamfilmen gewidmet sind. Die Tatsache, dass diese Filme etwas tollpatschig gemacht sind und üblicherweise keine besonders attraktiven Körper zeigen, scheint nicht als negativ erlebt zu werden. Der Punkt ist nicht, *was* die Zuschauer *sehen*, sondern dass Amateurdarsteller*innen *zeigen*. Es ist die Identifikation mit diesen sich zeigenden Amateur*innen, die das Zuschauen zu einer erotischen Erfahrung macht, eine Erfahrung,

and clumsily made. Being aware of the fact that these images were made, knowing by whom, where and from which position, makes the reality effect only stronger, for the production of these images stems from real life, and not from professional studios, where the production process can be made invisible.[16] The success of the webcam since its invention in the mid-1990s is in a double sense co-responsible for the explosion of information defining that decade. First of all because they are now everywhere—installed in or attached to computers, they distribute filmed information over the World Wide Web. But this quantitative explosion of information also has a qualitative dimension: as comprehensive and complete as the infomation spread by webcams may be, most of it is irrelevant, boring and ignored by the viewer. That is why the webcam is not only exemplary for the 1990s explosion of information but also for the implosion of meaning. As I argued before, with the webcam there are for the first time more people who want to be looked at than people who want to look. It is precisely in this displacement from voyeurism to exhibitionism that the intensities of affective mechanisms are released. When using the terms voyeurism and exhibitionism, I am no longer applying them in the more limited erotic sense, as I did in my example of amateur pornography. I use them in a more general sense, indicating a distinction between a passive consumerist attitude and a more active attitude of self-positioning of those distributing the information. This can be erotic, but is not necessarily so.

For the viewer of these images is not looking for their meaning, but gets access to them by means of identification with the exhibitionistic impulse behind them. Watching them is less a matter of signifying transactions than of an event that one experiences directly or bodily. In the case of webcam images the affective process of identification leads to feelings such as excitement or anxiety. This counters the affect of boredom produced on the level of signification. The fact that many people continue to look at webcam images (apart from very practical situations of surveillance) should be understood in terms of the affects they produce and enable, without being overshadowed by meanings they nevertheless offer.

Although not having shared the erotic conditions of pornographic images, something similar can be argued about Ruff's *jpeg* series. In this monumental series of 2007 he explores the distribution and reception of images in the digital age. The selected images show beautiful, untouched landscapes, and scenes of war and natural disasters. The images are primarily taken from the Web, and then enlarged to gigantic scale. Whereas the enlargements of the pornographic images resulted in images characterised by blurs, the enlargements of the pixel patterns of the web images result in sublime geometric displays of colour. Only from a distance do these coloured patterns become like a blur. When we take the distribution and reception of these images into consideration, it has repercussions for the installed mode of looking. The emphatically poor images do not function like windows through which the viewer voyeuristically gazes at sublime scenes of nature and war. They are rather opaque screens onto which the viewer can project his fantasies or memories, allowing to be part of the

die affektiv aufregender ist, als voyeuristisch attraktiven Körpern beim Vorführen sexueller Akte zuzuschauen.[15] Dieser Unterschied ist fundamental, denn er verschiebt das Wesen unserer Beziehung zu derartigen Bildern: Sie ist nun nicht mehr voyeuristisch, sondern exhibitionistisch.

Der Reiz pornografischer und anderer Webcambilder wird vor allem von ihrem starken Realitätseffekt ausgelöst. Denn er ist stärker und von einer anderen Art als der von konventionellen filmischen und fotografischen Bildern („reiche Bilder"), und zwar paradoxerweise, weil sie unbearbeitet und grob gemacht sind. Die Tatsache, dass uns bewusst ist, dass diese Bilder gemacht wurden, und von wem und wo, und aus welcher Position, verstärkt den Realitätseffekt nur noch, denn die Produktion dieser Aufnahmen findet im echten Leben statt und nicht in professionellen Studios, wo der Produktionsprozess unsichtbar gemacht werden kann.[16] Der Erfolg der Webcam seit ihrer Erfindung Mitte der 1990er Jahre ist in einem doppelten Sinne mitverantwortlich für die Explosion von Information, die diese Dekade definiert. Zunächst, weil sie nun überall sind; in Computer eingebaut oder an Computer angeschlossen, verbreiten sie gefilmte Information über das Internet. Aber diese quantitative Explosion von Information hat auch eine qualitative Dimension: Die Art von Information, die von Webcams verbreitet wird, ist komplett und umfassend. Aber so umfassend und komplett wie die Information der Webcam sein kann, ist sie doch meistens irrelevant und langweilig und wird von Betrachter*innen ignoriert. Deshalb ist die Webcam nicht nur exemplarisch für die Explosion von Informationen in den 1990er Jahren, sondern auch für die Implosion der Bedeutung. Wie ich zuvor argumentiert habe, gibt es mit der Webcam zum ersten Mal mehr Menschen, die angeschaut werden wollen, als solche, die schauen wollen. Genau in dieser Verschiebung vom Voyeurismus zum Exhibitionismus werden die Intensitäten affektiver Mechanismen freigesetzt. Wenn ich hier die Begriffe Voyeurismus und Exhibitionismus verwende, verstehe ich sie nicht mehr in dem begrenzten erotischen Sinn wie in meinem Beispiel der Amateurpornografie. Ich verwende sie in einem allgemeineren Sinn und verweise so auf eine Unterscheidung zwischen einer passiven konsumorientierten Einstellung und einer aktiveren Haltung der Selbstpositionierung derjenigen, die die Information verbreiten. Dies kann erotisch sein, ist es aber nicht notwendigerweise.

Denn die Betrachter*innen dieser Bilder suchen nicht nach deren Bedeutung, sondern erhalten über eine Identifikation mit dem hinter ihnen stehenden exhibitionistischen Impuls Zugang zu ihnen. Sie zu betrachten ist weniger eine Frage bedeutender Vorgänge als vielmehr eine Frage eines Ereignisses, das man direkt oder körperlich erlebt. Im Fall der Webcambilder führt der affektive Prozess der Identifikation zu Gefühlen wie Anregung oder Beklemmung. Dies wirkt dem Affekt der Langeweile, die auf der Ebene der Bedeutung produziert wird, entgegen. Die Tatsache, dass viele Menschen weiterhin Webcambilder betrachten (abgesehen von sehr praktischen Situationen der Überwachung), sollte hinsichtlich der Affekte, die sie produzieren und ermöglichen, verstanden werden, nicht im Schatten der Bedeutungen, die sie nichtsdestotrotz bieten.

scene s/he watches. Comparable to the position of exhibitionism, the viewer imagines her- or himself to be in the poorly represented scene. It is only through this act of the imagination that these poor images come to life, resulting in affects such as awe, anxiety or horror. As I argued earlier, the poverty of the image is an important precondition for this transformation of window into screen, and for the affective production.

Most of the artworks in the exhibition *Affect Me* use social media images of which the first priority was to be shown rather than to be looked at. Images of the "Arab Spring", of the war in Syria do not differ in this respect from other images with less political implications posted on Facebook or Instagram. The people involved in these violent conflicts, who took the images, want the rest of the world to know about their suffering and what is going on in their part of the world. On Facebook and other social media, the users build and stuff their identities by showing what they have seen, what they have done and what they have eaten. Although deprived of eroticism, this kind of visual culture is also fuelled by the impulse of exhibitionism. It is on the platforms of social media that the transformation of a voyeuristic visual culture into an exhibitionistic one is taking place. This adds a new dimension to war images: not making them erotically attractive, but emphasising that they want to be seen.

1 Susan Sontag, *Against Interpretation*, in: idem, *Against Interpretation and other Essays,* London 1967, pp. 3–14, here p. 3.
2 Ibid., p. 3.
3 Ibid., p. 14.
4 Ibid., p. 13.
5 For a more elaborate account of affect, theories of affect and the urgency to better understand what affect is and how it works, Ernst van Alphen, *Affective Operations of Art and Literature*, in: *RES* 53–54, Spring/Autumn 2008, pp. 20–30; and idem, *Explosions of Information, Implosions of Meaning, and the Release of Affects*, in: Patsy Spyer, Mary Steedly (eds.), *Images that Move*, Santa Fe 2013, pp. 219–236.
6 Brian Massumi, *The Autonomy of Affect*, in: Paul Patton (ed.), *Deleuze: A Critical Reader*, Oxford 1996, pp. 217–239, here p. 220.
7 For a discussion on medium specificity see Rosalind Krauss, *A Voyage on the North Sea. Art in the Age of the Post-Medium Condition*, London 1999.
8 https://en.oxforddictionaries.com/word-of-the-year/word-of-the-year-2016, n.p. (last access 20.5.2017).
9 Chantal Mouffe, *On the Political*, Routledge 2005, pp. 28, 31.
10 Maria Boletsi, *Crisis, Terrorism, and Post-Truth: Processes of Othering and Self-Definition in the Culturalization of Politics*, in: Maria Boletsi (ed.), *Subjects Barbarian, Monstrous and Wild: Encounters in the Arts and Contemporary Politics*, Leiden (in press).
11 Thomas Ruff, *Suchmaschinen. Ein Interview von Susanne Leeb*, in: *Texte zur Kunst*, 36, 1999, pp. 71–75, here p. 73.
12 Hito Steyerl, *In Defense of the Poor Image*, in: idem, *The Wretched of the Screen*, Berlin 2012, pp. 31–45.
13 Ibid., p. 32.
14 Bianca Stigter, *Staren naar een stuk kaas*, in: *NRC Handelsblad*, 2.5.2008, pp. 4–5.
15 For a critical reading of pornography, see Linda Williams, *Hard Core: Power, Pleasure and the Frenzy of the Visible*, Berkeley 1989.
16 For an analysis of how webcams affect the relationship between private and public, self and other, see José van Dijck, *Mediated Memories: Personal Cultural Memory in the Digital Age*, Stanford 2007.

Obwohl sie die erotischen Bedingungen pornografischer Bilder nicht teilt, lässt sich Ähnliches über Ruffs *jpeg*-Serie sagen. In dieser monumentalen Serie von 2007 setzt er sich mit der Verbreitung und Rezeption von Bildern im digitalen Zeitalter auseinander. Die ausgewählten Bilder zeigen wunderschöne, unberührte Landschaften und Kriegsszenen sowie Naturkatastrophen. Die Bilder stammen hauptsächlich aus dem Netz und wurden dann auf ein gigantisches Format vergrößert. Während die Vergrößerungen der pornografischen Bilder zu Bildern führte, die sich durch Unschärfe auszeichnen, erweisen sich die Vergrößerungen der Pixelmuster der Netzbilder als erhabene geometrische Darstellungen von Farben. Nur aus einer Entfernung werden diese farbigen Muster unscharf. Wenn wir die Verbreitung und Rezeption dieser Bilder bedenken, hat dies Konsequenzen für den installierten Modus des Schauens. Die emphatisch „armen Bilder" fungieren nicht als Fenster, durch die die Betrachter*innen erhabene Kriegs- und Naturszenen voyeuristisch anblicken. Sie sind eher opake Bildschirme, auf die die Betrachter*innen ihre Fantasien oder Erinnerungen projizieren können, Teil der von ihnen betrachteten Szene zu sein. Vergleichbar mit der Position des Exhibitionismus, stellen sich die Betrachter*innen selbst in der schlecht dargestellten Szene vor. Es ist nur durch diesen Akt der Imagination, dass diese „armen Bilder" zum Leben erwachen, was zu Affekten wie Ehrfurcht, Beklemmung oder Schrecken führt. Wie bereits oben ausgeführt, ist die „Armut" des Bildes eine wichtige Vorbedingung für diese Transformation von Fenster zu Bildschirm, und für die affektive Produktion.

Die meisten Kunstwerke in der Ausstellung *Affect Me* benutzen Bilder aus den sozialen Medien, deren erste Priorität es war, gezeigt und nicht gesehen zu werden. Bilder des „Arabischen Frühlings" oder des Kriegs in Syrien unterscheiden sich in dieser Hinsicht nicht von anderen Bildern mit weniger politischen Implikationen, die auf Facebook oder Instagram gepostet werden. Menschen, die in diese gewaltvollen Konflikte involviert sind und die diese Bilder aufgenommen haben, wollen, dass der Rest der Welt von ihrem Leid und den Ereignissen in ihrem Teil der Welt erfährt. Auf Facebook und anderen sozialen Medien bauen die Nutzer*innen Identitäten auf, indem sie zeigen, was sie gesehen haben, was sie getan haben und was sie gegessen haben. Obwohl Erotik hier keine Rolle spielt, ist diese Art von visueller Kultur vom Impuls des Exhibitionismus befeuert. Auf den Plattformen der sozialen Medien findet die Transformation einer voyeuristischen Bildkultur in eine exhibitionistische statt. Dies fügt Kriegsbildern eine neue Dimension hinzu: Sie werden zwar nicht erotisch attraktiv gemacht, aber es wird unterstrichen, dass sie gesehen werden wollen.

1 Susan Sontag, *Gegen Interpretation*, in: dies., *Kunst und Antikunst: 24 literarische Analysen*, deutsch von Mark W. Riehn, München 1980, S. 9–18, hier S. 10.
2 Ebd., S. 13.
3 Ebd., S. 10.
4 Ebd., S. 18.

5 Für eine ausführlichere Darstellung von Affekt, Affekttheorien und die Dringlichkeit eines besseren Verständnisses von Affekten und wie sie funktionieren, vgl. Ernst van Alphen, *Affective Operations of Art and Literature*, in: *RES* 53–54, Spring/Autumn 2008, S. 20–30; und ders., *Explosions of Information, Implosions of Meaning, and the Release of Affects*, in: Patsy Spyer, Mary Steedly (Hg.), *Images that Move,* Santa Fe 2013, S. 219–236.

6 Brian Massumi, *The Autonomy of Affect*, in: Paul Patton (Hg.), *Deleuze: A Critical Reader*, Oxford 1996, S. 217–239, hier S. 220.

7 Für eine Erörterung von Medienspezifizität siehe Rosalind Krauss, *A Voyage on the North Sea. Art in the Age of the Post-Medium Condition*, London 1999.

8 https://en.oxforddictionaries.com/word-of-the-year/word-of-the-year-2016 (letzter Zugriff 20.05.2017).

9 Chantal Mouffe, *On the Political*, Routledge 2005, S. 28 und 31.

10 Maria Boletsi, *Crisis, Terrorism, and Post-Truth: Processes of Othering and Self-Definition in the Culturalization of Politics*, in: Maria Boletsi (Hg.), *Subjects Barbarian, Monstrous and Wild: Encounters in the Arts and Contemporary Politics*, Leiden (im Erscheinen).

11 Thomas Ruff, *Suchmaschinen. Ein Interview von Susanne Leeb*, in: *Texte zur Kunst*, 36, 1999, S. 71–75, hier S. 73.

12 Hito Steyerl, *In Defense of the Poor Image*, in: *The Wretched of the Screen*, Berlin 2012, S. 31–45.

13 Ebd., S. 32.

14 Bianca Stigter, *Staren naar een stuk kaas*, in: *NRC Handelsblad*, 02.05.2008, S. 4–5.

15 Für eine kritische Interpretation von Pornografie siehe Linda Williams, *Hard Core: Power, Pleasure and the Frenzy of the Visible*, Berkeley 1989.

16 Für eine Analyse, wie Webcams die Beziehung zwischen privat und öffentlich, sich selbst und anderen beeinflussen, siehe José van Dijck, *Mediated Memories: Personal Cultural Memory in the Digital Age*, Stanford 2007.

Lara Baladi
Irene Chabr
Forensic Architecture
Lynn Hershman Leeson
Thomas Hirschhorn
Randa Maroufi
Rabih Mroué
Thomas Ruff
D. H. Saur

Lara Baladi

The Egyptian revolution of 2011 is presumably the best-documented event of the 21st century, for thousands of people in Tahrir Square in Cairo and all across the country had used their mobile phones to photograph and film the incidents. The Egyptian-Lebanese artist Lara Baladi initiated *Vox Populi* (http://tahrirarchives.com), an ongoing digital archiving project dedicated to such images "straight from the people", that follows the political principle of "Archiving as an Act of Resistance."[1] One motive behind this

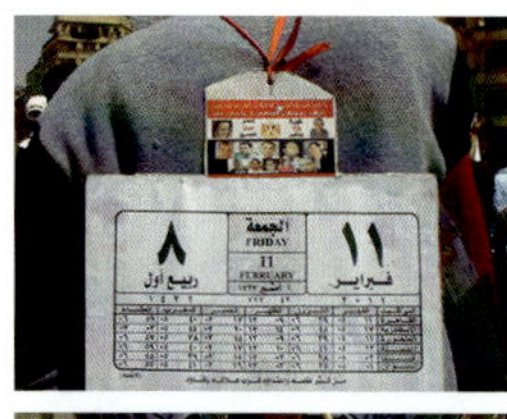

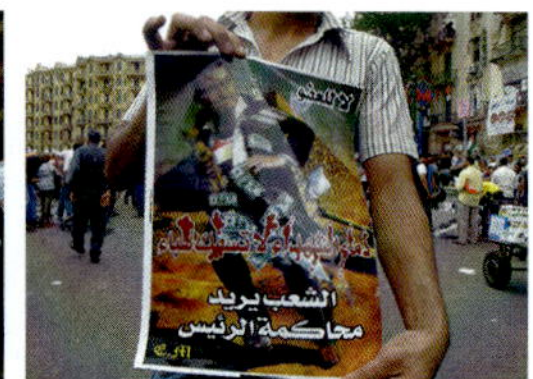

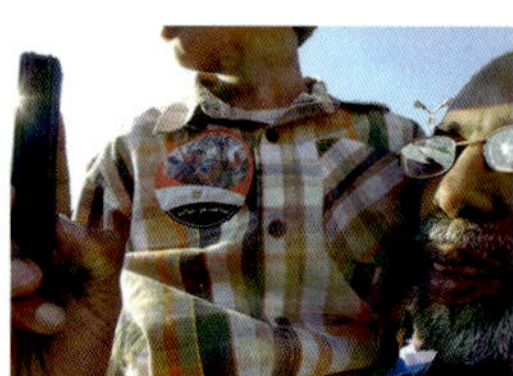
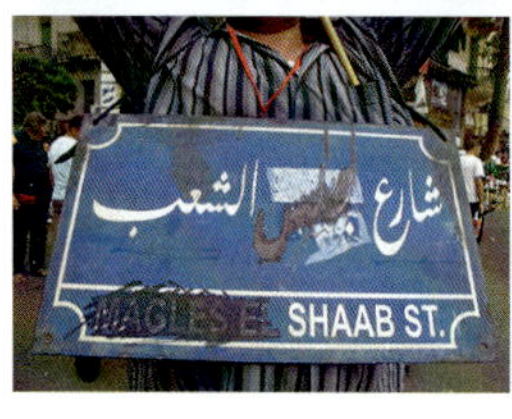

was that, in many cases, the images which were disseminated on the Web and had moved people all over the world are no longer available online today. Baladi is concerned with the broader issue of finding ways to preserve such civic footage, as image testimonies of protest against state repression, and explores in which way it can enter the historical narrative—a multi-perspectival narrative that includes the voice of the people. Her own image archive, which her works have derived inspiration from since 2011, goes far beyond the context of the Egyptian revolution. The three-channel video work *Alone, Together, … In Media Res* (2012) combines videos of the protests in Egypt with other found material from YouTube, like clips from animated films, feature films and music videos, clips from political or philosophical speeches and historical uprisings. This links the protests in Egypt with other socio-political movements, with their canon of motifs and their image politics. "It was as though Sartre was protesting with us in Tahrir,"[2] the artist writes and thus addresses the issue of YouTube as a "contact zone" of images that seem to be affecting one another across time and space. In the video installation, famous shots from a bird's eye view of the Tahrir Square filled to the brim with demonstrators are presented together with a scene from *Alice in Wonderland*, which Baladi employs as a metaphor: "[…] I, like Alice in Wonderland, fell into a hole: YouTube."[3] In this media-reflective work, Marshall McLuhan, who in the 1960s had coined the famous dictum of "The Medium is the Message," also has an appearance. Baladi not least questions the channels through which images are disseminated, including the status of the images themselves and their promise of authenticity,

Ana Masri (I am Egyptian), 2011, excerpt

Lara Baladi

Die Revolution in Ägypten 2011 ist das wohl am besten dokumentierte Ereignis des 21. Jahrhunderts. Denn tausende von Menschen auf dem Tahrir-Platz in Kairo und an anderen Orten im Land fotografierten und filmten die Geschehnisse mit ihren Mobiltelefonen. Die libanesisch-ägyptische Künstlerin Lara Baladi verfolgt mit *Vox Populi* (http://tahrirarchives.com/) ein fortlaufendes digitales Archivierungsprojekt, das sich diesen Bildern „des Volkes" widmet und dem politischen Leitgedanken „Archiving as an Act of Resistance"[1] folgt. Denn die Bilder der Proteste, die im Netz zirkulierten

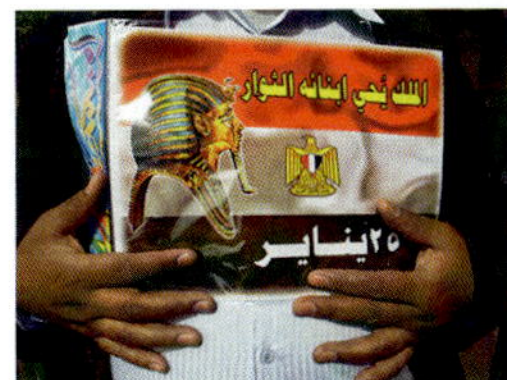

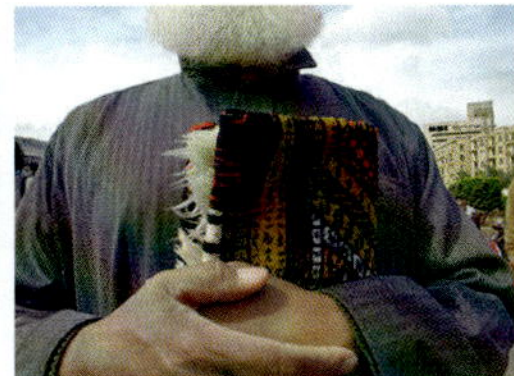
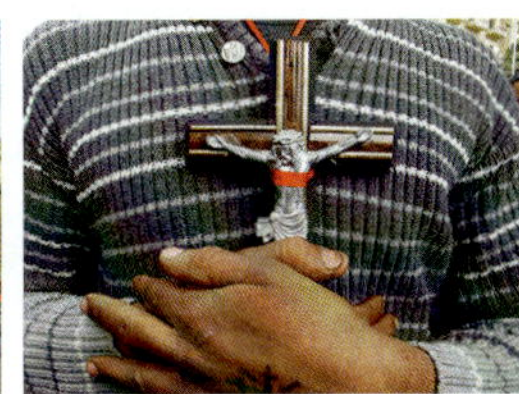

und weltweit die Menschen bewegten, sind heute oftmals nicht mehr online zugänglich. Baladi treibt die generelle Frage um, wie man die zivilgesellschaftlichen Bildzeugnisse der Auflehnung gegen staatliche Repression bewahren kann und wie sie in die Geschichtsschreibung – eine multiperspektivische Geschichte, die auch vom Volk erzählt wird – eingehen können. Ihr eigenes Bildarchiv, aus dem sich ihre Arbeiten seit 2011 speisen, geht jedoch weit über den Kontext der ägyptischen Revolution hinaus. Die Dreikanal-Videoarbeit *Alone, Together, … In Media Res* (2012) kombiniert Videos der Proteste in Ägypten mit anderen YouTube-Fundstücken wie Ausschnitten von Zeichentrickfilmen, Spielfilmen, Musikvideos, Clips von politischen oder philosophischen Reden und historischen Revolten.
Die Aufstände in Ägypten werden so mit anderen sozialen Bewegungen, ihrem Motivkanon und ihren Bildpolitiken in Verbindung gebracht. „It was as though Sartre was protesting with us in Tahrir"[2], schreibt die Künstlerin und thematisiert damit auch YouTube als „contact zone" von Bildern, die einander über Zeit und Raum hinweg zu affizieren scheinen. Die berühmten Aufnahmen des von Demonstrierenden gefüllten Tahrir-Platzes aus der Vogelperspektive werden in der Videoinstallation zusammen mit einer Szene aus *Alice im Wunderland* gezeigt, die Baladi als Metapher verwendet: „[…] I, like Alice in Wonderland, fell into a hole: YouTube."[3] In dieser medienreflexiven Arbeit hat auch Marshall McLuhan einen Auftritt, der in den 1960er Jahren das berühmte Diktum „The Medium is the Message" geprägt hat. Die Künstlerin befragt nicht zuletzt die Kanäle, über die die Bilder verbreitet werden, wie auch den Status der Bilder selbst und ihr

Ana Masri (I am Egyptian), 2011, Exzerpt

by way of blending fiction and documentation. The comparison of YouTube and "Wonderland" with all its paradoxes and absurdities, where one may dreamingly lose grip of reality, is ambiguous and telling.

Lara Baladi's recent project is an interactive timeline echoing the events in Egypt and their repercussions. This encompassing index surely can be considered as the core of *Vox Populi*, and it is being presented for the first

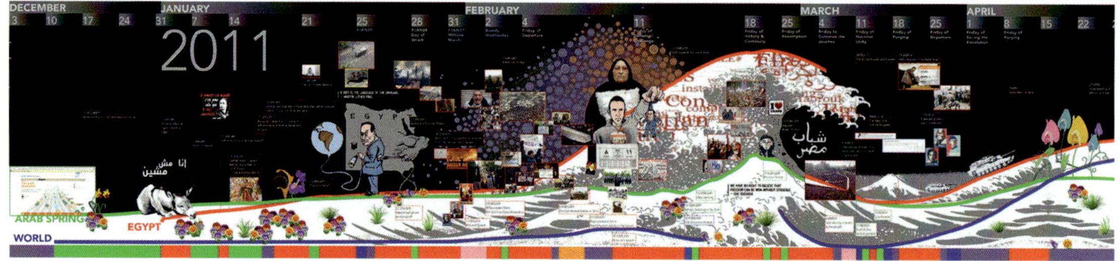

time at KAI 10. Here, we encounter Alice once more, who guides us along the timeline as an observer (or perhaps as the artist's alter ego). With her

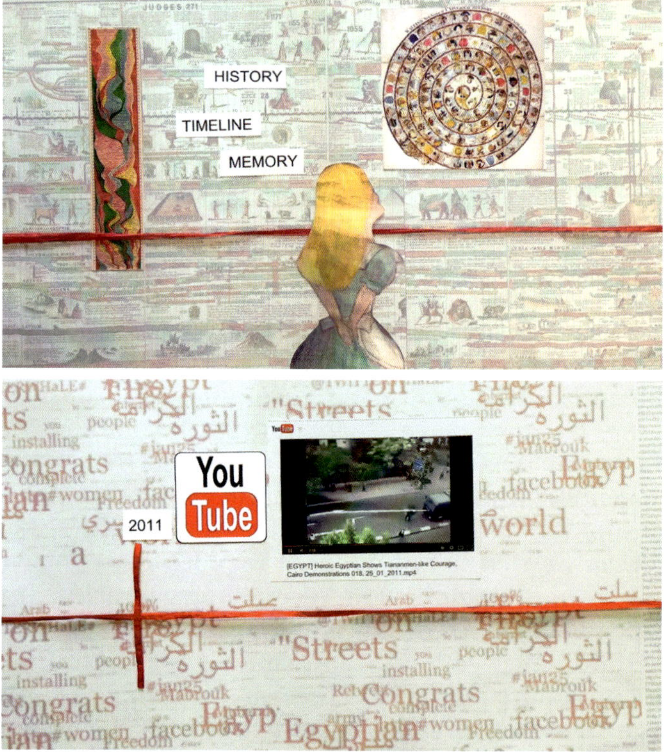

we can review the harrowing as well as the euphoric moments of the revolution. The digital footage collected from social platforms allows us to intensely experience the affective potential of images, when, for instance, the video *Tiananmen-like courage in Cairo*[4] is played. The blurred and pixelated mobile phone video that recorded the forming street protests from the elevated perspective of a window or balcony features a man who

Vox Populi, since 2011, study for the timeline

Paper prototyp for *Vox Populi*, 2015, video stills

Authentizitätsversprechen, indem sie Fiktion und Dokumentation miteinander verschränkt. Der Vergleich von YouTube und dem „Wunderland“ mit seinen Paradoxien und Absurditäten, in dem man sich träumend verliert, ist vieldeutig.

Lara Baladis neues Projekt ist eine interaktive Timeline der Ereignisse in Ägypten und ihren Folgen, die sicherlich als Herzstück von *Vox Populi* gelten kann und in KAI 10 erstmals ausgestellt wird. Erneut begegnen wir Alice, die uns als Betrachterin (vielleicht auch als Alter Ego der Künstlerin)

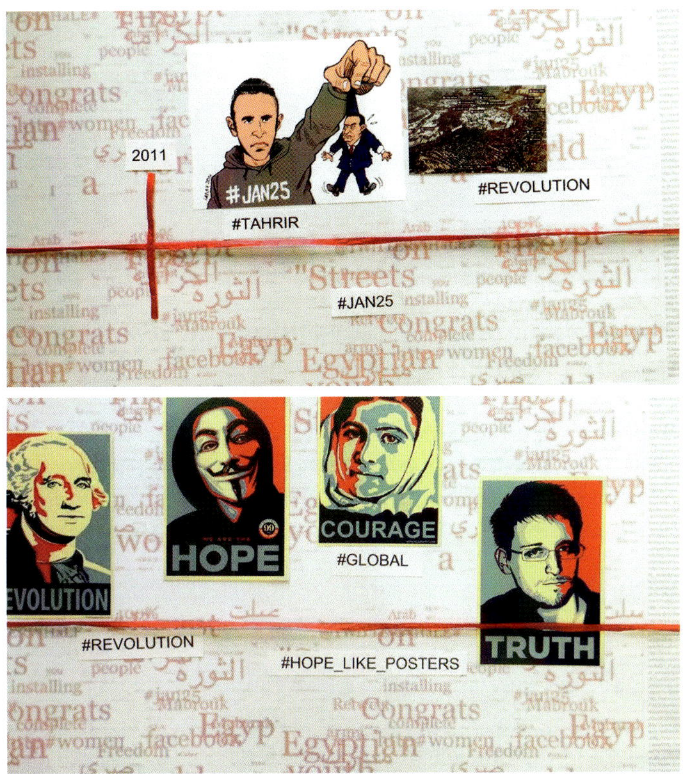

durch die Timeline führt. Mit ihr können wir die aufreibenden, erschütternden und euphorischen Momente der Revolution Revue passieren lassen. Das im Social Web gesammelte Material macht das Affizierungspotenzial der Bilder noch einmal intensiv erfahrbar, wenn etwa das Video *Tiananmen-like courage in Cairo*[4] abgespielt wird. Das verwackelte und pixelige Handyvideo, das aus der erhöhten Perspektive eines Fensters oder Balkons die

Papierprototyp für *Vox Populi*, 2015, Videostills

confronted a military riot-control vehicle equipped with a water cannon. The spectacular scene immediately recalls the iconic "Tank Man" of the Tiananmen Square in Beijing in 1989; the act of resistance and visual formula are being repeated here. One hears the shouts and cries of the people on the street, but the excitement of the person filming the scene is also mediated impressively. The video went viral instantly when it was uploaded on January 25, 2011. For the incident took place on the day that is known as the beginning of the "18 Days" (until Mubarak's resignation) and, based on the hashtag #Jan25, was to give the revolution its name (ثورة 25 يناير, January 25 Revolution).

For this exhibition Baladi developed the timeline project further by extending it as a multimedia installation composed of a neon sign with lettering, several murals and displays featuring the actual timeline.

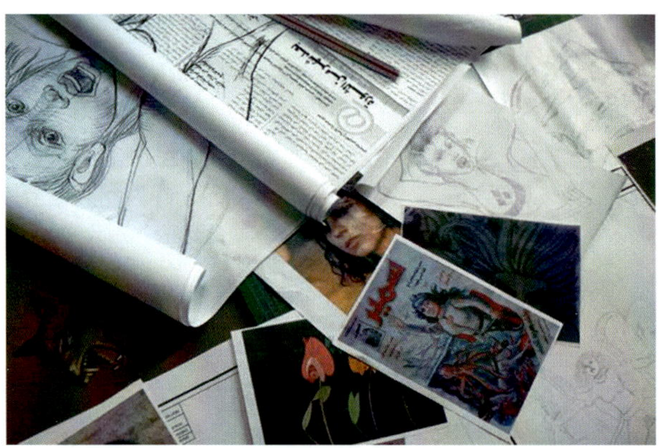

The lettering quotes the famous and frequently appropriated saying by Che Guevara, "Let's be realistic, demand the impossible!", which became the slogan of the 1968 movement in France. Baladi translates this revolutionary, utopian guiding principle to the Egyptian context. She thus comments on both the political events and the image economies involved, portraying them as a historical process of negotiation: What is reality; what is illusion? What is possible; what is unlikely? What is true and authentic and what isn't?

Kerstin Schankweiler

1 Lara Baladi, *Archiving a Revolution in the Digital Age, Archiving as an Act of Resistance*, in: *Ibraaz*, 28.7.2016, www.ibraaz.org/essays/163 (last access 3.8.2017).
2 Lara Baladi, *Alone, Together*, in: *Guernica. A Magazine of Art & Politics*, 25.1.2013, www.guernicamag.com/daily/lara-baladi-alone-together/ (last access 13.10.2017).
3 Ibid.
4 https://www.youtube.com/watch?v=q1m4_q_HP5o (last access 18.9.2017).

Be Realistic, Ask for the Impossible, study for a mural, 2017

sich formierenden Straßenproteste festgehalten hat, zeigt einen Mann, der sich einem Militärfahrzeug mit Wasserwerfer entgegenstellt. Die spektakuläre Szene erinnert unwillkürlich an den ikonischen „Tank Man“ vom Tian’anmen-Platz in Beijing 1989; widerständische Aktion und Bildformel werden hier wiederholt. Man hört die Schreie der Menschen auf der Straße, aber auch die Aufgeregtheit des Videografen vermittelt sich eindrücklich. Das Video ging augenblicklich viral, als es am 25. Januar 2011 hochgeladen wurde. Denn der Vorfall ereignete sich an jenem Tag, der als Beginn der „18 Tage“ (bis zum Rücktritt Mubaraks) gilt und mit dem Hashtag #Jan25 namensgebend wurde (ثورة 25 يناير, Revolution des 25. Januar).

Baladi hat das Timeline-Projekt für die Ausstellung als Multi-Media-Installation weiterentwickelt, die aus einem Leuchtschild mit Schriftzug, mehreren Wandgemälden und Displays mit der eigentlichen Timeline besteht.

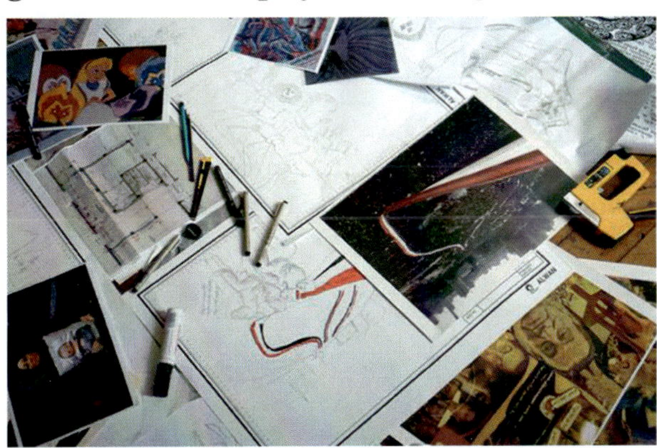

Der Schriftzug zitiert den berühmten und vielfach angeeigneten Ausspruch Che Guevaras „Seien wir realistisch, fordern wir das Unmögliche!“, der auf Französisch zum Slogan der 1968er Bewegung in Frankreich wurde. Baladi überträgt diesen revolutionären, utopischen Leitgedanken auf den ägyptischen Kontext. Sie kommentiert damit die politischen Ereignisse wie auch die damit einhergehenden Bildökonomien als einen historischen Prozess der Aushandlung: Was ist Realität, was ist Illusion? Was ist möglich, was ist unwahrscheinlich? Was ist wahr und authentisch, was nicht?

Kerstin Schankweiler

1 Lara Baladi, *Archiving a Revolution in the Digital Age, Archiving as an Act of Resistance*, in: *Ibraaz*, 28.07.2016, www.ibraaz.org/essays/163/ (letzter Zugriff 03.08.2017).
2 Lara Baladi, *Alone, Together*, in: *Guernica. A Magazine of Art & Politics*, 25.01.2013, www.guernicamag.com/daily/lara-baladi-alone-together/ (letzter Zugriff 13.10.2017).
3 Ebd.
4 https://www.youtube.com/watch?v=q1m4_q_HP5o (letzter Zugriff 18.09.2017).

Be Realistic, Ask for the Impossible, Studien zu Wandgemälde, 2017

Irene Chabr

Why do so many photos that appear on the Facebook newsfeed or Instagram look alike? The iconic mirror selfie, the plate of delicious food, a sunset, the finger pointing to a small, disgusting flaw in the hotel's bathroom. Images encourage the production of ever more images—and they all seem to refer back to a canonized pool of genres and gestures. The artistic and scientific approach of Irene Chabr is based on her interest in precisely these image practices in social networks. She has put together an extensive archive of users' photos that she describes as an "atlas of gestures." Chabr works on her project, *Wandernde Gesten. Eine künstlerisch-kultur-analytische Untersuchung von Bildmigrationen* (Wandering Gestures. An artistic and cultural-analytical inquiry of image migrations), at the Zurich University of the Arts. She analyses the way in which users pick up on visual repertoires and indicating gestures in their reenactments or Internet memes. She thereby questions the allegedly authentic nature of the images as well as their promise of contributing to the emergence of new global communities. From her archive, she continually produces new combinations as "work in progress," which she presents in installations of image boards. A new version of her series, *Wandernde Gesten* (2015–2017), which collects selfies from

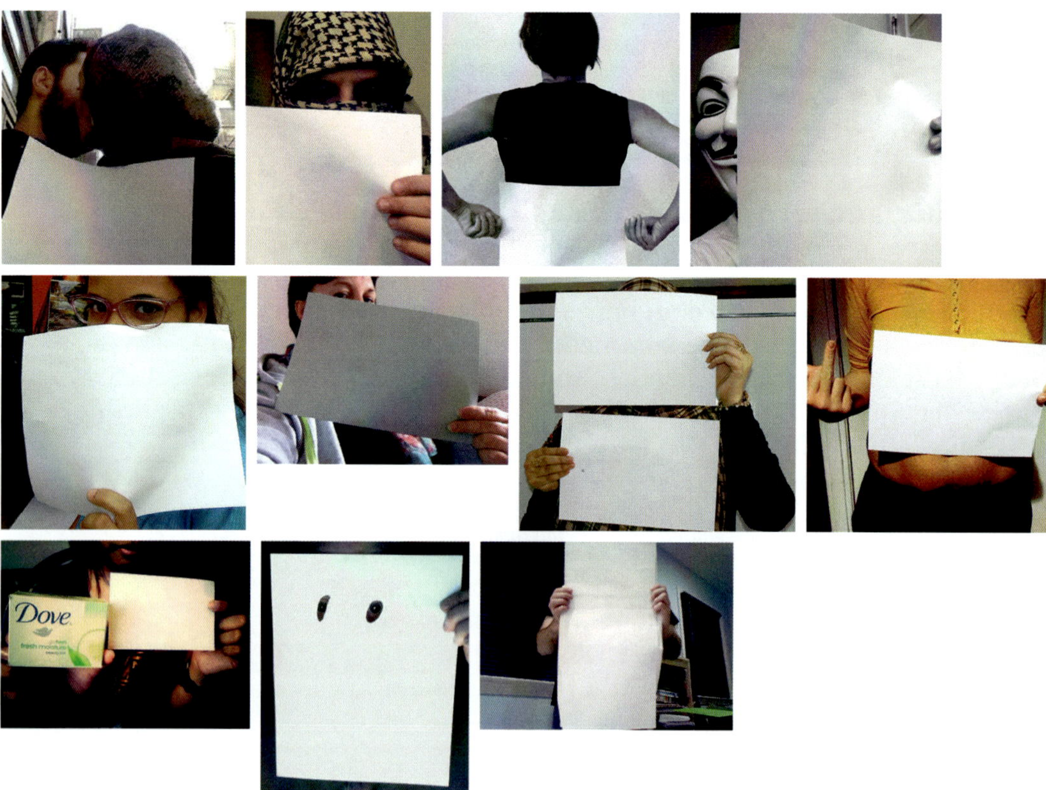

Wandernde Gesten, 2015–2017, details

Irene Chabr

Warum ähneln sich viele Fotos von Freund*innen, die im Newsfeed von Facebook oder auf Instagram auftauchen? Das ikonische Spiegel-Selfie, der Teller mit köstlichen Speisen, ein Sonnenuntergang, der ausgestreckte Zeigefinger, der auf eklige Mängel im Bad des Hotelzimmers hinweist. Bilder regen die Produktion immer neuer Bilder an – und sie alle scheinen auf einen kanonisierten Fundus von Genres und Gesten zu rekurrieren. Die künstlerische und wissenschaftliche Praxis der Künstlerin Irene Chabr basiert auf ihrem Interesse an eben diesen Bildpraktiken in sozialen Netzwerken. Sie hat ein umfangreiches Archiv von User*innen-Fotografien angelegt, das sie als „Atlas der Gesten" beschreibt. Chabr bearbeitet ihr Projekt *Wandernde Gesten. Eine künstlerisch-kulturanalytische Untersuchung von Bildmigrationen* an der Zürcher Hochschule der Künste. Ihre Analyse widmet sich der Art und Weise, wie User*innen Bildrepertoires und Gesten des Zeigens in Reenactments oder Internet-Memes aufgreifen. Dabei hinterfragt sie den vermeintlichen Authentizitätscharakter der Bilder ebenso wie ihr Versprechen, zur Entstehung neuer globaler Communities beizutragen. Aus ihrem Archiv entstehen als „work in progress" immer neue Zusammenstellungen, die Chabr als Installationen von Bildtafeln präsentiert. Eine neue Version ihrer Serie *Wandernde Gesten* (2015–2017) ist in der

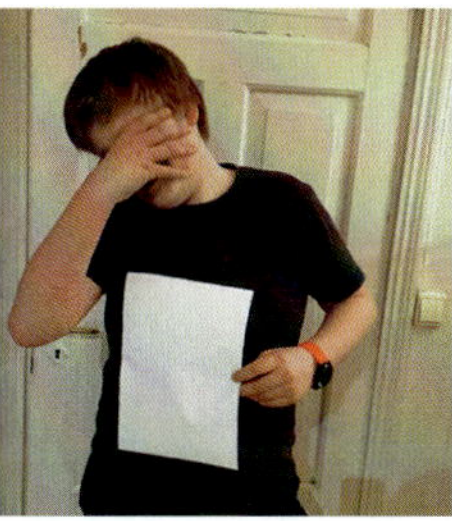
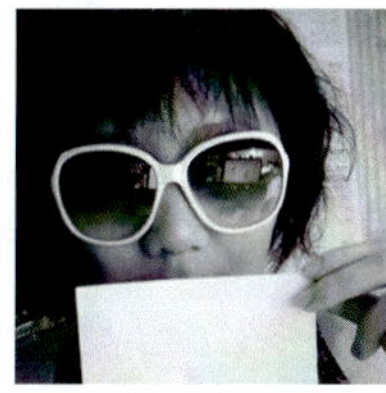
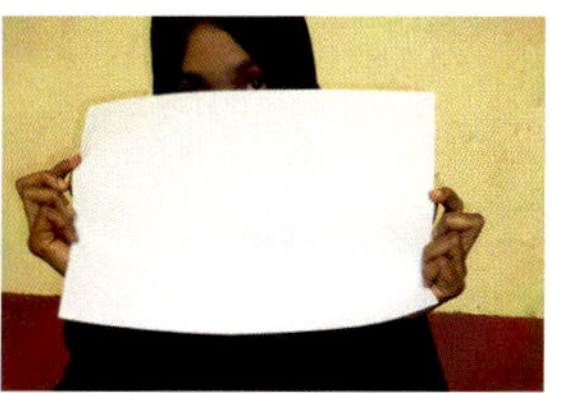
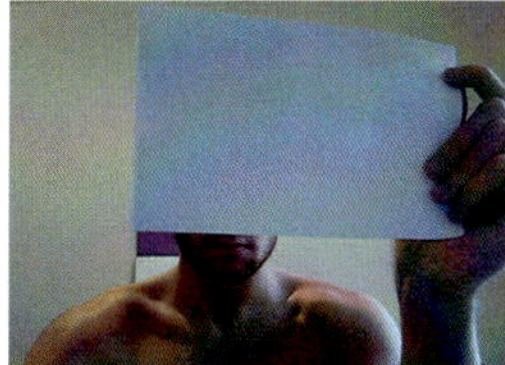
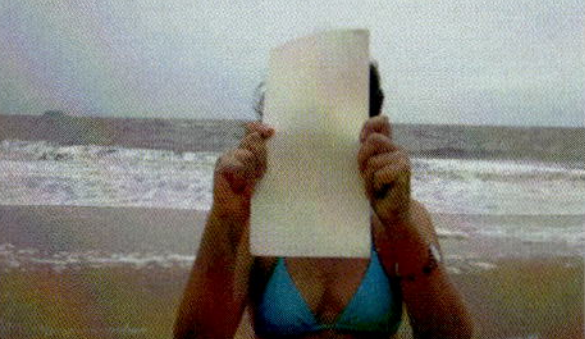
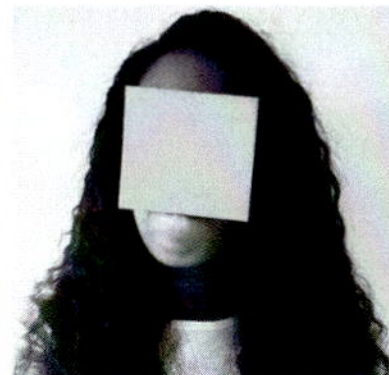
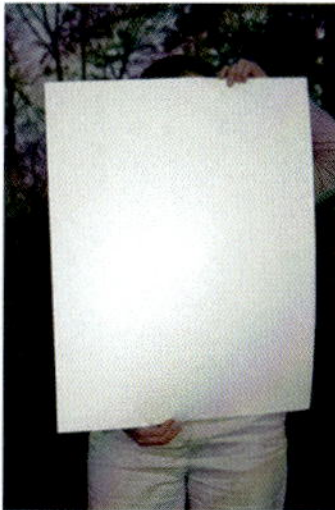

Wandernde Gesten, 2015–2017, Details

various protest campaigns, is presented in the exhibition. The visual convention conveys itself in a second: someone holds a sign with a protest slogan (usually with the hashtag of the relevant campaign) in front of the camera. This image formula continually changes, further develops and expands, for example, through additional protest gestures such as the fist stretching upwards or the victory sign. Sometimes people make themselves anonymous by holding the protest sign in front of their faces.

Irene Chabr edits this visual material and obliterates the original message on the sign. This intervention directs the viewer's attention more to the collective gestures of those photographed as well as their surroundings, which often reveal cultural and social differences. There is one photo, for example, in Chabr's 2015 installation, which shows Michelle Obama taking

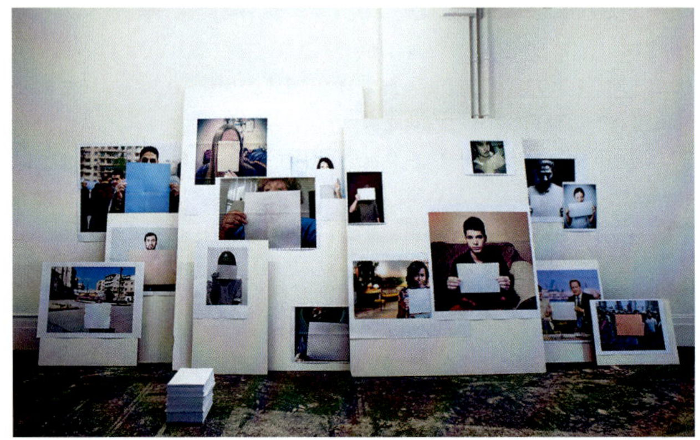

part in the online protest #BringBackOurGirls—probably the most retweeted photo in a selfie campaign. The perfect staging of the First Lady in the White House stands in stark contrast to a selfie of Syrian journalist Zaina Erhaim in war-torn Aleppo, which is also part of the work. Erhaim had participated in the "Je suis Charlie" campaign with this photo posted on her blog. After the attack on the editorial office of *Charlie Hebdo* in Paris, Erhaim's act was not just one of solidarity but also a reference to the

Wandernde Gesten I, 2015

Ausstellung zu sehen und versammelt Selfies aus unterschiedlichen Protest-Kampagnen. Die klassische Bildformel vermittelt sich auf einen Blick: Eine Person hält ein Schild mit einem Protestslogan (meist das Hashtag der jeweiligen Kampagne) in die Kamera. Diese Formel wird beständig verändert, weiterentwickelt und erweitert, etwa durch zusätzliche Protestgesten, wie die emporgereckte Faust oder das Victory-Zeichen, manchmal anonymisieren sich die Personen, indem sie zum Beispiel das Protestschild vor das Gesicht halten. Irene Chabr bearbeitet das Bildmaterial und löscht die ursprünglich auf die Schilder geschriebene Botschaft aus. Durch diesen Eingriff richtet sich die Aufmerksamkeit der Betrachter*innen stärker auf die kollektiven Gesten der Fotografierten sowie auf die sie umfangende Szenerie, die oftmals soziale und kulturelle Unterschiede offenbart. Chabrs Installation von 2015 zeigt etwa ein Foto, mit dem Michelle Obama

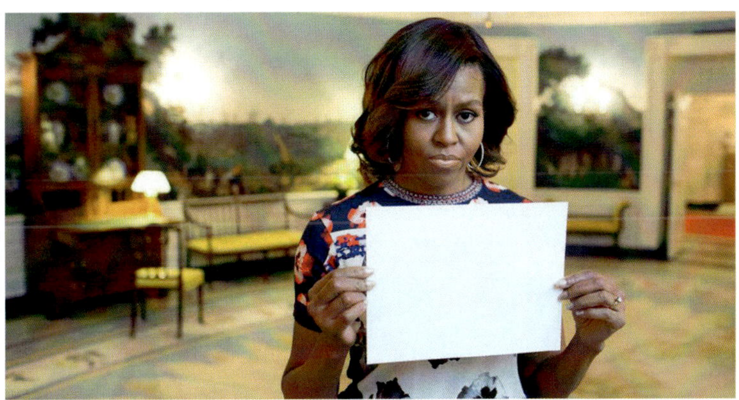

am Online-Protest #BringBackOurGirls teilnahm – das wohl am meisten re-tweetete Bild einer Selfie-Kampagne. Die perfekte Inszenierung der First Lady im Weißen Haus steht in harschem Kontrast zum ebenfalls in der Arbeit zitierten Selfie der syrischen Journalistin Zaina Erhaim im kriegsversehrten Aleppo. Erhaim hatte mit diesem Foto, das sie auf ihrem Blog

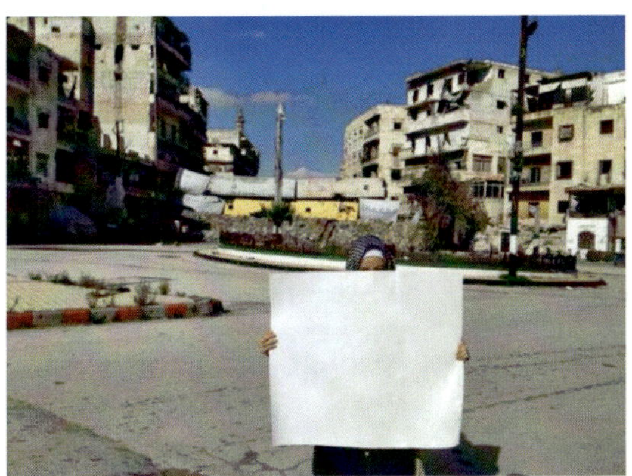

postete, an der Kampagne „Je suis Charlie“ teilgenommen. Nach der Attacke auf die Redaktion der Zeitschrift *Charlie Hebdo* in Paris war dies nicht nur ein Akt der Solidarität, sondern gleichzeitig ein Hinweis auf die

Wandernde Gesten I, 2015, Detail
Wandernde Gesten I, 2015, Detail

adverse conditions in Syria under which she has to work. Chabr also integrates into her montages commercial templates from the advertising industry, which have seized on the visual language of the selfie protests. She does not, however, misappropriate the contexts of the individual images; rather she makes the sources, messages and hashtags of the images available to the exhibition viewers in the form of a factual list so that her research and reworking can be identified.

A second work in the exhibition that Irene Chabr made together with Noëmie Stähli also strategically separates text and image. The video piece is based on an archive of YouTube clips that both artists created on the phenomenon of the "Harraga." They are recordings produced shortly after

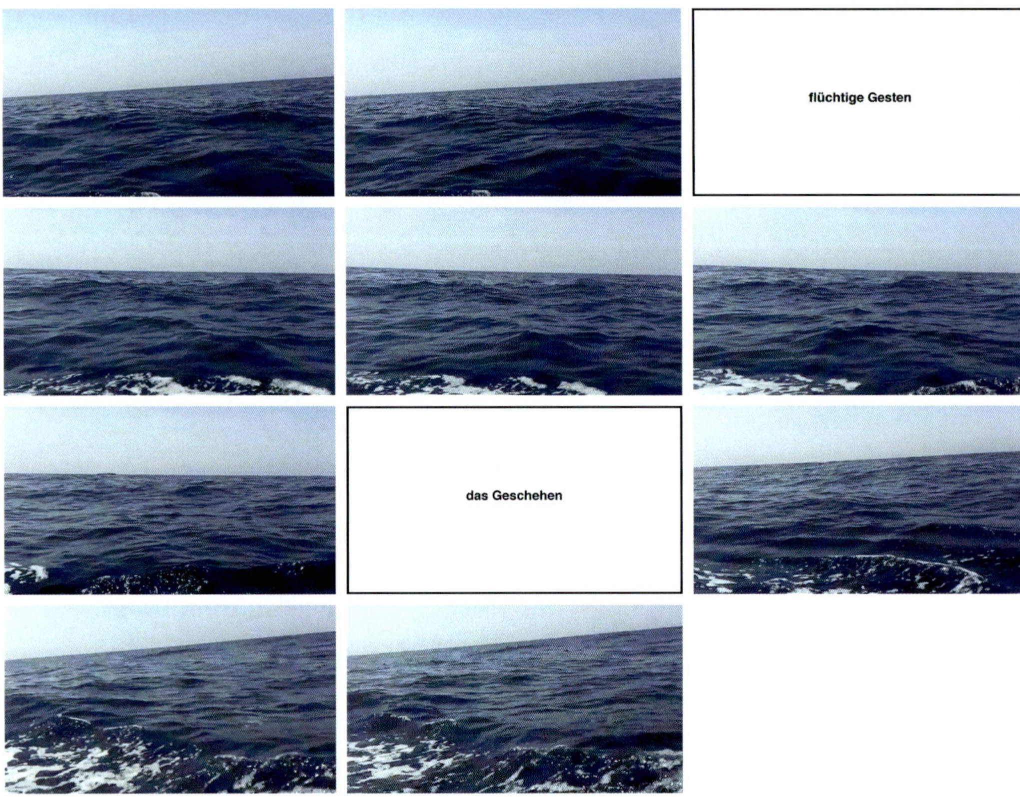

the so-called Arab Spring made by young men from the Maghreb states with their mobile phone cameras while crossing the Mediterranean Sea. This form of narrating migration is unusual, as we are typically confronted only with stereotypical representations of migrants. The two-channel video projection, however, does not present the videos as authentic evidence of migration but deconstructs the material into image and text. The actions and gestures of those in the boat are translated into text; the viewer is thus visually deprived of them. The edited video, on the other hand, shows only the view over open sea filmed from a careening, skewed perspective from the small boat. The shaky images become metaphors for the passengers'

Harraga (www.youtube.com/watch?v=TT2ijWrTUr4; www.youtube.com/watch?v=eWvvRF3Y-S8; www.youtube.com/watch?v=36kbTfnVkg), 2013, video stills

widrigen Umstände, unter denen sie in Syrien arbeiten muss. Irene Chabr integriert aber auch kommerzielle Templates aus der Werbeindustrie in ihre Montagen, die die Bildsprache der Selfie-Proteste gekapert haben. Die Kontexte der einzelnen Bilder unterschlägt die Künstlerin dabei nicht, sie stellt die Quellen, Botschaften und Hashtags der Bilder den Betrachter*innen im Ausstellungsraum in Form einer sachlichen Liste zur Verfügung, die ihre Recherchen und Bearbeitungen nachvollziehbar macht.

Auch eine zweite Arbeit, die in der Ausstellung zu sehen ist und die Irene Chabr mit Noëmie Stähli zusammen produziert hat, nimmt eine strategische Trennung von Text- und Bildebene vor. Die Videoarbeit basiert auf einem Archiv von YouTube-Clips, das die beiden Künstlerinnen zum Phänomen der „Harraga" angelegt haben. Es handelt sich um Aufnahmen,

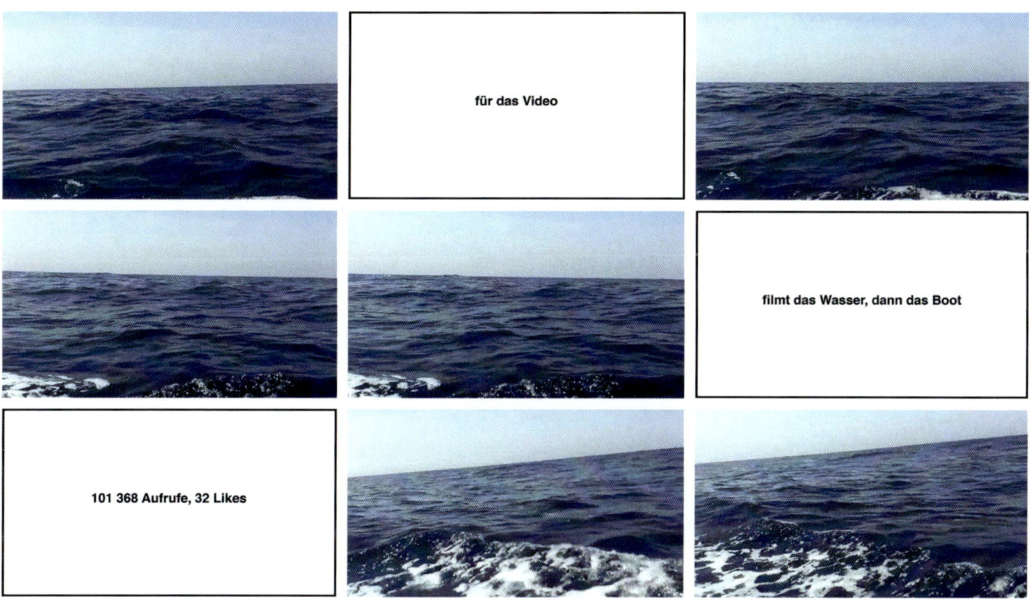

die kurz nach dem sogenannten Arabischen Frühling entstanden sind und mit denen junge Männer aus den Maghreb-Staaten ihre Überfahrt über das Mittelmeer mit Handykameras selbst dokumentierten. Dies ist insofern bemerkenswert, als wir in den Medien meist nur mit stereotypen Fremdrepräsentationen von Migrant*innen konfrontiert sind. Die Zweikanal-Videoprojektion präsentiert uns die Videos jedoch nicht als authentische Zeugnisse der Migration, sie zerlegt das Material in einen Bild- und einen Textstrang. Die Handlungen und Gesten der Akteure im Boot werden in Text übersetzt und damit den Betrachter*innen visuell entzogen. Das edierte Video hingegen zeigt nur noch den Blick auf das offene Meer, das

Harraga (www.youtube.com/watch?v=TT2ijWrTUr4; www.youtube.com/watch?v=eWvvRF3Y-S8; www.youtube.com/watch?v=36kbTfnVkg), 2013, Videostills

discomfort and existential anxiety, which the viewer can feel almost physically.

Irene Chabr questions representations through a strategy of abstraction to which the removal of the video's emotionalising soundtrack belongs. The affective dynamic of the images are thus reduced and allow a more analytical viewpoint—but as viewers, we cannot completely distance ourselves from their affective potential.

Kerstin Schankweiler

aus einer schwankenden und schrägen Perspektive aus dem kleinen Boot heraus gefilmt wurde. Die verwackelten Bilder werden zu Metaphern für das Unbehagen und die existentiellen Ängste der Bootsinsassen, die beim Anschauen fast körperlich spürbar werden.

Irene Chabr hinterfragt diese Repräsentationen durch eine Strategie der Abstrahierung, zu der auch das Wegschneiden der emotionalisierenden Audiospur des Videos gehört. Die affektiven Dynamiken der Bilder werden dadurch reduziert und geben einem stärker analytischen Blick Raum – und doch können wir als Betrachter*innen uns dem Affizierungspotenzial der Bilder nicht ganz entziehen.

Kerstin Schankweiler

Forensic Architecture

On September 24, 1914, shortly after the onset of the First World War, the composer Arnold Schoenberg was watching the clouds. He interpreted their ephemeral formation before the backdrop of a blue sky and their colouring as signs of the upcoming: an "impending catastrophe"[1] or war as a catharsis—for Schoenberg this at first was undecided. Defying the powerlessness of the unknown, "[a]t the moment of indeterminate danger, of an irritation suspending all known parameters of knowledge, he begins to observe, to draw and to record whatever he can discern in the sky."[2] The cloud drawings in Schoenberg's *Kriegs-Wolken-Tagebuch* (War Clouds Diary) are projected into the future of world conditions, "finding forms for something yet to be determined."[3] While in this case the tension created from the expectation of things to come points towards the future, the current cloud models by the collective Forensic Architecture, based at Goldsmiths, University of London, are traces existing "after the fact". The research team of architects, artists, filmmakers, journalists, scholars, lawyers and activists visualises incidents which, though they lie in the past, remain uncertain regarding their course of events. Based on photographic and film media shared in social networks, their 3D-printed models and filmic animations reconstruct bombings and war-related events that otherwise would fade into the obscurity of a lack of responsibility.

Air Strike Atimah (2015). On March 8, 2015 three bombs were dropped near the Syrian-Turkish border between the town of Atimah and a refugee camp with more than 30,000 people, killing six civilians. The lack of transparency regarding the event and the missing acceptance of responsibility by the military had led the casualty-monitoring group Airwars to commission Forensic Architecture with an investigation. The sources for the subsequent reconstruction were video and photo material distributed on the Internet by citizens who had recorded the bomb detonations from different points of view. In order to analyse the specific danger for the civilians, the locations of the cameras were reconstructed using photogrammetric measuring methods and compared with satellite images. Additionally, comparisons were made between the smoke emission caused by the detonation and archival images, enabling the identification of the bomb type as a one-tonne bomb. Based on this reconstruction it became evident that the bombs had struck only 900 metres away from the refugee camp, and near residential homes and public buildings of the town of Atimah. Forensic Architecture supposes that the U.S. military planned the bombing as an attack against al-Qaeda fighters operating in the area.[4]

Forensic Architecture fills the knowledge gap of the circumstances surrounding the event, which was visible only indirectly in the form of three cloud formations, through an investigative practice relying on the analysis of subsequent traces. In *Air Strike Atimah* the gaseous cloud was measured with the aid of technical images, allowing to unequivocally determine the time and place of events. The group's multimedia production of evidence based on images and models is presented as political work, undertaken as

Forensic Architecture

Am 24. September 1914, kurz nach Beginn des Ersten Weltkrieges, beobachtete der Komponist Arnold Schönberg die Wolken. Ihre ephemere Formation vor blauem Himmel, ihre Färbung las er als Zeichen des Kommenden: „drohende Katastrophe“[1] oder Krieg als Katharsis – dies war für Schönberg anfangs noch nicht entschieden. Gegen die Ohnmacht des Unwissens, „[i]m Moment einer unbestimmten Gefahr, einer Irritation, die alle bekannten Parameter des Wissens aussetzt, fängt er an zu beobachten, zu zeichnen und aufzuschreiben, was er irgend am Himmel erkennen kann.“[2] Die Wolkenzeichnungen in Schönbergs *Kriegs-Wolken-Tagebuch* sind in die Zukunft der Weltverhältnisse hineinprojiziert und „finden Formen für etwas, das noch offen ist.“[3] Während die Spannung in Erwartung der Ereignisse hier in die Zukunft weist, sind die aktuellen Wolkenmodelle des Kollektivs Forensic Architecture vom Goldsmiths, University of London, Spuren „after the fact“. Die aus Architekt*innen, Künstler*innen, Filmemacher*innen, Journalist*innen, Wissenschaftler*innen, Jurist*innen und Aktivist*innen bestehende Forschungsgemeinschaft visualisiert Ereignisse, die zwar schon in der Vergangenheit liegen, deren Hergang jedoch unbestimmt ist. Ihre 3D-Modelle und filmischen Simulationen rekonstruieren aus fotografischen und filmischen Medien, die über soziale Netzwerke verbreitet wurden, Bombenanschläge und kriegerische Ereignisse, die sonst im Dunkel fehlender Verantwortlichkeit versinken würden.

Air Strike Atimah (2015). Am 8. März 2015 wurden drei Bomben an der syrisch-türkischen Grenze zwischen der Stadt Atimah und einem Flüchtlingslager mit mehr als dreißigtausend Menschen abgeworfen und töteten sechs Zivilist*innen. Die Unklarheit des Ereignisses und die fehlende Übernahme der militärischen Verantwortung brachte die casualty-monitoring group Airwars dazu, Forensic Architecture mit einer Untersuchung zu beauftragen. Die Quellen der nachträglichen Rekonstruktion waren im Netz verbreitete Videos und Fotos von Zivilist*innen, die von verschiedenen Standpunkten aus die Bombendetonationen aufzeichneten. Um die konkrete Gefahr für die Zivilbevölkerung zu analysieren, wurden die Kamerastandpunkte durch photogrammetrische Messmethoden rekonstruiert und mit Satellitenbildern abgeglichen. Zusätzlich wurde die Rauchentwicklung der Detonation mit Archiv-Bildern verglichen, wodurch die Identifizierung des Bombentyps einer „one-tonne bomb“ hergeleitet werden konnte. Durch diese Rekonstruktion wurde evident, dass die Bomben nur 900 Meter entfernt vom Flüchtlingslager und nahe von Wohnhäusern und öffentlichen Gebäuden der Stadt Atimah einschlugen. Forensic Architecture nimmt an, dass die Bombardierung vom US-Militär als Angriff gegen Al-Qaeda-Kämpfer geplant war, die in der Gegend operierten.[4]

Forensic Architecture füllt die Leerstelle im Wissen um die Umstände des Ereignisses, das nur indirekt in Form von drei Wolkenformationen sichtbar wurde, mit einer investigativen Praxis, die sich auf die Auswertung nachträglicher Spuren stützt. In *Air Strike Atimah* wurde die gasförmige Wolke mit Hilfe technischer Bildmedien vermessen, um Ort und Zeitpunkt

independent research for human rights organisations, courts and truth commissions. The term "forensic," which, according to Eyal Weizman, head of the group, in its original usage within the history of rhetoric pertained to the entire sphere of the political, legal and economics, was reduced to forensic processes of police force in the mid-19th century.[5] This monopolising of forensic practice through state authority is to be countered through the independent analysis of topographical situations, diffused images and photogrammetric methods of measurement. The resulting production of visual evidence, generates its distinctiveness from being embedded in the juridical context. Although virtual 3D models are being employed, the focus of this work is not on fictionalising computergenerated worlds. By evaluating metadata and employing documentary material as operational images, the collective rather reconstructs real events in order to establish political responsibility in an unclear state of facts. The 3D model of the clouds featured in the exhibition is a chiffre for foggy, military violence in a space in which

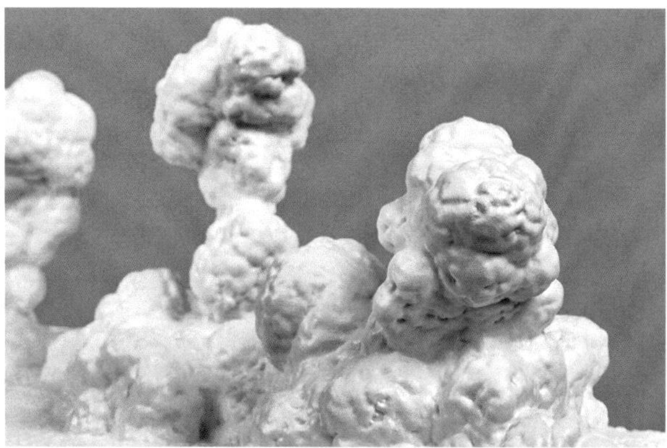

an architectural form transforms into destruction. At the same time, it serves as an anchor point for the subsequent evaluation of an ephemeral incident: "A bomb cloud is made of everything a building once was—concrete, plaster, soil, glass, bodies—and is thus architecture in gaseous form, an event as monument that exists for seven to ten minutes."[6]

Katja Müller-Helle

1 Ute Holl, *Traum, Wolken, Off, Exil(-remix)*, in: *Diaphanes Magazin*, Spring 2017, Issue 1, p. 100. Schönberg's *War Clouds Diary* (1914) can be accessed under: http://www.schoenberg.at/index.php/de/schoenberg/bildnerischeswerk/skizzen/tage-und-notizbuecher-kalender (last access 31.7.2017).
2 Ibid.
3 Ibid.
4 Eyal Weizman, *Forensic Architecture. Violence at the Threshold of Detectability*, New York 2017, p. 104.
5 Eyal Weizman, *Forensis. The Architecture of Public Truth*, Berlin 2015, pp. 9 and 746.
6 *Bomb Cloud Atlas, Forensic Architecture, 2016, Dissecting the violence of war*, https://dublin.sciencegallery.com/designandviolence/exhibits/bomb-cloud-atlas.html (last access 29.7.2017).

Air Strike Atimah, 2015

der Ereignisse eindeutig zu bestimmen. Die multimediale Evidenzerzeugung durch Bilder und Modelle wird von der Gruppe als politische Arbeit präsentiert, die sie als unabhängige Forschung für Menschenrechtsorganisationen, Gerichte und Wahrheitskommissionen versteht. Der Begriff „Forensic", der nach Eyal Weizman, dem Kopf der Gruppe, in seinem ursprünglichen Wortgebrauch innerhalb der Rhetorik die gesamte Sphäre des Politischen, des Rechts und der Ökonomie betraf, erfuhr eine Verengung in der Mitte des 19. Jahrhunderts auf forensische Verfahren der Polizeigewalt. Dieser Monopolisierung forensischer Praxis durch Staatsgewalt soll durch die unabhängige Analyse topografischer Gegebenheiten, zirkulierender Bilder und photogrammetrischer Messmethoden begegnet werden.[5] Das Spezifische an der visuellen Evidenzerzeugung, die für diese Zwecke entwickelt wird, generiert sich aus ihrer Einbettung in den juridischen Kontext. Auch wenn mit virtuellen 3D-Modellen operiert wird, geht es nicht um die Fiktionalisierung computergenerierter Welten; durch die Auswertung von Metadaten und die Behandlung von dokumentarischem Material als operative Bilder rekonstruiert das Kollektiv reale Ereignisse, um politische Verantwortlichkeit in unklarer Faktenlage herzustellen. Das 3D-Modell der Wolke in der Ausstellung steht als Chiffre für diffuse,

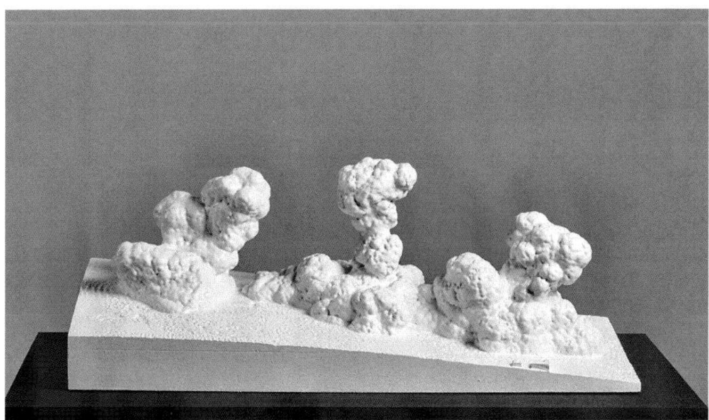

militärische Gewalt im Raum, in der sich die architektonische Form ins Destruktive transformiert. Gleichzeitig bildet es den Ankerpunkt für die nachträgliche Vermessung des ephemeren Geschehens: „A bomb cloud is made of everything a building once was – concrete, plaster, soil, glass, bodies – and is thus architecture in gaseous form, an event as monument that exists for seven to ten minutes."[6]

Katja Müller-Helle

1 Ute Holl, *Traum, Wolken, Off, Exil(-remix)*, in: *Diaphanes Magazin*, Spring 2017, Issue 1, S. 100. Schönbergs *Kriegs-Wolken-Tagebuch* (1914) ist abrufbar unter http://www.schoenberg.at/index.php/de/schoenberg/bildnerischeswerk/skizzen/tage-und-notizbuecher-kalender (letzter Zugriff 31.07.2017).
2 Ebd.
3 Ebd.
4 Eyal Weizman, *Forensic Architecture. Violence at the Threshold of Detectability*, New York 2017, S. 104.
5 Eyal Weizman, *Forensis. The Architecture of Public Truth*, Berlin 2015, S. 9 und 746.
6 *Bomb Cloud Atlas, Forensic Architecture, 2016, Dissecting the violence of war*, https://dublin.sciencegallery.com/designandviolence/exhibits/bomb-cloud-atlas.html (letzter Zugriff 29.07.2017).

Air Strike Atimah, 2015

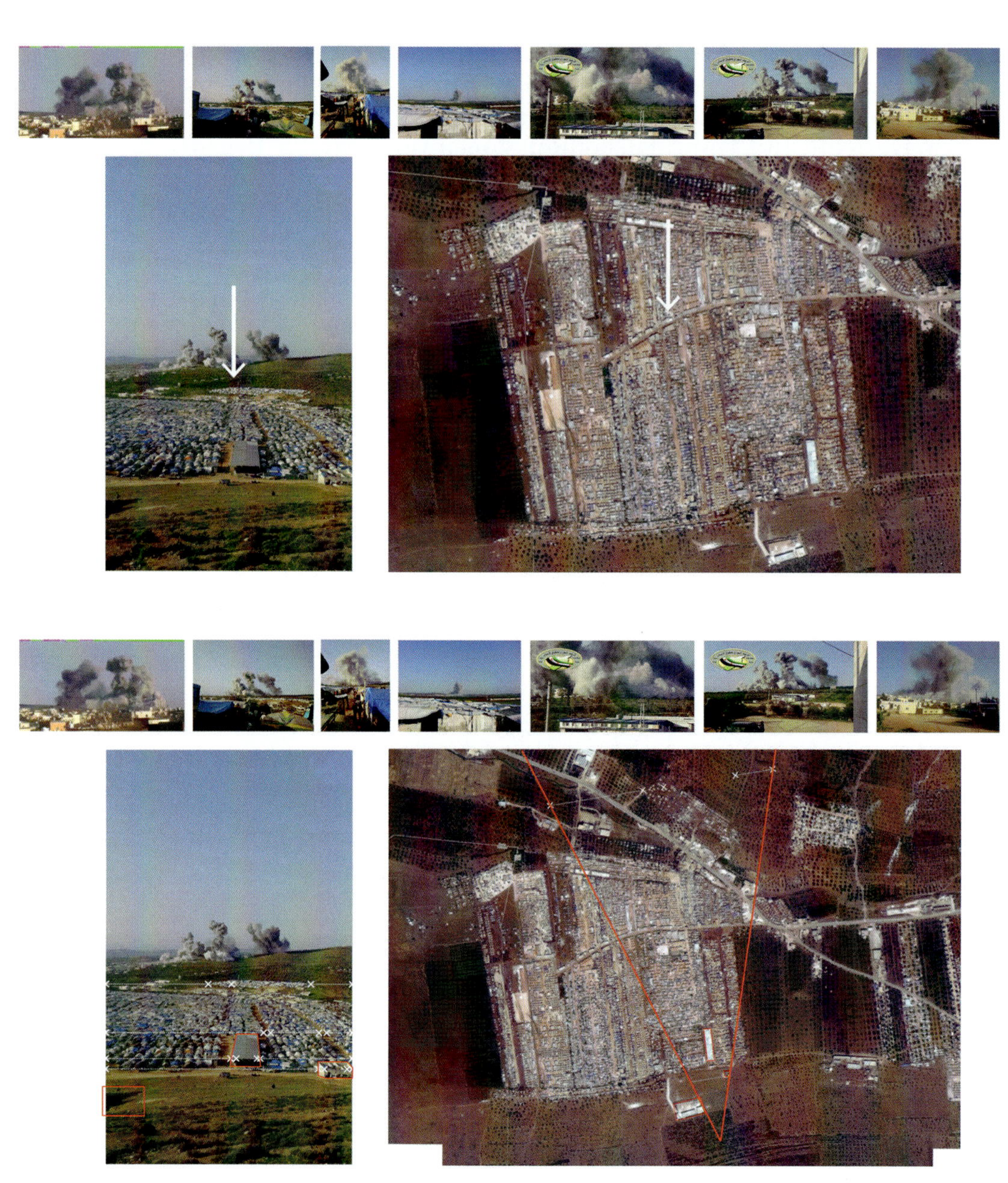

Air Strike Atimah, 2015, video stills

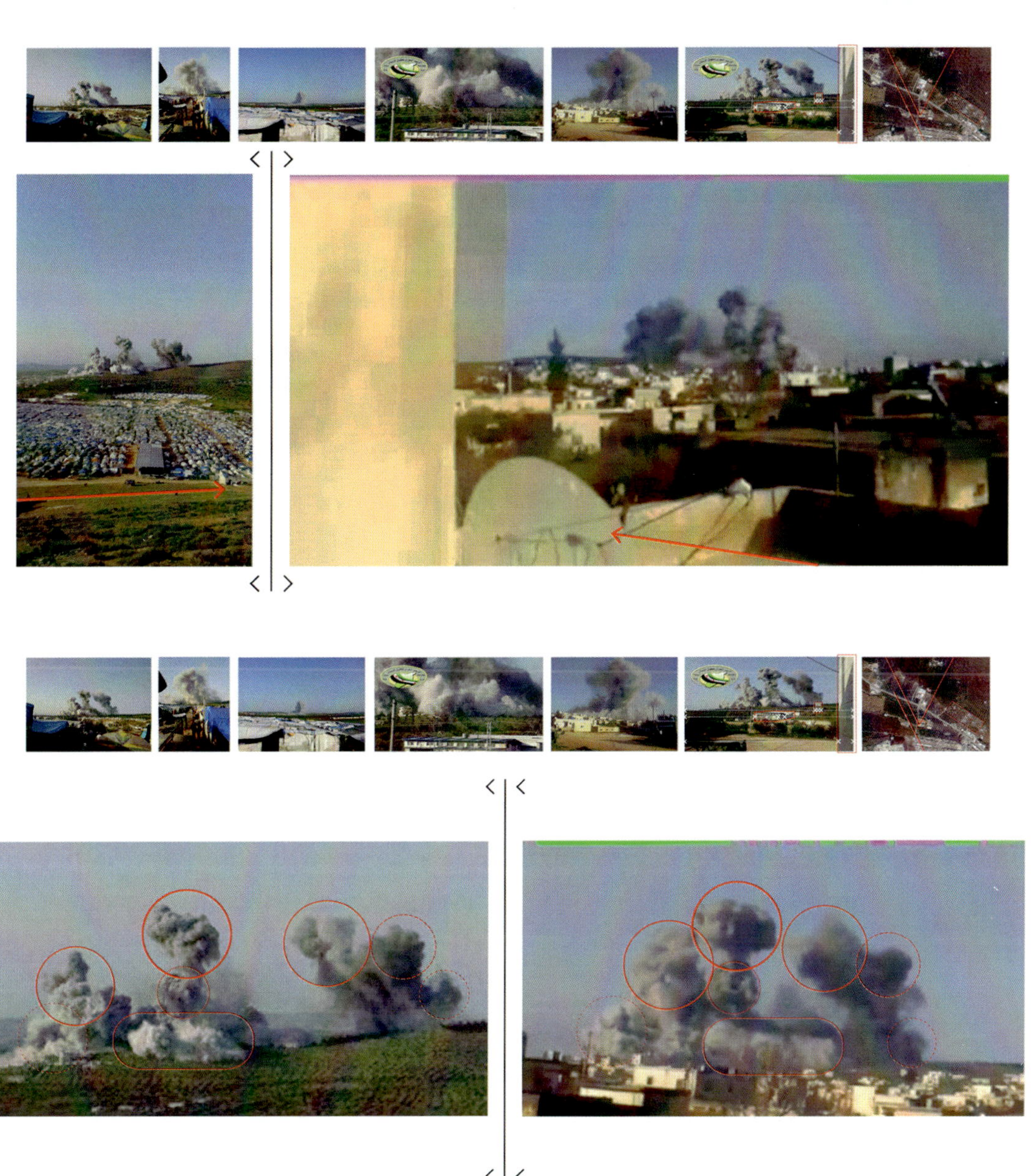

Air Strike Atimah, 2015, Videostills

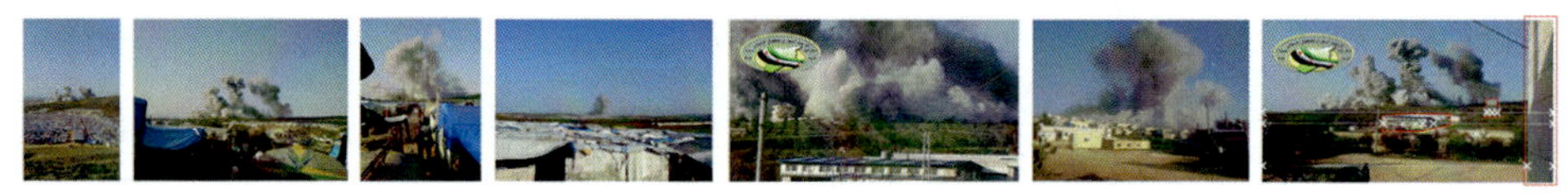

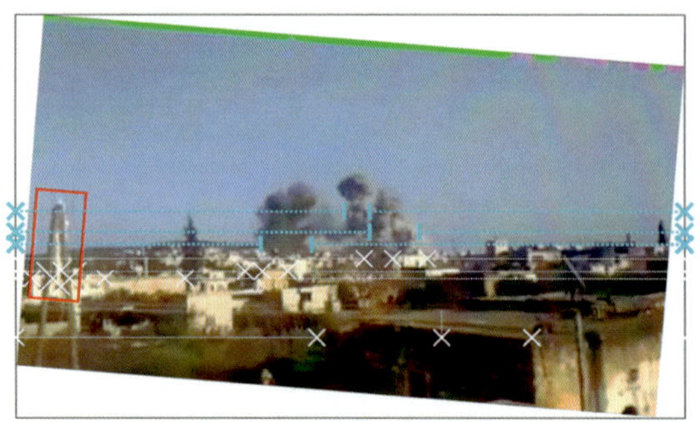

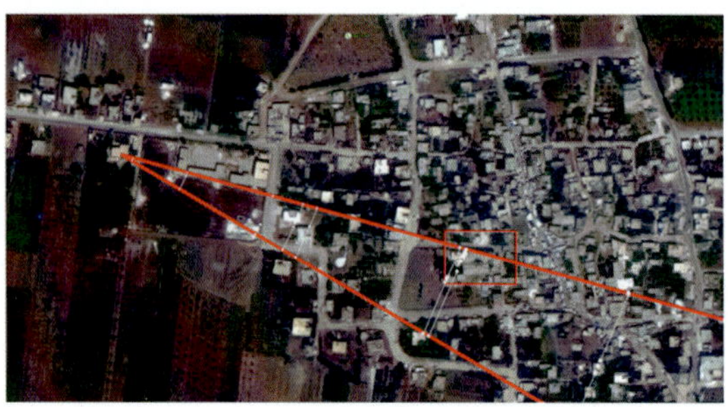

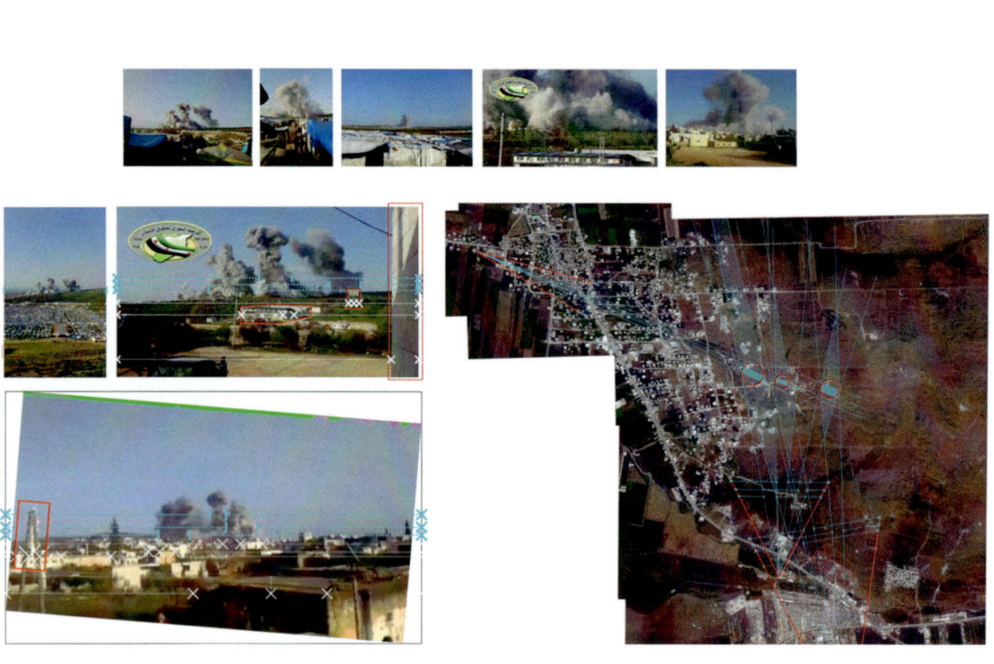

Air Strike Atimah, 2015, video stills

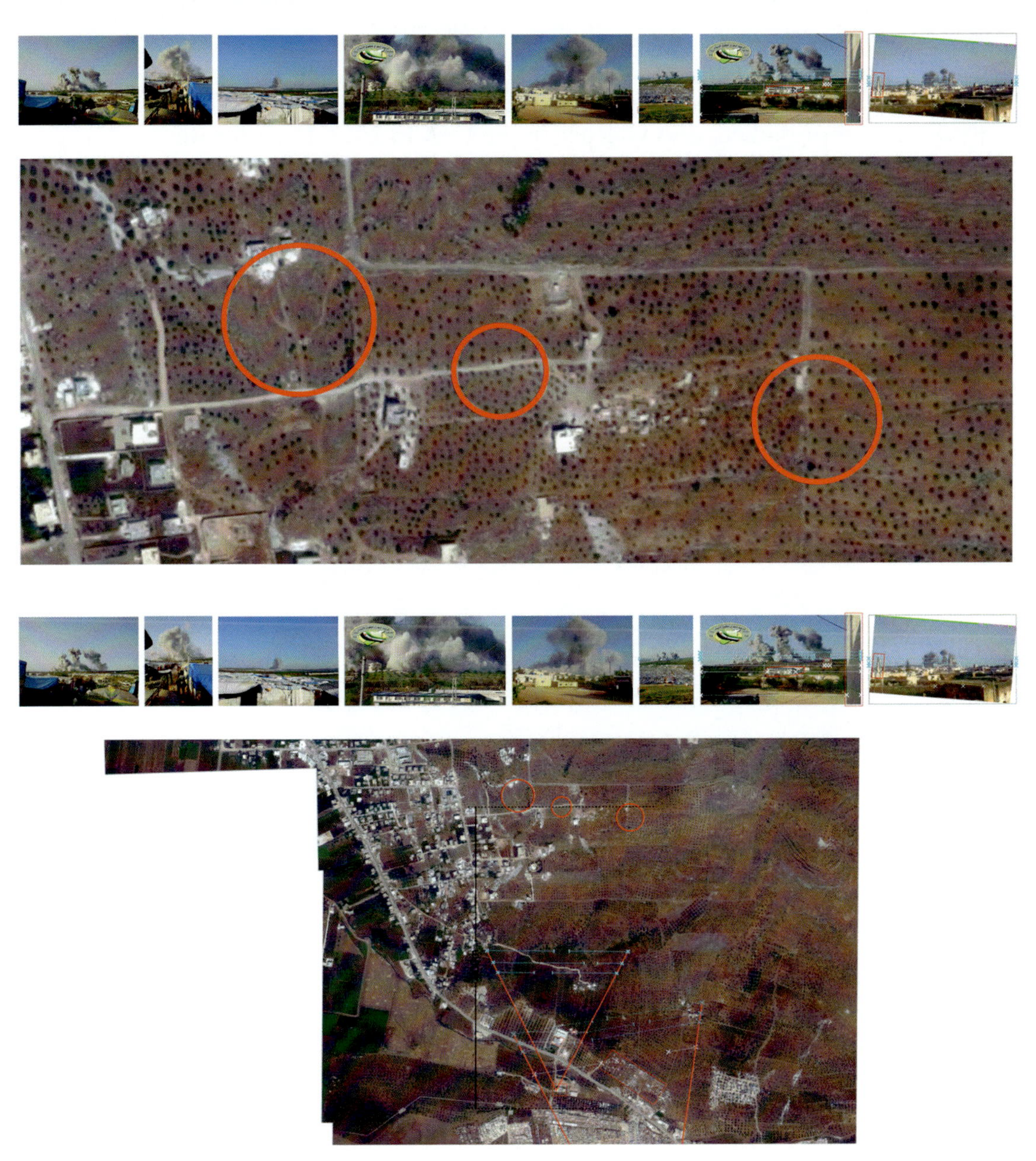

Air Strike Atimah, **2015, Videostills**

Lynn Hershman Leeson

Hooded sweatshirts became a ubiquitous symbol of protest against racially motivated prejudices and violence in the USA in 2012. Even senators in congress wore "hoodies" after the shooting of 17-year-old Trayvon Martin by the self-appointed neighbourhood watchman, George Zimmerman. Based on a black and white photo showing Martin in a hooded sweatshirt —as he was clothed the night he got shot—numerous powerfully emotionalising reenactments by dark-skinned toddlers, hashtag #IAmTrayvon, circulated in social media. The hooded sweatshirt that made Martin look "suspicious"[1] became an icon against racial profiling.[2] The explosiveness and significance of the public participation, culminating with Zimmerman's acquittal in 2013, created the #BlackLivesMatter movement as a result of the online traffic.

In her series, *Disaster Aesthetics*, U.S. American artist, Lynn Hershman Leeson, uses images of great affective potential that are circulating online, such as those reporting on the Martin case. In digital collages, she mounts images of civil uprisings or the humanitarian aftermaths of natural catastrophes with shots of shattered iPhone displays. The smartphone, which records and transfers these incidents at a rapid speed, is not only medium and carrier but has become an integral part of the image and its message. Its damage reflects the drama of the event—as if the telephone was wrecked in the heat of the moment.

The digital print, *Big Hoodie* (2016), shows a smashed screen on which a still from the Netflix series, *Luke Cage*, is juxtaposed with a street scene

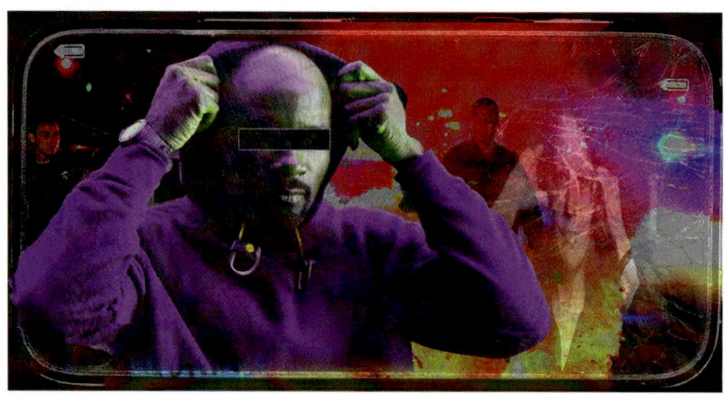

***Big Hoodie*, 2016**

Lynn Hershman Leeson

Kapuzenpullover wurden 2012 in den USA zum allgegenwärtigen Symbol des Protestes gegen rassistisch motivierte Vorurteile und Gewalt. Nach der Erschießung des 17-jährigen Trayvon Martin durch den selbsternannten Nachbarschaftswachmann George Zimmerman trugen selbst Senatoren im Kongress „Hoodies“. Ausgehend von einem Schwarzweiß-Foto, das Martin wie in der Tatnacht im Kapuzenpullover zeigte, kursierten in den sozialen Medien zahlreiche, stark emotionalisierende Reinszenierungen von dunkelhäutigen Kleinkindern mit dem Hashtag #IAmTrayvon. Der Kapuzenpullover, der Martin „verdächtig“[1] gemacht hatte, wurde zum Zeichen des Widerstandes gegen Racial Profiling.[2] Die Brisanz und Tragweite der öffentlichen Teilhabe in den sozialen Netzwerken kulminierten schließlich mit dem Freispruch Zimmermans im Jahr 2013, woraufhin sich unter dem Hashtag #BlackLivesMatter die gleichnamige Bewegung gründete.

Die US-amerikanische Künstlerin Lynn Hershman Leeson verwendet in ihrer Serie *Disaster Aesthetics* online kursierende Bilder mit hohem

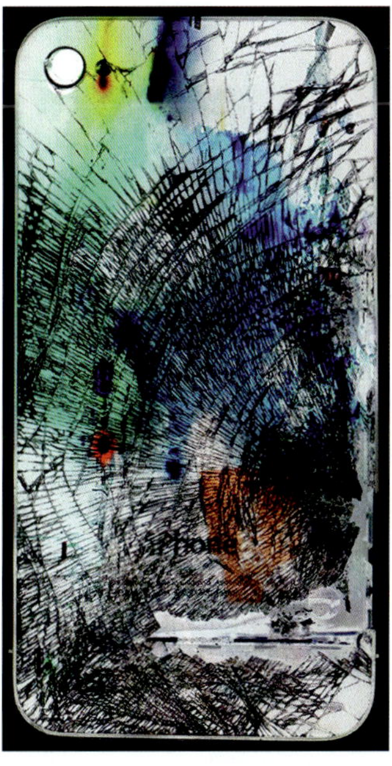

Affizierungspotenzial wie jene, die vom Fall Martin berichten. In digitalen Collagen montiert sie die Bilder von zivilgesellschaftlichen Aufständen oder den humanitären Folgen von Naturkatastrophen mit Aufnahmen zersplitterter iPhone-Displays. Das Smartphone, das die Vorfälle in rasantem Tempo einfängt und überträgt, ist nicht mehr nur Medium und Bildträger, sondern wird fester Bestandteil des Bildes und seiner Aussage. Die Zerstörung spiegelt die Dramatik des Ereignisses – als wäre das Telefon im Eifer des Gefechtes demoliert worden.

Der Digitalprint *Big Hoodie* (2016) kombiniert auf dem zerschmetterten Screen ein Still der Netflix-Serie *Luke Cage* mit einer Straßenszene, die

Image Capture on Discarded Broken Cell Phone after Trayvon Martin Riots, 2012

after Zimmerman's acquittal. The foreground shows the contemporary adaptation of Marvel's first black superhero, *Luke Cage* (1972); but, instead of the yellow shirt of the comic character, the actor in 2016 wears a purple hooded sweatshirt–in memory of Trayvon Martin. Transferred into popular culture, the iconic piece of clothing reverberates the collective shock unleashed by the original incident. The visual attraction and power of the original images predestines them for appropriation. The night-time police scene in the background could be part of the series but in fact originates from a news broadcast.

Furthermore, an image from Hershman Leeson's *Cut and Paste* series (2012–2013) is placed on the right-hand side. In the transparent photograph (as if made with double exposure), she deals with the manipulation of selfies. For her media self-representation, she smooths out her face, presenting a fixed gaze. By including the portrait, she declares herself, as it were, a witness of the event.

In social media, it is no longer only about seeing but also about being seen—intentionally or not. The sentence, "The Water is Rising Pleas," sprayed

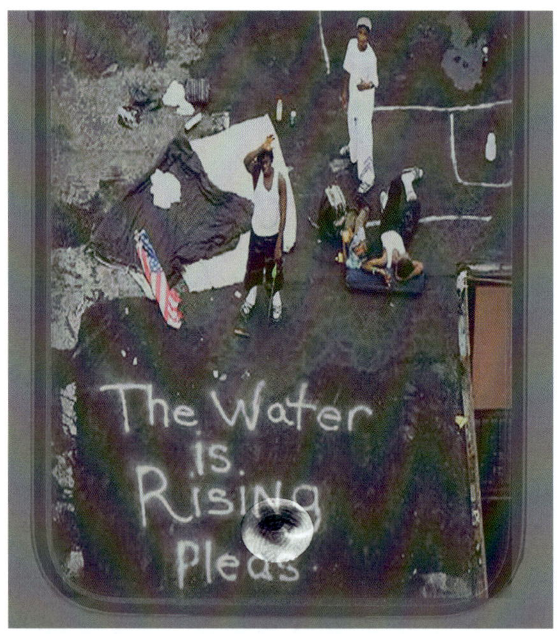

on a flat roof, thus addresses itself directly to the viewers of the aftermath of Hurricane Katrina.[3] In another work from this series, one can read "Don't Shoot" on posters. This imperative escalated into a widespread, vociferous call to protest after the shooting of unarmed, 18-year-old Michael Brown by a white policeman in August 2014. Hershman Leeson focuses on the issue of seeing and being seen, transparency and surveillance in our digital time through the interlacing of different viewpoints. In both works, eyes look at us from the round iPhone keys.

Final water is rising, 2016

nach dem Freispruch Zimmermans entstand. Der vordere Bildausschnitt zeigt eine aktuelle Adaption von Marvels erstem schwarzen Superhelden *Luke Cage* (1972), doch statt des gelben Hemdes der Comicfigur trägt der Schauspieler im Jahr 2016 eine violette Kapuzenjacke – in Erinnerung an Trayvon Martin. In die Populärkultur überführt, vergegenwärtigt das ikonische Kleidungsstück die kollektive Betroffenheit, die das ursprüngliche Ereignis international auslöste. Die visuelle Sogkraft prädestiniert die ursprünglichen Bilder für diese Aneignung. Die nächtliche Polizeiszene im Hintergrund, die tatsächlich ein Nachrichtenbild ist, könnte auch der Actionserie entstammen.

Weiterhin ist ein Bild aus Hershman Leesons *Cut and Paste* Serie (2012–2013) in die rechte Bildhälfte gesetzt. In dem transparenten, wie durch Doppelbelichtung entstandenen Foto beschäftigt sie sich mit der Manipulation von Selfies. Sie zieht sich darauf mit starrem Blick das eigene Gesicht für die mediale Selbstinszenierung glatt. Mit der Montage erklärt sie sich gleichsam zur Zeugin der Ereignisse.

In den sozialen Medien geht es nicht mehr nur um das Sehen, sondern auch um das – gewollte oder ungewollte – Gesehenwerden. So richtet sich der auf ein Flachdach gesprühte Schriftzug „The Water is Rising Pleas“

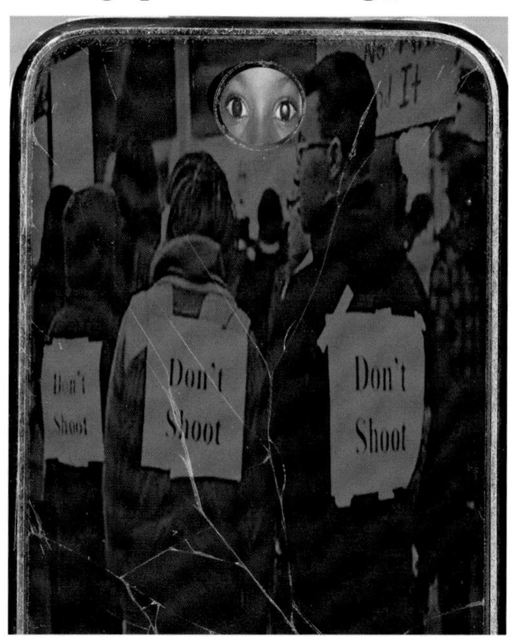

direkt an die Betrachter*innen der katastrophalen Folgen von Hurricane Katrina.[3] In einem anderen Werk der Serie ist auf Plakaten der Imperativ „Don’t Shoot“ zu lesen, der mit der Erschießung des unbewaffneten 18-jährigen Michael Brown durch einen weißen Polizisten im August 2014 lautstark zum übergreifenden Protestruf anstieg. Sehen und gesehen werden, Transparenz und Überwachung im digitalen Zeitalter thematisiert Lynn Hershman Leeson durch die Verschränkung unterschiedlicher

Cyclops of the anthropocine 1, 2016

In the installation, *iPhone Crack (August Moon)* (2014), this "observation

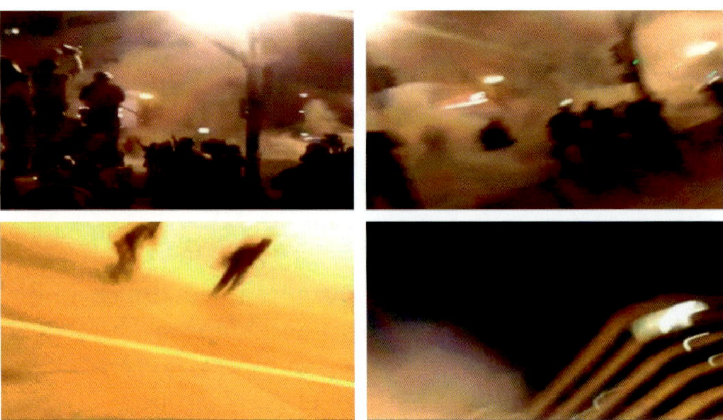

of the viewer" is actively integrated into the piece. As soon as the spectator draws near, the projection surface changes from a milky, clouded pane to a shattered iPhone. The video showing the smoke bombs and gunshots of a

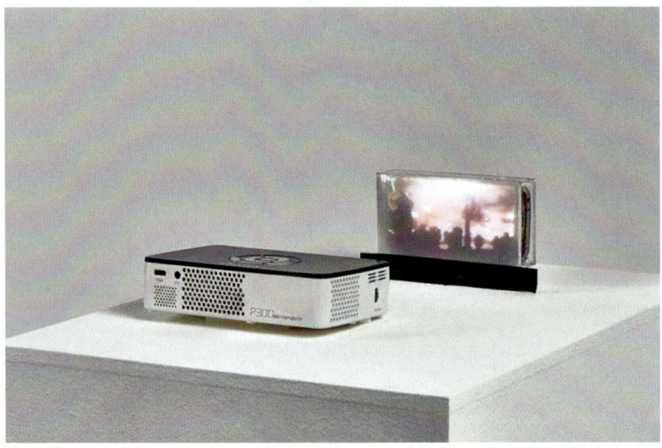

street fight does not stop, even when a wounded woman is carried away. The viewer, registered by the motion sensor, follows the events, so to speak, "live."

Lynn Hershman Leeson is known as one of the first media artists worldwide. She has significantly shaped the feminist discourse in art and is dealing artistically and theoretically with questions about the relationship between identity and modern technology for over fifty years. She has repeatedly been ahead of her time with her visionary thoughts about society-changing categories of technological innovations, which makes her one of the most influential contemporary artists.

Marion Eisele

1 In his call to the police, George Zimmerman spoke of a "real suspicious guy" and answered questions with "He looks black" and "[...] a dark hoodie, like a grey hoodie, and either jeans or sweatpants and white tennis shoes," on: https://www.youtube.com/watch?v=zj7qEcD8R-8 (last access 5.9.2017).

2 Cf. Rashawn Ray, *"If Only He Didn't Wear the Hoodie..." Selective Perception and Stereotype Maintenance*, in: Stephanie McClure, Cherise Harris (ed.), *Getting Real about Race: Hoodies, Mascots, Model Minorities, and Other Conversations,* Los Angeles 2015, pp. 81–93.

3 In the original pictorial material, "HELP", can be seen further towards the back.

iPhone Crack (August Moon), 2014, video stills

iPhone Crack (August Moon), 2014, installation view

Blickachsen. Denn in beiden Arbeiten blicken uns aus den runden iPhone-Tasten Augen an.

In der Installation *iPhone Crack (August Moon)* (2014) wird diese

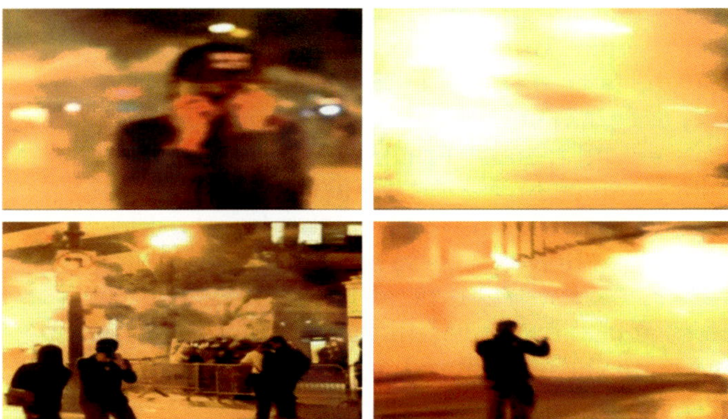

„Beobachtererfassung" aktiv ins Werk integriert. Sobald sich die Betrachter*-innen annähern, wechselt die Projektionsfläche von einer milchig trüben Scheibe auf ein zersplittertes iPhone. Das von Rauchbomben und Schüssen durchsetzte Handyvideo eines Straßenkampfes bricht selbst dann nicht ab,

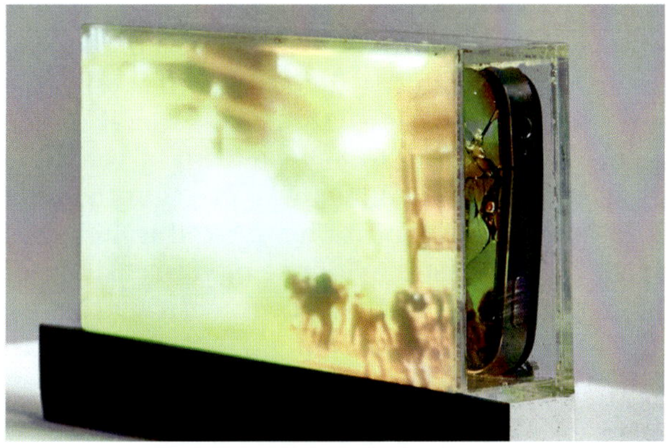

als eine angeschossene Frau abtransportiert wird. Die technisch erfassten Betrachter*innen sind sozusagen „live" dabei.

Lynn Hershman Leeson gilt als eine der ersten Medienkünstler*innen weltweit. Sie hat maßgeblich den feministischen Diskurs in der Kunst mitgeprägt und beschäftigt sich seit über fünfzig Jahren künstlerisch und theoretisch mit Fragen zum Verhältnis von Identität und moderner Technologie. Immer wieder denkt sie in ihrem vielschichtigen Werk gesellschaftsverändernde Kategorien technologischer Innovationen visionär voraus, was sie zu einer der einflussreichsten Künstler*innen der Gegenwart macht.

Marion Eisele

1 In seinem Anruf bei der Polizei spricht George Zimmerman von einem „real suspicious guy" und antwortet auf Nachfragen mit „He looks black." und „[…] a dark hoodie, like a grey hoodie, and either jeans or sweat-pants and white tennis shoes", auf: https://www.youtube.com/watch?v=zj7qEcD8R-8 (letzter Zugriff 05.09.2017).

2 Vgl. Rashawn Ray, *"If Only He Didn't Wear the Hoodie…" Selective Perception and Stereotype Maintenance*, in: Stephanie McClure, Cherise Harris (Hg.), *Getting Real about Race: Hoodies, Mascots, Model Minorities, and Other Conversations,* Los Angeles 2015, S. 81–93.

3 Im Originalbildmaterial steht weiter hinten noch „HELP".

iPhone Crack (August Moon), 2014, Videostills

iPhone Crack (August Moon), 2014, Detail

Thomas Hirschhorn

We are right in the thick of it, in a network of refugee misery, international terrorism, catastrophic civil wars and the disastrous impacts of an increasingly deteriorating environment. But we look the other way. Certainly, news feeds from the press keep us up to date by the second on each of the latest manoeuvres of power-hungry autocrats in the most remote corners of our global village. But the information policy of the media is based on confronting us only with those pictures that the news channels consider to be approvable. Smashed skulls from which the brains are flowing out, intestines squeezed out of open bodies—these are not the kind of images that belong to the repertoire of news reports, although they are equally being produced by the second. So we are, on the one hand, more informed now than ever before, yet on the other hand, we are conditioned to turn our back on the suffering in the world.

Thomas Hirschhorn challenges us to look. Like a thread running through his oeuvre are images that deliver the unfiltered drama of human existence, placing it right before our very eyes. The artist thus questions the sovereignty of interpretation of those information media that channel images in terms of their content by supplementing contextualizing explanations. According to Hirschhorn, this weakens the status of the image itself and, at the same time, prevents a direct encounter with it, which would confront viewers with their "own responsibility for the act of seeing."[1]

In line with Hirschhorn's notion of images, the era of social media is reinforcing photography's claim of speaking to us as a kind of vehicle of truth.[2] At first sight, this may seem paradoxical: as there are countless images circulating on the Web, whose origin and conditions of production are not traceable and which, in terms of journalistic evidence of sources, are of dubious character. And yet it is these images that become direct testimonies of events. They are true—for as image phenomena lacking context, they represent nothing but themselves.

What such images convey, above all, is the intensity of events, released in the artist's works in a rigorous, almost ecstatic manner. The viewers respond to such intensity with a wide range of emotions reaching from anger, disgust or shock to feelings of guilt. This is also apparent in the series *The Subjecters*. The title refers to a number of mannequins, which Hirschhorn

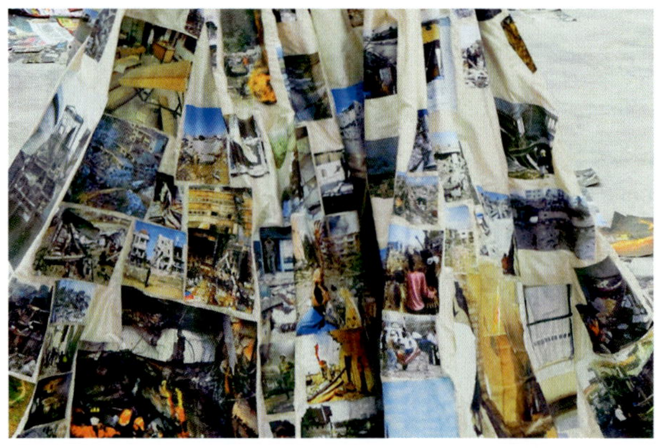

Subjecter (Katastrophé), 2010, detail

Thomas Hirschhorn

Wir befinden uns mitten drin, in einem Netzwerk aus Flüchtlingselend, internationalem Terrorismus, katastrophalen Bürgerkriegen und den desaströsen Folgen einer zunehmend kollabierenden Umwelt. Doch wir schauen nicht hin. Die Newsfeeds der Presseorgane halten uns zwar im Sekundentakt über jedes neue Manöver machtbesessener Autokraten in den entferntesten Winkeln unseres globalen Dorfs auf dem Laufenden. Aber die Informationspolitik der Medien beruht darauf, dass wir nur mit jenen Bildern konfrontiert werden, welche die Nachrichtenkanäle für goutierbar halten. Zertrümmerte Schädel, aus denen Gehirnmasse fließt, aus offenen Körpern hervorquellende Eingeweide – solche Bilder gehören nicht zum Repertoire der Nachrichtensendungen, obschon sie ebenfalls im Sekundentakt entstehen. So sind wir also einerseits aufgeklärt wie nie zu vor, andererseits dazu konditioniert, uns abzuwenden vom Elend der Welt.

Thomas Hirschhorn fordert uns auf hinzuschauen. Wie ein roter Faden ziehen sich Bilder durch sein Werk, die das Drama menschlicher Existenz ungefiltert vor uns ausbreiten. Er stellt damit die Deutungshoheit jener Informationsmedien in Frage, die Bilder durch kontextualisierende Erklärungen inhaltlich kanalisieren. Folgt man Hirschhorn, so wird dadurch sowohl der Status des Bildes geschwächt als auch eine direkte Auseinandersetzung mit ihm verhindert, die die Betrachter*innen mit ihrer „eigenen Verantwortung für den Akt des Sehens konfrontier[en]“[1] würde.

Das Zeitalter der sozialen Medien bekräftigt den Anspruch der Fotografie, im Sinne Hirschhorns als eine Art Vehikel der Wahrheit[2] zu uns zu sprechen. Das mag zunächst paradox erscheinen: denn durch das Netz zirkulieren massenweise Bilder, deren Herkunft und Entstehungsbedingungen nicht nachvollziehbar sind und die somit im Sinne journalistischer Beweisführung zweifelhaften Charakter haben. Gerade aber diese Bilder werden zu unmittelbaren Zeugen von Ereignissen; sie sind wahr, weil sie als kontextlose Bildphänomene für nichts anderes stehen, als für sich selbst.

Was diese Bilder vor allen anderen Dingen transportieren, ist die Intensität der Ereignisse, die sich in den Werken des Künstlers geradezu rauschhaft entlädt und bei den Betrachter*innen auf ein weites Feld von Emotionen trifft, die von Wut, Ekel, Erschrecken bis hin zu Schuldgefühlen reichen. Dies wird anhand der Werkgruppe *The Subjecters* deutlich.

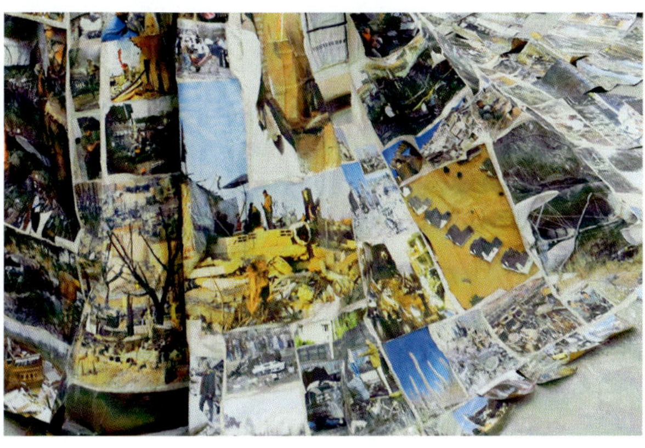

Subjecter (Katastrophé), 2010, Detail

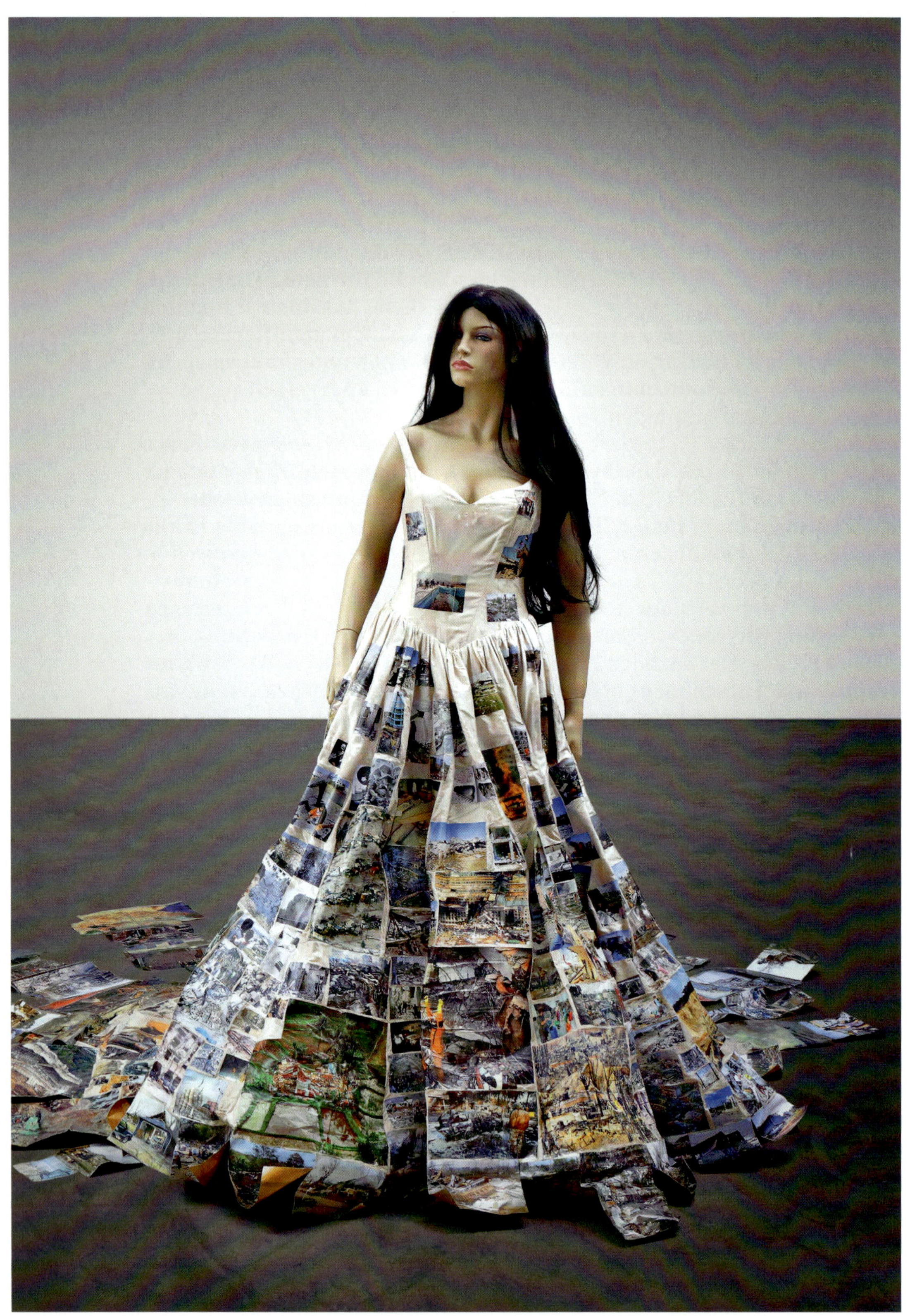

Subjecter (Katastrophé), 2010

Der Titel bezeichnet eine Reihe von Schaufensterpuppen, denen Hirschhorn Brautkleider übergestreift hat und auf die er Unmengen jenes kontextlosen, jedoch inhaltlich „hochexplosiven“ Bildmaterials appliziert. Die Bilder bezieht er aus Tageszeitungen, aber auch aus dem Internet und dort zunehmend von den Plattformen der sozialen Medien.

An Kleid und Schleppe der Puppe in KAI 10 mit dem Titel *Subjecter (Katastrophé)* von 2010 haften solche, in den Massenmedien tagtäglich zirkulierenden Bilder, welche die dramatischen Folgen von Naturkatastrophen auf urbanes Leben und menschliche Siedlungsräume zeigen. Die Bilder

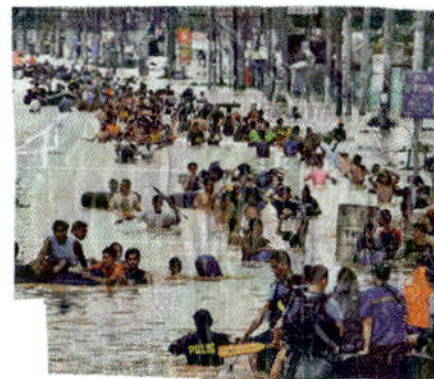

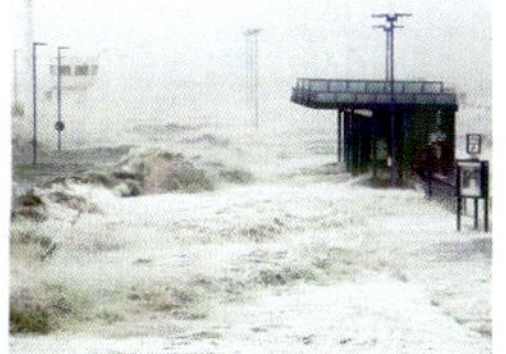

von Extremsituationen treffen die Betrachter*innen unmittelbar, da Hirschhorn sie bewusst aus dem Informationszusammenhang gerissen hat. Dadurch ist es unmöglich, einzelne Ereignisse und deren Hintergründe herauszufiltern und die Bildereignisse im Sinne üblicher Nomenklaturen zu dekodieren.

Andererseits hält uns Hirschhorn in Distanz zu dem, was wir sehen. Dabei spielt auch eine Rolle, dass er als zentrales Objekt eine Schaufensterpuppe gewählt hat. Hirschhorn versteht die Schaufensterpuppe dabei als „[...]die dürftige, zeitgenössische, amoralische, nichtreligiöse Version von jemandem oder etwas [...], der oder das anstelle eines Anderen etwas erträgt [...]“[3]. Dieser modellhafte Stellvertreter-Körper an Stelle echter Subjektivität erschwert die Identifikation, aber verstärkt die Logik der applizierten Bilder: angesichts der Flut ähnlicher Motive ist man unentschieden, wo man zuerst hinschauen soll – und schaut irgendwann gar nicht mehr. Ein Bilderstrom wie ein kalter Windzug, der uns nicht wirklich betroffen macht, sondern uns nur kurz Frösteln lässt, um dann folgenlos vorüber zu ziehen. Dieses Wechselspiel zwischen emotionaler Ergriffenheit und Apathie wird mit der rasanten Verbreitung von Bildern in den sozialen Medien verstärkt.

Hirschhorns Arbeiten vergegenwärtigen eindringlich, wie Affekte in Bildern gebunden sind und wie diese sich wahlweise beim Gegenüber entladen – oder man sich dagegen abschottet. Im Kern konfrontieren sie uns mit dem Akt des Sehens selbst. Das Sehen macht uns immer zu Kompliz*innen des Bildes und des dort Sichtbaren, das uns in letzter Konsequenz herausfordert, Position zu beziehen.

Julia Höner

Subjecter (Katastrophé), 2010, Details

has dressed in wedding gowns, and onto which he affixed a superabundance of just this kind of autonomous, yet "explosive" image material. He uses images from newspapers combined with images drawn from the Internet, reverting increasingly to social media platforms.

Attached to the dress and train of the mannequin at KAI 10, titled *Subjecter (Katastrophé)* (2010), are the kind of images found circulating day in, day out in the mass media that illustrate the dramatic effects of natural disasters on urban life and human settlements. The spectators are affected by such images of extreme situations with a striking immediacy, for Hirschhorn has deliberately isolated them from their informational context. This makes it impossible to single out particular incidents along with their backgrounds or to decode the visual experiences in the usual sense of conventional nomenclatures.

Then again Hirschhorn keeps us at a distance from what we are seeing. Choosing a mannequin as a central object contributes to this impression. Hirschhorn perceives the mannequin as the "meager, contemporary, amoral, non-religious version of someone or something […], who or which endures something in the place of another […]."[3] This exemplary substitute body, taking the place of real subjectivity, impedes identification, yet at the same time enhances the logic behind the affixed images: at the sight of such a flood of similar motifs, one is undecided about where to look first—and sooner or later tends not to look at all. A stream of images, like a cold gust of wind that doesn't really arouse our concern, just gives us a brief chill to then continue on without affecting us. This interplay between emotional involvement and apathy is enhanced by the rapid dissemination of images in social media.

Hirschhorn's works insistently point out to which extent affects are bound up with images and how they either discharge themselves onto the viewer—or one shuts them out. Essentially, these works confront us with the act of seeing itself. Seeing always makes us accomplices of the image and of what is visible there, which as a last consequence challenges us to take a stand.

Julia Höner

1 Hirschhorn also works against the hierarchisation of information by presenting images in swarms, thus working against the idea of a unique, representative image icon.

2 In many of his statements Hirschhorn makes reference to the truth content inherent in each image, regardless of its context, for instance when he says: "I […] believe the image, because I know that the image isn't lying, an image never lies. Even a staged or simulated picture doesn't lie; it only shows what it is." Thomas Hirschhorn in an interview with Sebastian Egenhofer in the booklet accompanying the exhibition at Galerie Susanna Kulli, Zurich 2012, unpaged.

3 Thomas Hirschhorn in an interview with Sarah Douglas, on: http://ende.blouinartinfo.com/features/article/10763-thomas-hirschhorn (last access 18.9.2017).

1 Einer Hierarchisierung von Informationen arbeitet Hirschhorn auch dadurch entgegen, dass Bilder bei ihm in Schwärmen auftreten und er so der Vorstellung von der einen, repräsentativen Bildikone entgegenwirkt.

2 In vielen seiner Äußerungen bezieht sich Hirschhorn auf den Wahrheitsgehalt, der jedem Bild, losgelöst von seinem Kontext, zugrunde liege, etwa wenn er sagt: „Ich […] glaube dem Bild, weil ich weiss, dass das Bild nicht lügt, ein Bild lügt nie. Auch ein gestelltes oder vorgetäuschtes oder retuschiertes Bild lügt nicht, es zeigt immer nur das, was es ist." Thomas Hirschhorn im Interview mit Sebastian Egenhofer im Begleitheft zur Ausstellung in der Galerie Susanna Kulli, Zürich 2012, unpaginiert.

3 Thomas Hirschhorn im Interview mit Sarah Douglas, auf: http://ende.blouinartinfo.com/features/article/10763-thomas-hirschhorn (letzter Zugriff 18.09.2017).

Randa Maroufi

“How does he want the photo? Ask him how he wants the photo, so I can do it right now,” a protagonist demands of director, Randa Maroufi in her film, *Le Park* (2015). The camera meanders parallel through the derelict rooms of an empty building in Yasmina Park in Casablanca that Maroufi has chosen as the setting for her work. The former leisure park in the city centre has now fallen into disrepair and is being used as a retreat, especially by adolescents. They are now the protagonists in Maroufi’s *Le Park*.

The camera tentatively explores the architecture and surfaces. On its journey, it keeps encountering these youths, who appear frozen in their interactions. Like tableaux vivants, they restage scenes based on Maroufi’s prior research on social media. In these social media posts, the youths recreate either violent scenes from film and media sources or present themselves in expensive, branded clothing. Such images are shared and imitated en masse on the Internet.

How can their success be explained? Why do they fascinate both sender as well as recipient? To pursue this question, Maroufi and her protagonists re-stage the virtual world of images back in the analogue space of the park. The camera ceaselessly circles scenes of raw violence and self-staging, scans bodies, gestures and faces and offers different perspectives of the same set. The view is thus not limited solely to the detail of the two men with machetes raised against each other; it shows the whole picture: the horror in a few faces as well as gestures of encouragement from bystanders. The illusion of the uniqueness of this one moment captured by the photo dissolves into a holistic panorama. The longer we study the protagonists in this way, the more the camera turns itself on us: what is performed here are clichés of violence and the stigmatisation of a particular group of people as its cause. These have become so ingrained in the semiotics of our media that the producers —the youths and the media—as well as consumers—other youths and we ourselves—hardly question them anymore. The pictorial codes repeatedly confirm themselves in the virtual, infinite loop and thereby reveal their emotionalising and affective potential.

In her tableaux vivants, Maroufi brings this fixed order out of balance. Minimal body movements become visible. The areas around the eyes are deliberately and almost imperceptibly pixelated, thereby raising the question: who is revealing or hiding which information here, and for what reason? The soundtrack also contributes to the deconstruction of this formulaic pictorial world. Different voices come from off camera: a newsreader, the youths from the park, the director herself—fragments of information that, however, never lead to a meaningful connection. The film’s soundtrack, composed specifically for this work, whizzes through the space like images on the Internet, it creates tension that is never released and offers no orientation. The deconstruction, however, reveals that it is precisely the unfathomable in the images that makes them so desirable.

Le Park belongs to Maroufi’s interdisciplinary works, as do photography and sculpture as well as performance and sound pieces. The focal point of

Randa Maroufi

„How does he want the photo? Ask him how he wants the photo, so I can do it right now“, verlangt ein Protagonist in Randa Maroufis Film *Le Park* (2015) von der Regisseurin. Die Kamera mäandert parallel durch die verfallenen Räume eines der leer stehenden Gebäude im Yasmina Park in Casablanca, den Maroufi als Schauplatz für ihre Arbeit ausgewählt hat. Der ehemalige Vergnügungspark inmitten der Stadt ist heute im Verfall begriffen und wird besonders von jungen Heranwachsenden als Rückzugsort genutzt. In *Le Park* werden diese nun zu Protagonist*innen auf Maroufis Filmset.

Die Kamera, die sich suchend und tastend durch die Architekturen und über die Oberflächen bewegt, trifft in ihrer Fahrt immer wieder auf diese Jugendlichen, die in ihrer Interaktion eingefroren scheinen. Vergleichbar tableau vivants bilden sie Szenen nach, die Maroufi zuvor in den sozialen Netzwerken recherchiert hat. Es sind Bilder, in denen Jugendliche entweder Gewaltszenen aus Film und Medien nachstellen oder sich in teurer Markenkleidung inszenieren. Sie werden massenhaft im Netz geteilt und nachgeahmt.

Wie erklärt sich der Erfolg dieser Bilder, welche Faszination geht von ihnen sowohl für die Sender*innen als auch die Empfänger*innen aus? Um dieser Frage nachzugehen, re-inszeniert Maroufi die virtuelle Bildwelt gemeinsam mit ihren Protagonist*innen und bringt sie zurück in den analogen Raum des Parks. Unaufhörlich umkreist die Kamera Szenen aus roher Gewalt und Selbstinszenierung, scannt Körper, Gesten und Gesichter und bietet immer wieder neue Perspektiven auf ein und dieselbe Szene an. Das Bild beschränkt sich so nicht mehr allein auf den Ausschnitt der beiden Männer mit den gegeneinander erhobenen Macheten. Es zeigt das gesamte Bild, das den Schrecken in einigen Gesichtern ebenso einschließt wie die anfeuernden Gesten der Beistehenden. Die Illusion der Einmaligkeit des einen, im Foto festgehaltenen Augenblicks wird aufgelöst in ein ganzheitliches Panorama. Je länger wir den Protagonist*innen auf diese Weise begegnen, desto mehr wendet sich der Blick der Kamera auf uns selbst: Was hier vorgeführt wird, sind Klischees von Gewalt und die Stigmatisierung einer bestimmten Gruppe von Menschen als Auslöser dieser Gewalt. Diese haben sich derart in die Semiotik unserer medialen Sprachwelt eingeprägt, dass sie sowohl für die Produzent*innen – die Jugendlichen und die Medien – als auch die Konsument*innen – andere Jugendliche und wir selbst – kaum mehr hinterfragt werden. In der virtuellen Dauerschleife bestätigen sich diese Bildformeln immer wieder selbst und offenbaren damit ihr emotionalisierendes und affizierendes Potenzial.

Maroufi bringt in ihren tableau vivants diese festgefügte Ordnung ins Wanken. Minimale Bewegungen der Körper werden sichtbar. Augenpartien werden willkürlich und kaum merklich verpixelt und damit die Frage in den Raum gestellt, wer hier eigentlich welche Information zu welchem Zweck offenlegt oder verbirgt. Und auch die Tonebene arbeitet an der Dekonstruktion dieser formelhaften Bildwelt. Aus dem Off liefern uns unterschiedliche

all her works is social reality as a construct, which she repeatedly questions with every means available. She especially looks at the pivotal role images play in this construction of the social. In previous works such as *Reconstitutions* (2013), a series of photographs as well as a video, the performance, *Attempts of seduction* (2013), or the performative video work, *Mantons* (2011), she also investigates the construction of gender roles and reveals the mechanisms underlying them. Here, too, are repeated moments of latent violence, expressed through the body as well as the glance and the therein hidden perceptions that Maroufi unmasks. Finally, she interrupts for a moment the circulation of ever more similar stereotypes and leaves us with alternative views of this particular reality.

Tasja Langenbach

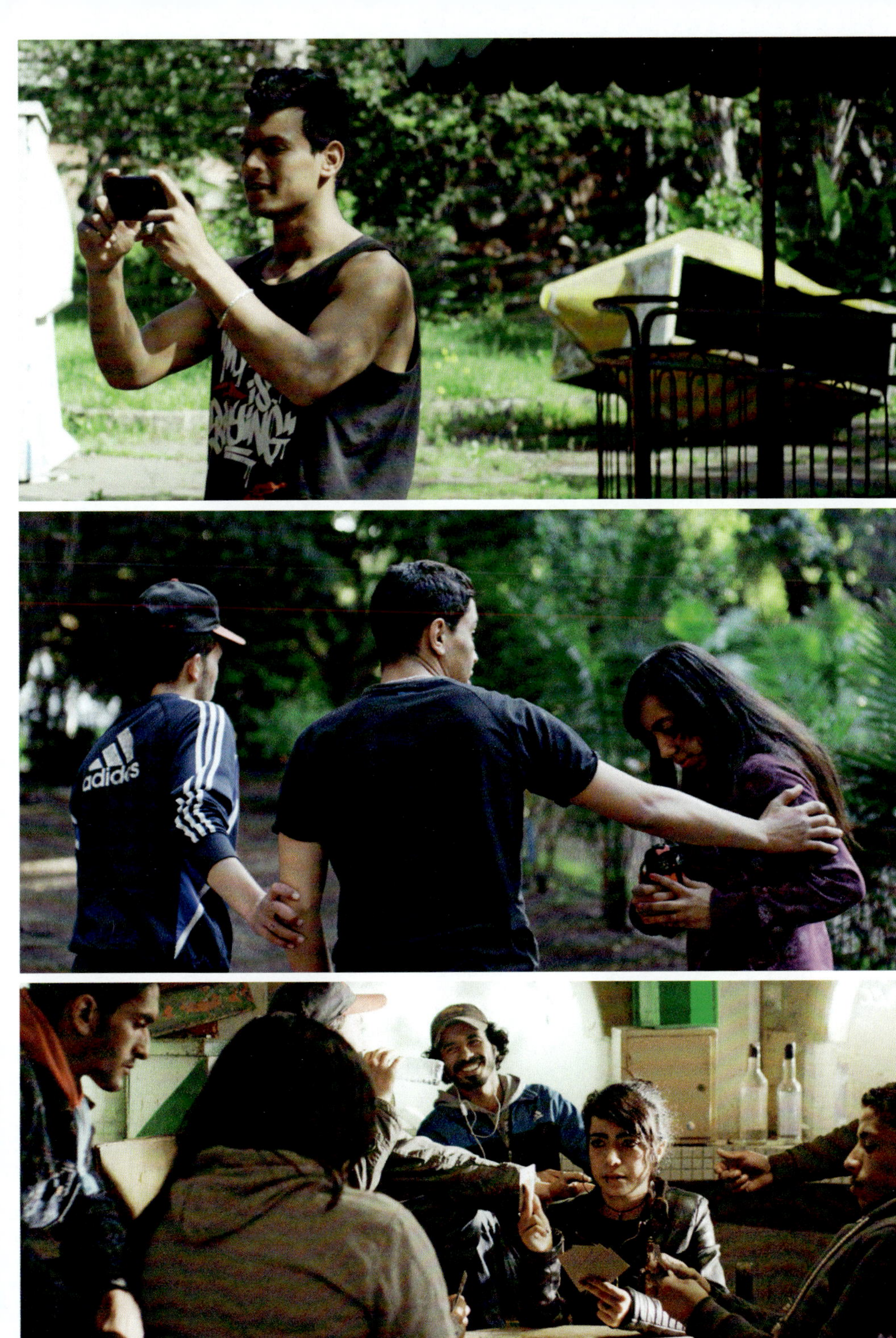

Le Park, 2015, Filmstills

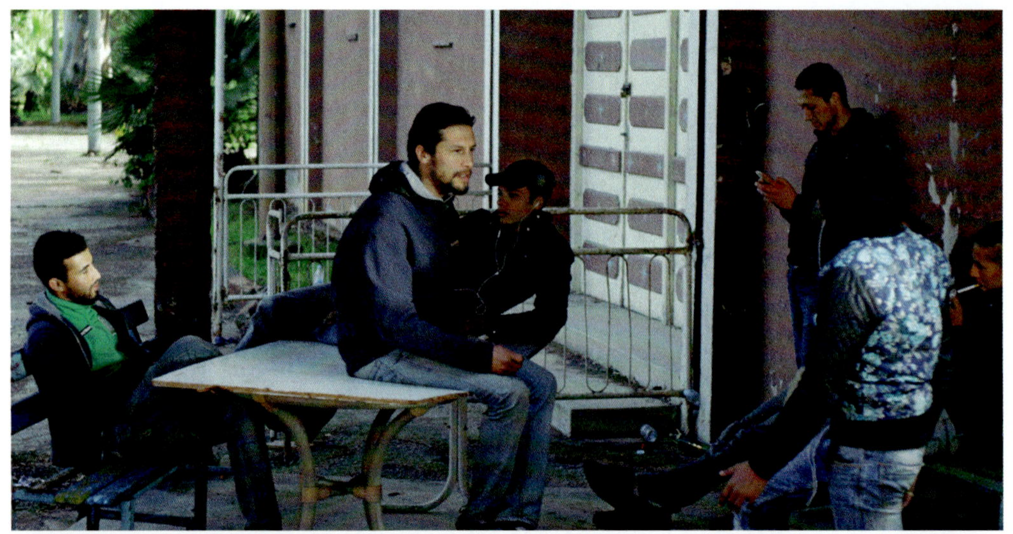

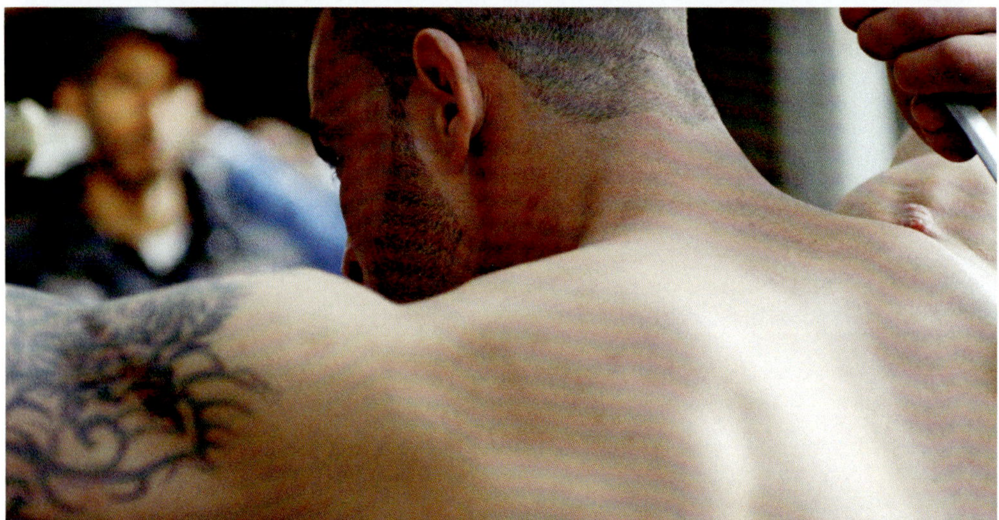

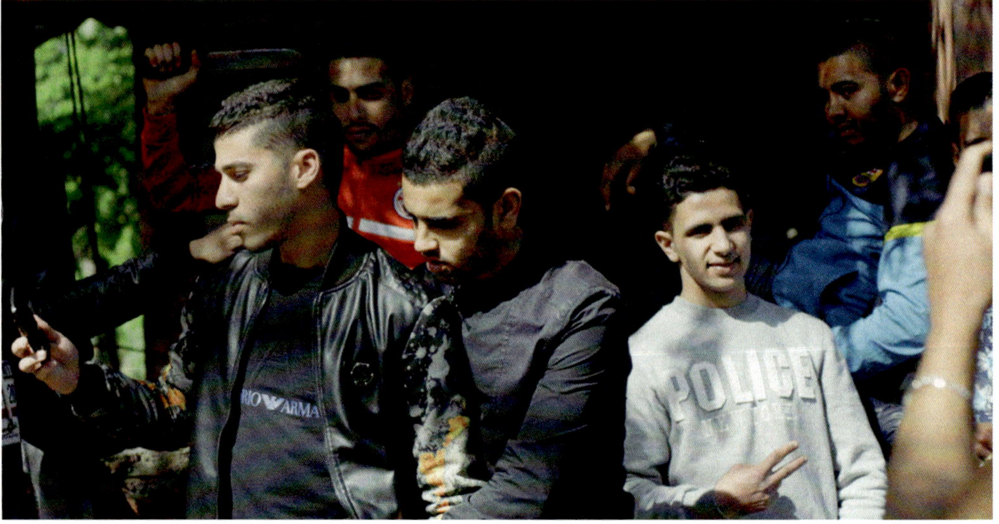

Le Park, 2015, film stills

Stimmen – eine Nachrichtensprecherin, die jungen Erwachsenen aus dem Park, die Regisseurin selbst – Versatzstücke an Informationen, die sich jedoch nie zu einem sinnvollen Zusammenhang fügen. Der Filmton, der eigens für die Arbeit komponiert wurde, flirrt durch den Raum wie die Bilder durchs Netz, baut Spannung auf, die sich nirgends entlädt und bietet keine Orientierung. In der Dekonstruktion wird jedoch auch deutlich, dass es gerade das für uns Unfassbare in diesen Bildern ist, das sie so begehrenswert macht.

Le Park reiht sich ein in Randa Maroufis interdisziplinäres Arbeiten, zu dem Fotografie und Skulptur ebenso zählen wie Performance und Soundarbeiten. Im Mittelpunkt aller Arbeiten steht die soziale Realität als Konstrukt, das es immer wieder und mit allen Mitteln zu hinterfragen gilt. Der Status der Bilder für dieses Konstrukt nimmt dabei eine zentrale Rolle ein. Schon in Arbeiten wie *Reconstitutions* (2013), einer Serie aus Fotografien sowie einem Video, der Performance *Attempts of seduction* (2013) oder der performativen Videoarbeit *Mantons* (2011) geht sie der Konstruktion von Geschlechterrollen nach und stellt die zugrundeliegenden Mechanismen zur Schau. Auch hier sind es immer wieder Momente von latenter Gewalt, ausgeübt sowohl durch Körper als auch durch Blicke und die darin verborgenen Sichtweisen, die Maroufi entlarvt. Letztendlich unterbricht sie so für einen Moment die Zirkulation immer gleicher Stereotype, die doch nur unsere Schaulust befriedigen und entlässt uns mit alternativen Blicken auf diese spezifische Wirklichkeit.

Tasja Langenbach

Rabih Mroué

“The Syrian protesters are recording their own deaths!”[1] The shock and-consternation resulting from this sudden realisation are the starting points for Rabih Mroué’s multi-media installation, *The Pixelated Revolution* (2012).

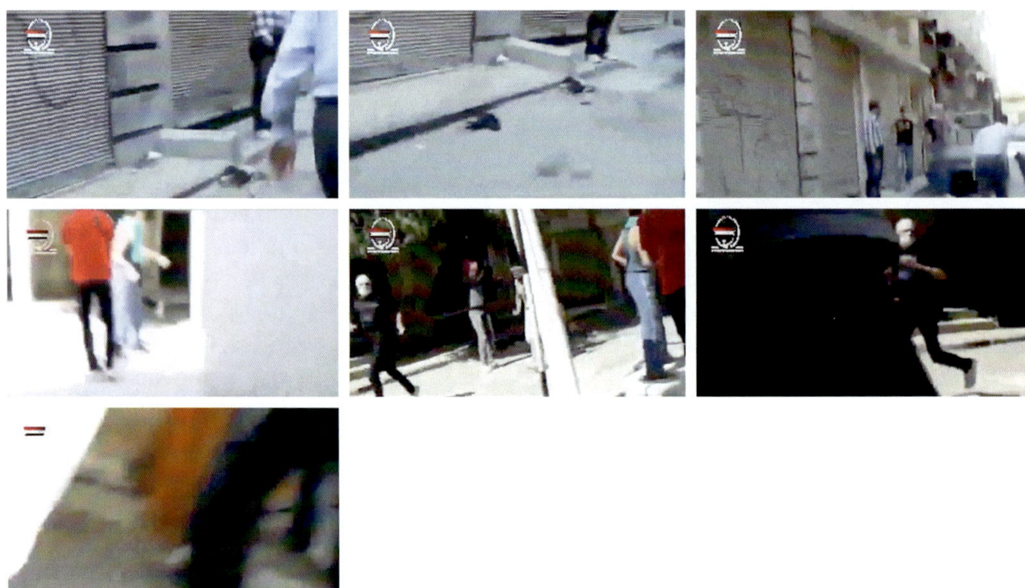

The Lebanese artist is drawing on video clips prevalent on the Internet’s social networks at the beginning of the Syrian revolution in 2011. They were made by Syrian demonstrators armed only with their mobile phone cameras, who confronted the alleged snipers of the Assad regime and filmed the (fatal?) shot aimed at their own bodies. One of these videos, a 1:23 minute short clip, shows the disturbing moment when the barrel of a sniper’s gun appears in the phone’s camera. Mroué describes this point in time as “Double Shooting. One person is shooting with a camera, and the other

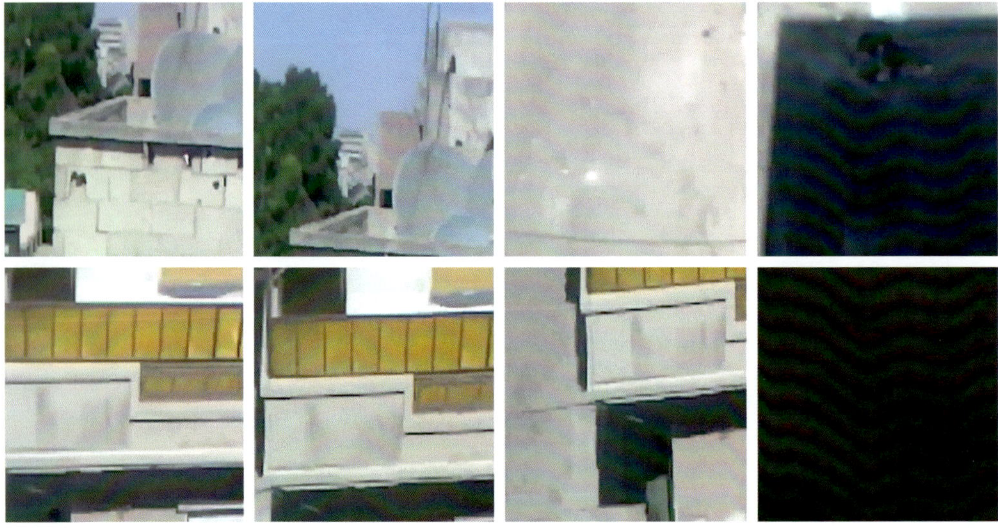

***The Pixelated Revolution*, 2012, video stills**

 ***The Pixelated Revolution*, 2012, video stills**

Rabih Mroué

„The Syrian protesters are recording their own deaths!“ [1] Der Schock und die Betroffenheit angesichts dieser Erkenntnis bilden den Ausgangspunkt für Rabih Mroués Multimedia-Installation *The Pixelated Revolution* (2012).

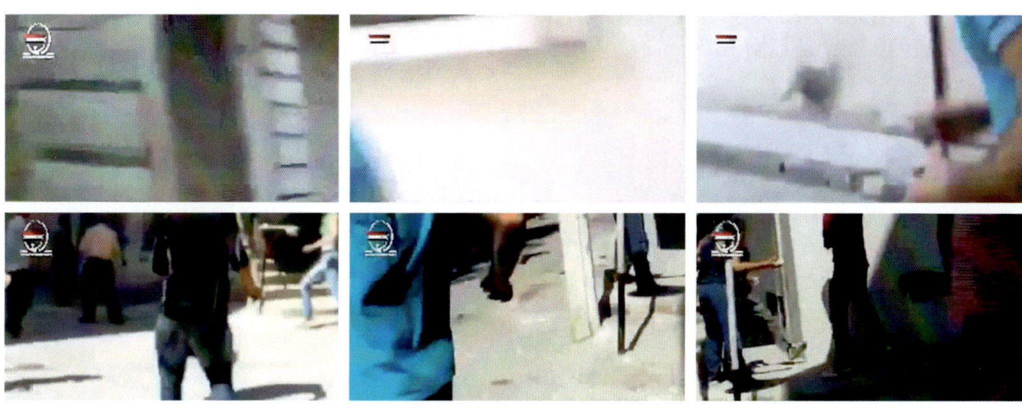

Der libanesische Künstler bezieht sich damit auf Videoclips, die zu Beginn der syrischen Revolution 2011 über soziale Netzwerke im Internet verbreitet wurden. Es handelt sich um Aufnahmen von syrischen Demonstrant*innen, die – lediglich mit ihren Handykameras bewaffnet – den mutmaßlichen Scharfschützen des Assad-Regimes gegenübertreten und letzten Endes auch den (tödlichen?) Schuss gegen ihren eigenen Körper filmisch festhalten. Eines dieser Videos, ein 1:23 Minuten kurzer Clip, zeigt den verstörenden Moment, als der Gewehrlauf des Scharfschützen ins Visier der Handykamera gerät. Mroué beschreibt diesen Zeitpunkt als „Double Shooting. One person

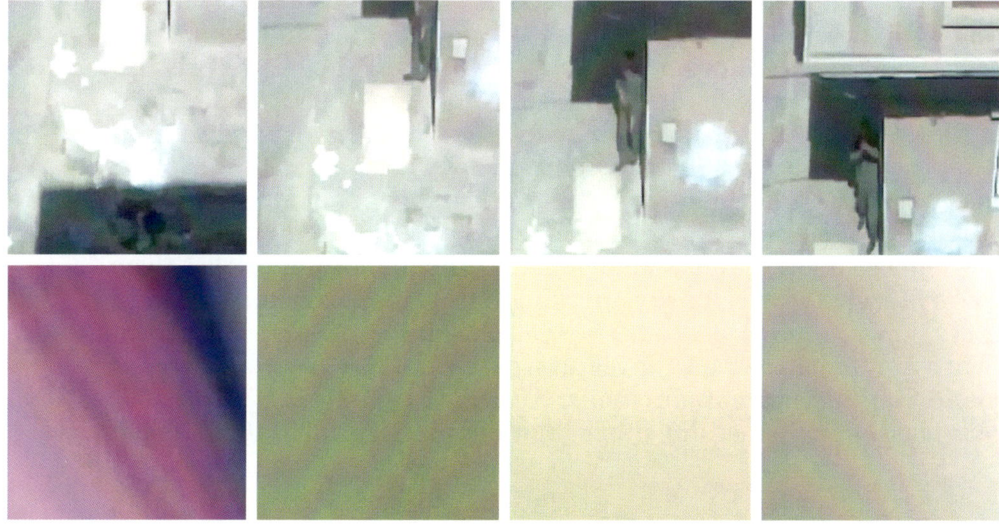

The Pixelated Revolution, 2012, Videostills

 The Pixelated Revolution, 2012, Videostills

is shooting with a rifle." The second the sound of the gunshot is heard the phone camera falls out of the filmmaker's hand onto the ground. The image loses control. From this moment on, we see only blurry fields of colour, flickering lights. We hear screams of pain and cries for help. Then the video stops. Does the abrupt end also mean the death of the person who was filming? We do not know. We also know little about the circumstances under which this material found its way into the public arena via social media.

The fact that we become witnesses here—via the camera—to a killing, is harrowing and disturbing. The video lets us see with the eyes of the person who is about to die. As observers, we also come into the cross hairs of the snipers. This is not least why the image material is so overwhelming and addresses us above all on an affective level. On the basis of these video clips, we are confronted with questions of the technological entanglements of image recording and killing. And thereby also with questions related to our position and role as observer.

These image theoretical and simultaneously existential questions are Rabih Mroué's concerns in many of his performances, video works and installations. He is often considered one of a generation of Lebanese artists who have experienced the civil war in Lebanon and now deal with the conditions of image-making in the context of war and violence. Mroué is not only interested in images that represent war, but also in the question of what war does to images, i.e., to what extent military violence changes and shapes image-making practices.

Mroué's artistic process is to be compared more with that of an image scientist: Instead of generating new images, Mroué starts with strategies of dissection, analysis and the deconstruction of found footage from the Internet. He has followed this course for more than ten years, especially in his "non-academic" lecture performances. Supposedly objective image analyses are confronted with personal, partly digressive speculations that question and contradict the format of the scientific lecture. The video of the Syrian demonstrators provides the opportunity for such a lecture, which can be viewed as a video recording during the exhibition. The physical disturbance and immediate affective reaction that we have to this "Double Shooting" is now countered by a frame-by-frame, detailed image analyses.

During his video lecture, Mroué repeatedly halts the hectic, breath-taking clips and enlarges details, seeking answers in the images. The large-format *Blow Up*s (2012) on paper of individual frames, in which the outline of the snipers can be seen, illustrates Mroué's desire to uncover the identity of the assailant. The digital and fleeting mobile phone images are materially fixed in the exhibition space, presented as portraits and "held liable."

The enlargement of the mobile phone pictures, however, makes them even more blurry: there is hardly anything to recognise. Zooming in on the spaces between the pixels could be seen as a desperate and doomed-to-failure attempt to counteract the helplessness we feel when both perpetrator and victim remain anonymous. At the same time, it is clear that Mroué is looking for something other than factual "truth" in these images.

is shooting with a camera, and the other is shooting with a rifle." Im selben Augenblick, als im Video das Abfeuern eines Schusses zu hören ist, fällt die Handykamera aus der Hand des Filmenden zu Boden. Das Bild entzieht sich seiner Kontrolle. Von diesem Moment an sehen wir nur noch verschwommene Farbfelder, flackernde Lichter, hören schmerzerfüllte Schreie, Hilferufe. Dann bricht das Video ab. Ist das abrupte Ende gleichbedeutend mit dem Tod des Filmenden? Wir wissen es nicht. Auch über die Umstände, wie das Bildmaterial seinen Weg über die sozialen Medien in die Öffentlichkeit gefunden hat, ist kaum etwas bekannt.

Die Tatsache, dass wir hier – vermittelt über die Kamera – zu Augenzeug*innen einer Tötung werden, ist erschütternd und aufwühlend. Das Videobild lässt uns mit den Augen dessen sehen, der gleich sterben wird. Als Betrachtende treten wir dadurch selbst ins Fadenkreuz der Scharfschützen. Nicht zuletzt deshalb wirkt das Bildmaterial so überwältigend und spricht uns vor allem auf einer affektiven Ebene an. Auf dem Grund dieser Videoclips begegnet uns die Frage nach den Verstrickungen zwischen den Technologien der Bildaufzeichnung und den Technologien des Tötens. Und damit auch die Frage nach unserer eigenen Position und Rolle als Betrachtende.

Diese bildtheoretischen und zugleich existenziellen Fragen treiben Rabih Mroué in vielen seiner Performances, Videoarbeiten und Installationen um. Er wird häufig zu einer Generation libanesischer Künstler*innen gezählt, die sich, ausgehend von den Erfahrungen des Bürgerkriegs im Libanon, mit den Bedingungen des Bildermachens im Kontext von Krieg und Gewalt beschäftigen. Mroués Interesse gilt dabei nicht nur Bildern, die Krieg repräsentieren, sondern der Frage, was Krieg mit den Bildern macht, also inwiefern sich militante Gewalt in Bildpraktiken selbst einschreibt, diese verändert und prägt.

Mroués künstlerische Herangehensweise ist daher eher mit der eines Bildwissenschaftlers zu vergleichen: Statt neue Bilder hervorzubringen, setzt Mroué auf Strategien des Sezierens, der Analyse und der Dekonstruktion von Found Footage aus dem Internet. Seit mehr als zehn Jahren verfolgt er dies vor allem im Rahmen seiner „nicht-akademischen" Lecture Performances. Scheinbar objektive Bildanalysen werden dabei von persönlichen, teils abwegigen Spekulationen abgelöst, die das Format des wissenschaftlichen Vortrags selbst in Frage stellen und konterkarieren. Das Video des syrischen Demonstranten bildete den Anlass für eine solche „lecture", die als Videoaufzeichnung in der Ausstellung zu sehen ist. Der geradezu körperlichen Betroffenheit und unmittelbar affektiven Reaktion, die wir als Betrachtende auf das „Double Shooting" haben, wird nun – Frame für Frame – mit einer detailierten Bildanalyse entgegnet.

Immer wieder stellt Mroué während seines Videovortrags die hektischen, atemlosen Videoclips still und vergrößert Details, um nach Antworten in den Bildern zu suchen. Auch die großformatigen, auf Papier aufgezogenen *Blow Up*s (2012) einzelner Frames, auf denen die Umrisse der Scharfschützen zu erkennen sind, verdeutlichen Mroués Verlangen, der Identität der Täter auf die Spur zu kommen. Die digitalen und flüchtigen Handybilder

He increasingly creates doubt about the border between fictional and non-fictional genres by confronting the mobile phone images with the affective registers and aesthetics of feature films. Mroué's searching movements *in* and *with* the images do not track down either perpetrator or victim. Instead, his approach to the videos appears to be one thing above all else: an approach to our own feelings of helplessness when confronted by the dead in Syria.

Verena Straub

1 **All quotes from: Rabih Mroué, *The Pixelated Revolution. A non-academic Lecture by Rabih Mroué*, video with sound, 21:59 Min, produced by dOCUMENTA 13, 2012.**

werden im Ausstellungsraum materiell fixiert, als Porträts präsentiert und „dingfest“ gemacht.

Doch das Vergrößern der Handybilder führt lediglich zu noch unschärferen Bildern, die kaum mehr etwas zu erkennen geben. Das Zoomen in den Zwischenraum der Pixel könnte als – verzweifelter und letztlich zum Scheitern verurteilter – Versuch gedeutet werden, der Ohnmacht angesichts der Anonymität von Täter und Opfer etwas entgegen zu setzen. Gleichzeitig wird deutlich, dass Mroué in den Handybildern eigentlich etwas Anderes sucht als eine faktische „Wahrheit“. Indem er die Handyvideos mit den affektiven Registern und der Ästhetik von Spielfilmen konfrontiert, zieht Mroué die Grenze zwischen fiktionalen und nichtfiktionalen Genres zunehmend in Zweifel. Mroués Suchbewegungen *in* und *mit* den Bildern kommen weder den Tätern noch den Opfern auf die Spur. Stattdessen scheint Mroués Annäherung an die Videos vor allem eins zu sein: eine Annäherung an unsere eigenen Gefühle der Hilflosigkeit beim Anblick der Toten in Syrien.

Verena Straub

1 Alle Zitate aus: Rabih Mroué, *The Pixelated Revolution. A non-academic Lecture by Rabih Mroué*, Video mit Ton, 21:59 Min, produziert von dOCUMENTA 13, 2012.

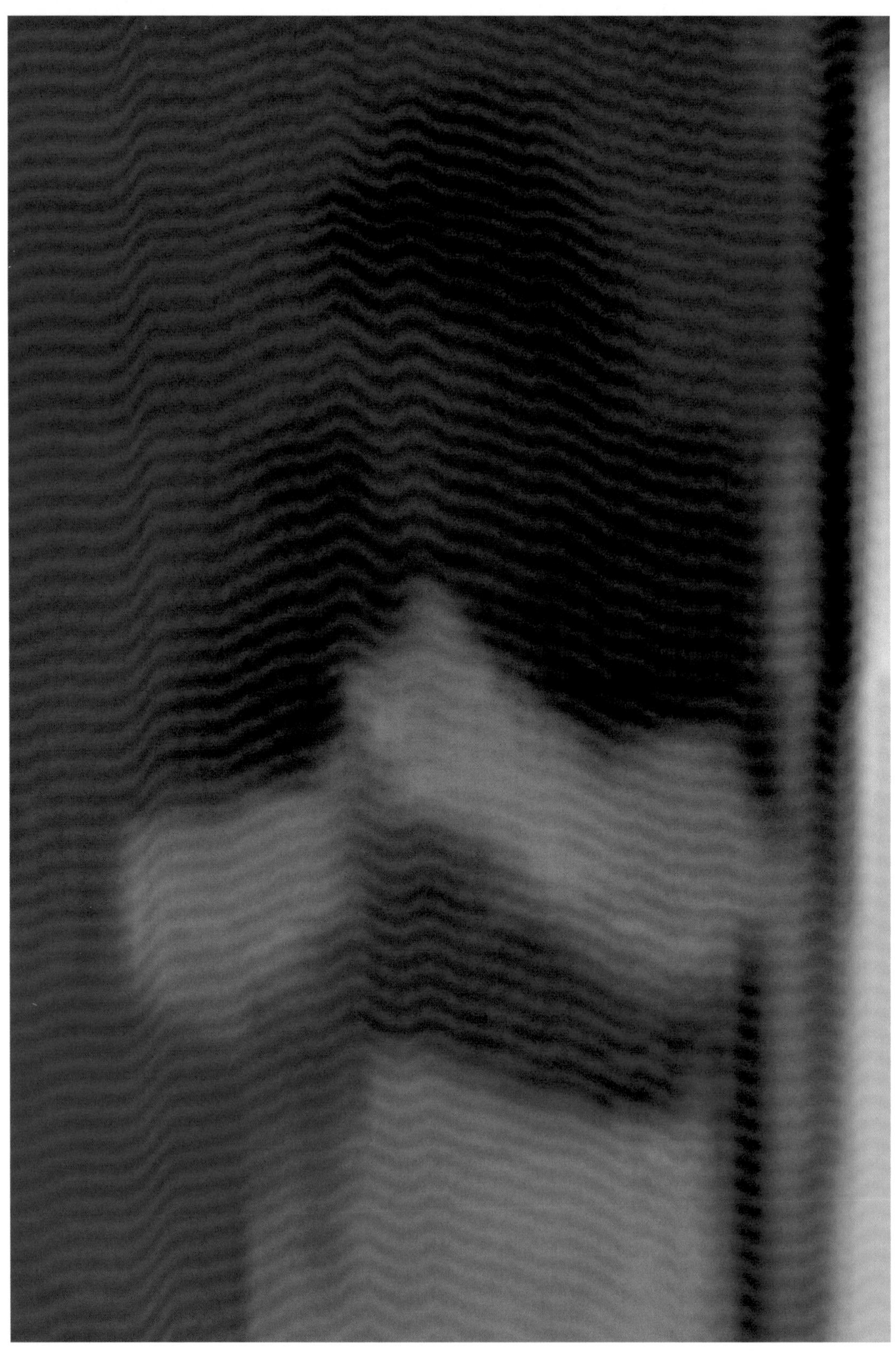

Blow Up 3, 2012

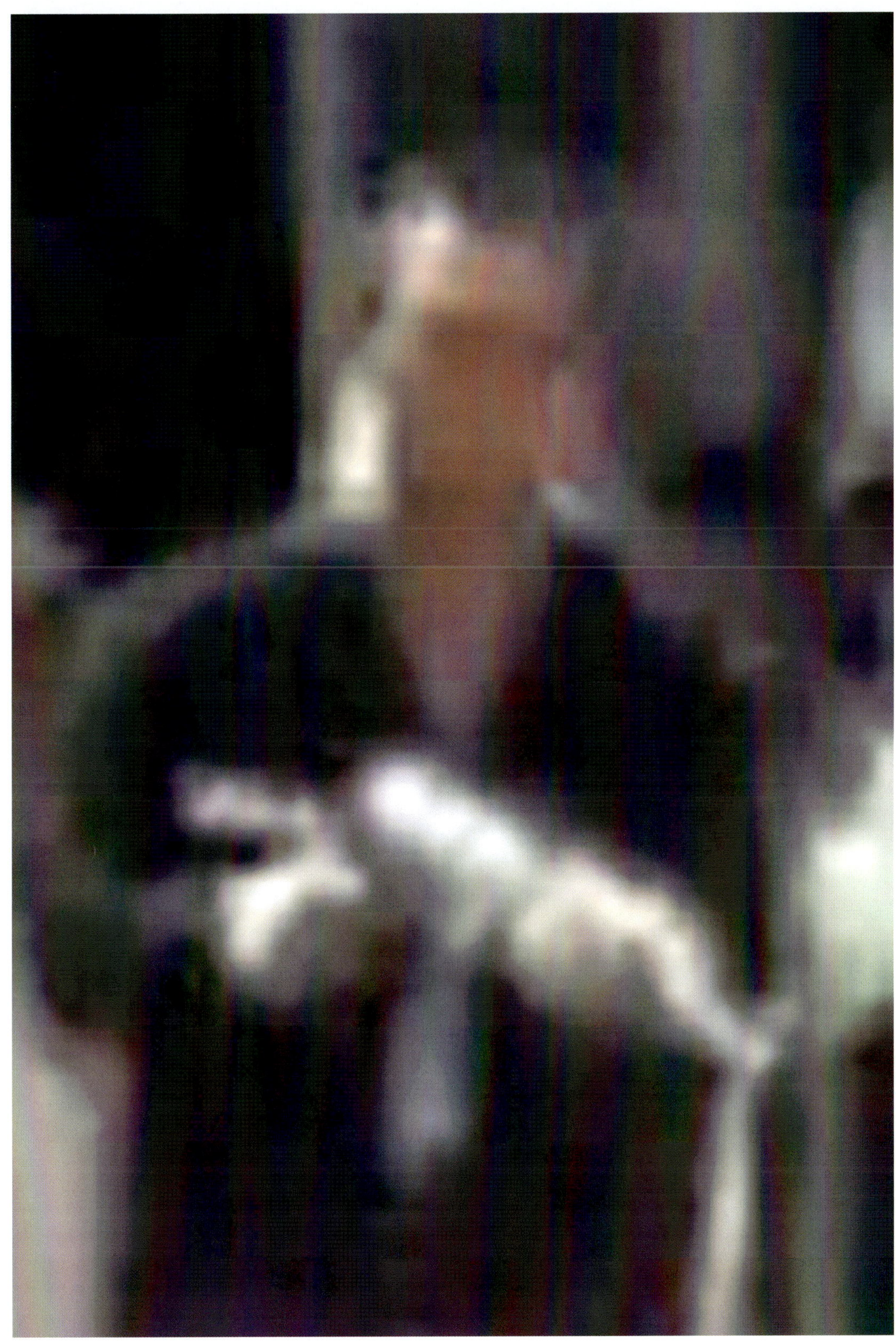

***Blow Up 4*, 2012**

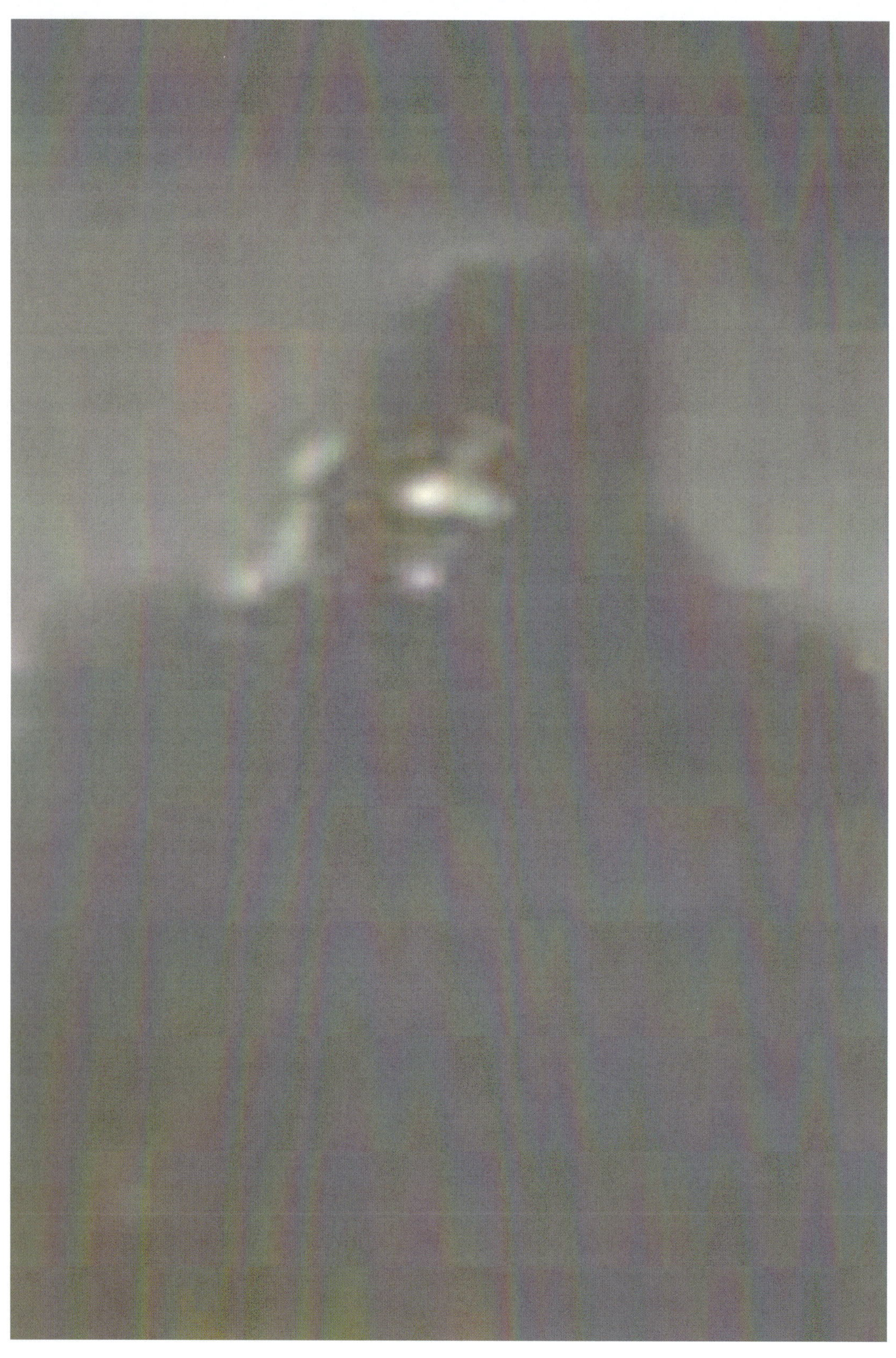

Blow Up 5, 2012

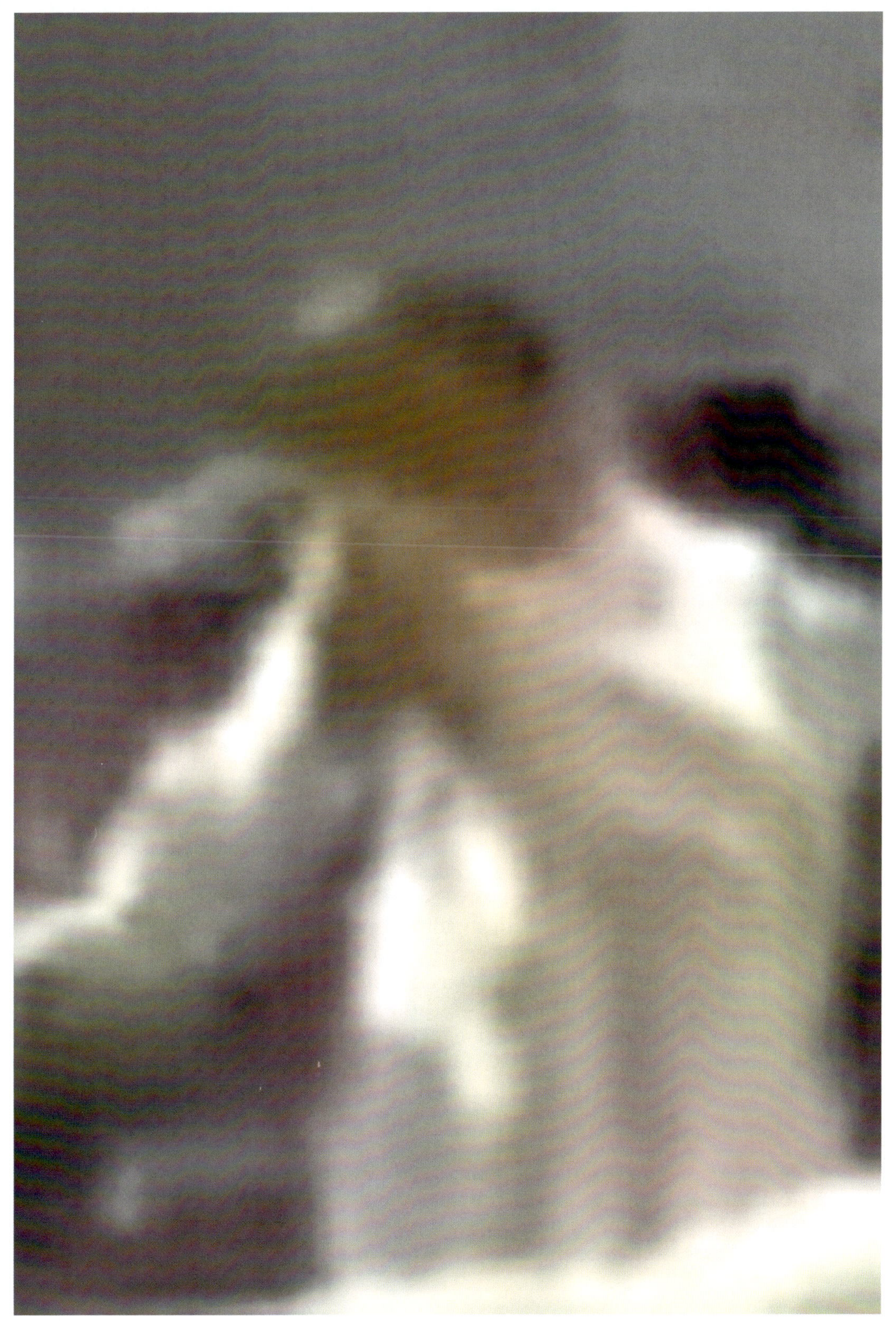

Blow Up 7, 2012

Thomas Ruff

The terrorist attacks on New York and Washington on September 11, 2001 were globally considered as a major catastrophe. Not only the events as such shocked the public, but also the dramatic images involved. The attacks were directed against the World Trade Center as a striking symbol of American capitalism. Its unexpected destruction took place right in front of the public and for all the world to see. Just a few minutes after the first kidnapped airplane hit one of the buildings, first recordings from the surveillance cameras were shown on American television. When the second airplane flew into the South Tower, it was broadcast in real time. This conveyed the eerie feeling of being directly involved in the terrorist attack to the TV audience. The terrorists had aimed at such images being spread on a global scale by the media to maximise the terror. Ever since, one speaks of "wars of images" to underline the increasing involvement of the public through images.

According to an anecdote, the artist Thomas Ruff was on the spot as an eyewitness on the said day. Like many others he took out his camera. But due to a technical defect his photos later turned out to be unusable. Personally affected by the event, the artist searched the Web for photographs of the attacks, started collecting them and later processed them in the *jpeg* series (2004–2007). Ruff is known for his artistic transformations of found photographic material, sourced from magazines, photo books and archives. With the Internet, the number of available images has multiplied; it therefore seems only logical that Ruff would also extend his media-reflective approach to comprise the Internet. The *jpeg* series thematises the power of images in the digital present. It focusses not only on specific motifs and forms, but likewise deals with the technical conditions that have enabled the globalisation of public communication.

In order to pointedly depict the technical context of production, Ruff employed a certain kind of image disturbance. Every artwork features a strong pixelation, resulting from an extreme enlargement of the digital images. The abbreviation JPEG stands for a procedure developed in the 1990s to allow the exchange of digital picture files via the Internet. To this aim data is reduced by means of different rendering algorithms, as reducing the file size enables a faster transfer. Ruff's post-processing and extreme enlarging of the source material reveal the loss of information involved, which mostly goes unnoticed in everyday usage. The large-format presentation leads to completely blurred pictures. Viewed from a distance, the motifs are still recognizable, but the more one approaches the work, the more its forms dissolve into abstract patterns. Details and contours become blurred, colours are simplified and moreover, the rasterization of the image—the process underlying the compression—appears in the form of squares.

But why this distortion? The disturbance rendered visible clearly decreases the documentary value of the images. The ruin of the World Trade Center in *jpeg ny11* (2006) may, in the context of the Internet, still qualify

Thomas Ruff

Die terroristischen Anschläge auf New York und Washington am 11. September 2001 wurden weltweit als eine Katastrophe besonderen Ausmaßes wahrgenommen. Die Ereignisse schockierten die Öffentlichkeit nicht nur, aber auch aufgrund der spektakulären Bilder. Die Angriffe richteten sich gegen das World Trade Center als ein prägnantes Symbol des amerikanischen Kapitalismus. Seine überraschende Zerstörung vollzog sich vor den Augen der Weltöffentlichkeit. Schon wenige Minuten nach dem Einschlag des ersten entführten Verkehrsflugzeugs hatte das amerikanische Fernsehen Aufnahmen aus Überwachungskameras zeigen können. Als das zweite Flugzeug dann in den Südturm flog, wurde in Echtzeit übertragen. Das vermittelte dem Publikum an den Fernsehgeräten das unheimliche Gefühl, bei dem Terrorangriff unmittelbar dabei zu sein. Die Terroristen zielten mit ihren Anschlägen auf eine globale Verbreitung der Bilder durch die Medien, um den Schrecken maximal zu verstärken. Seither spricht man auch von „Bilderkriegen", um die zunehmende Einbindung der Öffentlichkeit mittels Bildern zu betonen.

Einer Anekdote zufolge soll der Künstler Thomas Ruff am besagten Tag als Augenzeuge vor Ort gewesen sein. Wie viele andere griff auch er zur Kamera. Doch stellten sich seine Aufnahmen später auf Grund eines technischen Defekts als unbrauchbar heraus. Die persönliche Betroffenheit ließ den Künstler im Internet nach Fotografien von den Anschlägen suchen, die er zu sammeln begann und später in der Serie *jpeg* (2004–2007) verarbeitete. Ruff ist bekannt für seine künstlerischen Transformationen vorgefundener Fotografien, die er aus Zeitschriften, Fotobänden und Archiven bezieht. Mit dem Internet hat sich die Menge der zur Verfügung stehenden Bilder vervielfacht. Deshalb erscheint es nur logisch, dass Ruff seinen medienreflexiven Ansatz auch auf das Internet ausdehnt. Die Serie *jpeg* thematisiert die Macht der Bilder in der digitalen Gegenwart. Dabei geht es nicht allein um spezifische Motive und Formen, sondern ebenso um die technischen Voraussetzungen, die eine Globalisierung der öffentlichen Kommunikation ermöglicht haben.

Ruff bedient sich einer spezifischen Bildstörung, um den technischen Produktionszusammenhang demonstrativ ins Bild zu setzen. Jedes Werk zeigt eine starke Verpixelung, die ihre Ursache in der erheblichen Vergrößerung der digitalen Bilder hat. Die Abkürzung JPEG bezeichnet ein Verfahren, das in den 1990er Jahren für den Austausch von digitalen Bilddateien im Internet entwickelt wurde. Dabei werden Daten durch die Anwendung verschiedener Algorithmen reduziert, die Reduktion der Dateigröße ermöglicht einen schnelleren Transfer. Ruffs Nachbearbeitung und extreme Vergrößerung des Ausgangsmaterials offenbart den damit einhergehenden Informationsverlust, der im Alltagsgebrauch häufig gar nicht auffällt. Die großformatige Präsentation führt zu komplett unscharfen Bildern. Mit Abstand betrachtet sind die Motive noch gut erkennbar. Doch je näher man herantritt, desto stärker lösen sich die Formen in abstrakte Muster auf. Die Details und Konturen verschwimmen, die Farbwerte sind

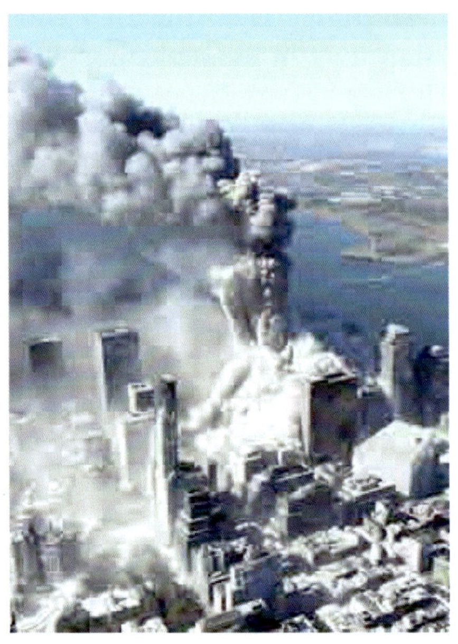

as a piece evidence from an eyewitness. The enlargement and the image transfer to the exhibition space, however, serve to reveal which technical processes of abstraction remain hidden in the depths of such pictures. Moreover, when compared to the photograph circulating on the Web that the artist presumably used as source material, changes become apparent. The picture was cut on the right side, removing the heroic figure of the fireman. This substantially alters the meaning. While the journalistic photo tells of the heroic effort, giving back some sense to the blow of fate, Ruff's version displays a landscape void of humans, adjoining the aesthetic category of the terrible-sublime. The question arises as to which images are actually suited to create emotional intensity and thus to enter our collective memory. Images may become iconic representatives of events through conciseness, aesthetic shaping, and last but not least through their repetition in different contexts.

Stefanie Stallschus

***jpeg ny14*, 2006**

vereinfacht, zudem tritt die quadratische Rasterung des Bildfeldes zutage, an der die Komprimierung ansetzt.

Wozu aber diese Verfremdung? Mit der sichtbaren Störung wird der dokumentarische Wert der Bilder zurückgedrängt. Die Ruine des World Trade Center in *jpeg ny11* (2006) mag im Kontext des Internets noch als

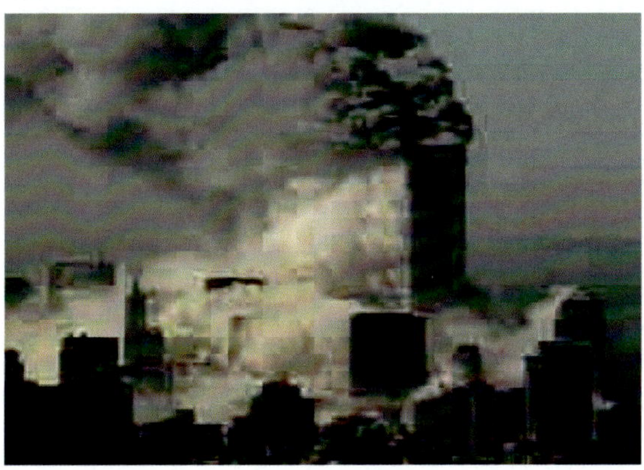

Beleg eines Augenzeugen durchgehen. Die Vergrößerung und der Transfer in den Ausstellungsraum machen jedoch sichtbar, welche technischen Abstraktionsprozesse am Grund der Bilder verborgen liegen. Im Vergleich mit der im Internet kursierenden Fotografie, die vermutlich vom Künstler als Ausgangsmaterial verwendet wurde, fallen die Veränderungen auf. Das Bild wurde auf der rechten Seite beschnitten, so dass die heroische Figur des Feuerwehrmannes entfernt wurde. Damit verändert sich die Bedeutung erheblich. Während im journalistischen Bild vom heldenhaften Einsatz erzählt wird, der dem Schicksalsschlag wieder einen Sinn gibt, zeigt die Fassung Ruffs eine menschenleere Landschaft, die an die ästhetische Kategorie des Schrecklich-Erhabenen anschließt. Das wirft die Frage auf, welche Bilder überhaupt emotionale Intensität erzeugen und ins kollektive Gedächtnis aufgenommen werden. Bilder werden zu ikonischen Stellvertretern von Ereignissen durch Prägnanz, ästhetische Stilisierung, und nicht zuletzt durch Wiederholung in unterschiedlichen Kontexten.

Stefanie Stallschus

jpeg ny02, 2006

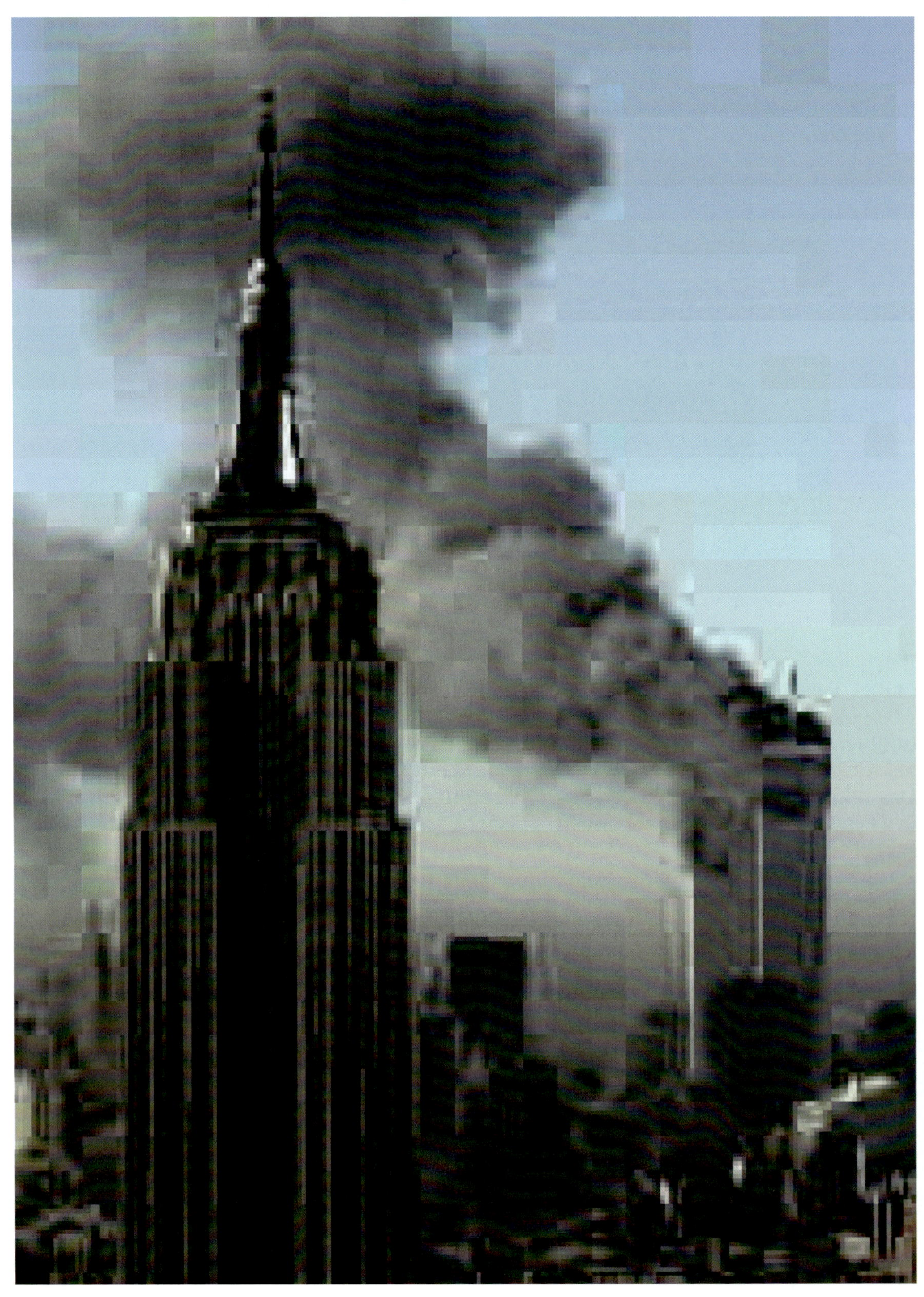

jpeg ny01, 2006

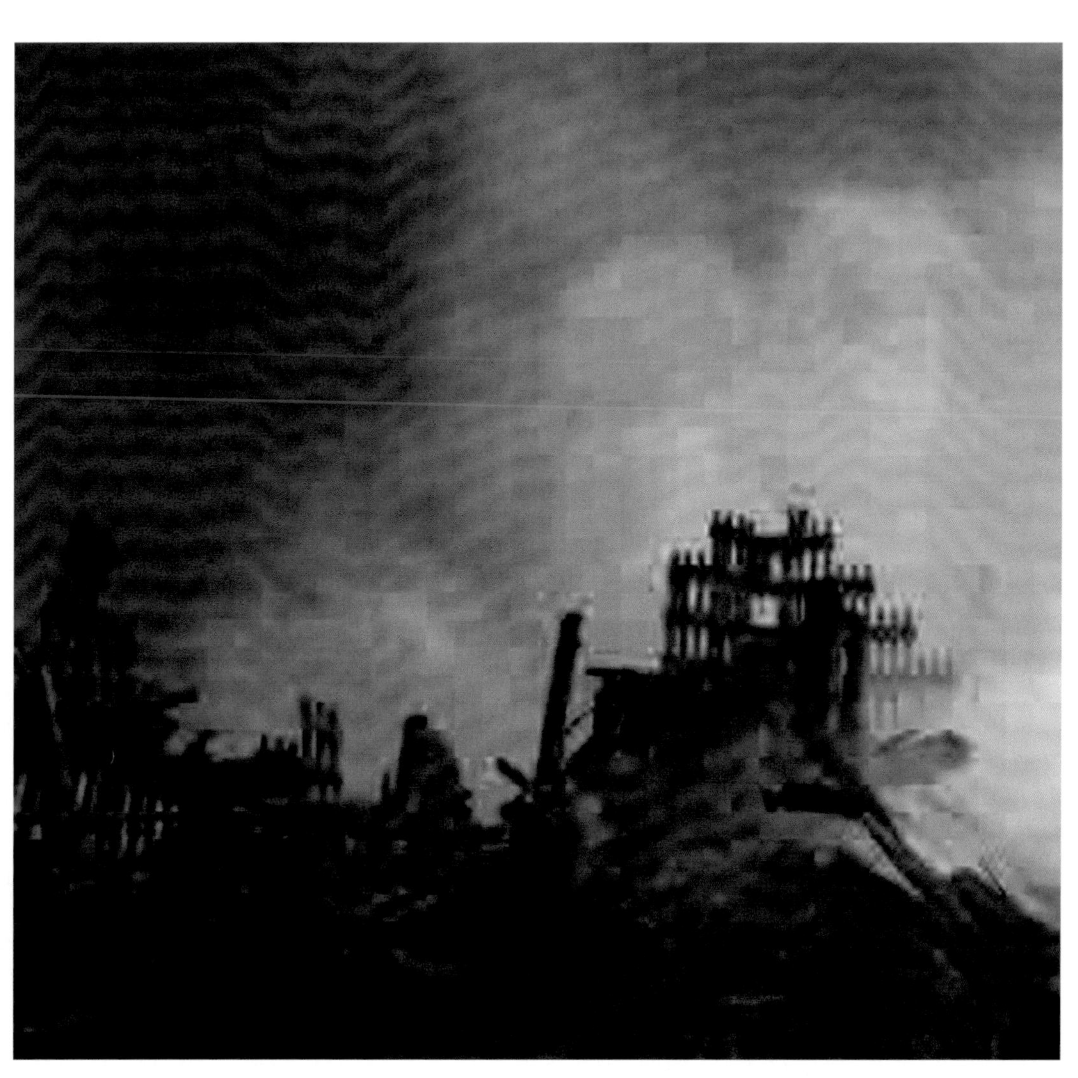

jpeg ny11, 2006

D. H. Saur

View, forward, rework, share and view again: the consumption and production of images are daily practices on the Internet. We all became "prosumers" a long time ago. In his works, *Hope 2008–2017* (2017) and *Facebook* (2011), the artist, D. H. Saur, examines how images catch our attention and thereby provoke a wave of reactions.

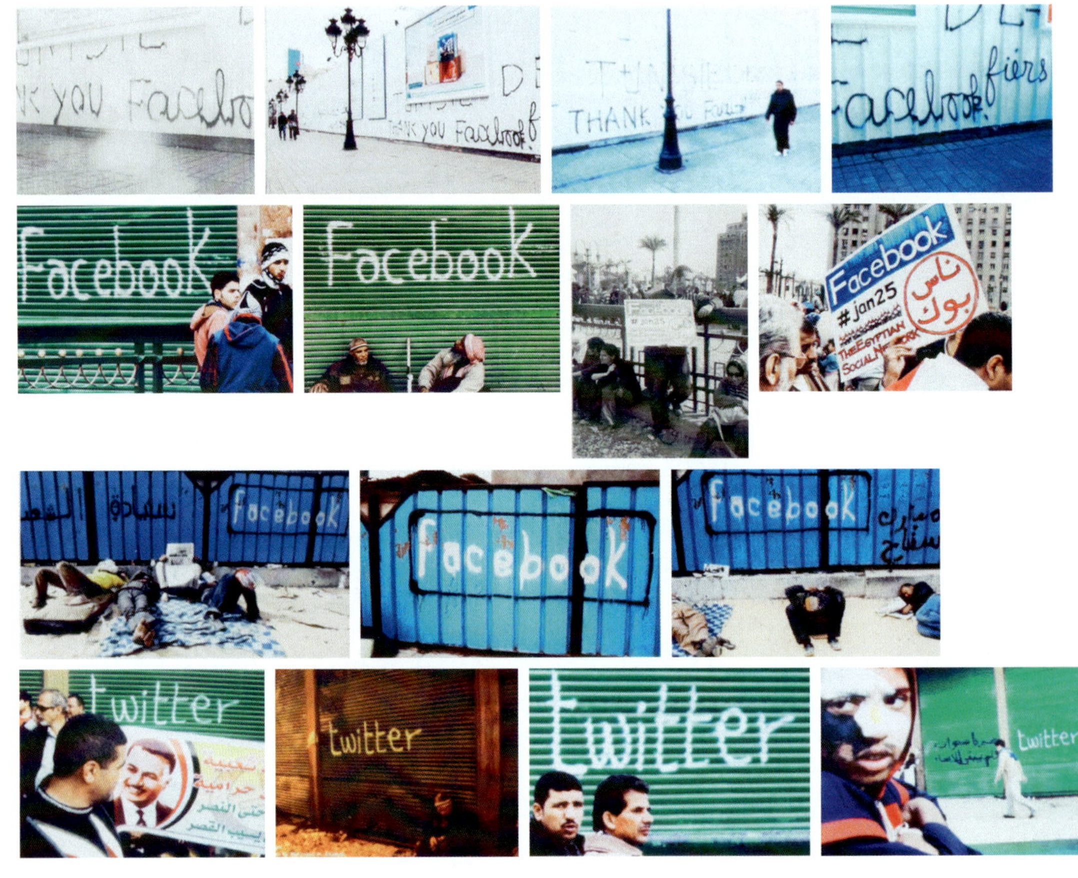

Saur collages photographs from different sources on large sheets of paper and adds hand-written notes explaining and locating them. Connected by pencil lines, the images are formed into groups. Out of date facts are covered, rubbed out or supplemented. The polycentric composition looks like an indirect reproduction of the cloud-like structure of the Internet—and just as the Internet keeps forcing us to select pictures and information from its stream, Saur's collages confront us with countless options for where we direct our attention.

In his long-term research *Hope 2008–2017*, Saur charts the emergence of and changes in the legendary "Hope" meme on the Internet. A meme never consists of a single image, as Limor Shifman points out, but "is a particular manifestation of a group of units that together can be described as a meme."[1]

***Facebook*, 2011, details**

D. H. Saur

Sehen, weiterleiten, bearbeiten, teilen, wiedersehen: Das Konsumieren und Produzieren von Bildern ist im Internet alltägliche Praxis. Schon längst sind wir alle zu „Prosument*innen“ geworden. Wie Bilder unsere Aufmerksamkeit erregen und dabei massenhaft Reaktionen provozieren, untersucht der Künstler D. H. Saur in seinen Arbeiten *Hope 2008–2017* (2017) und *Facebook* (2011).

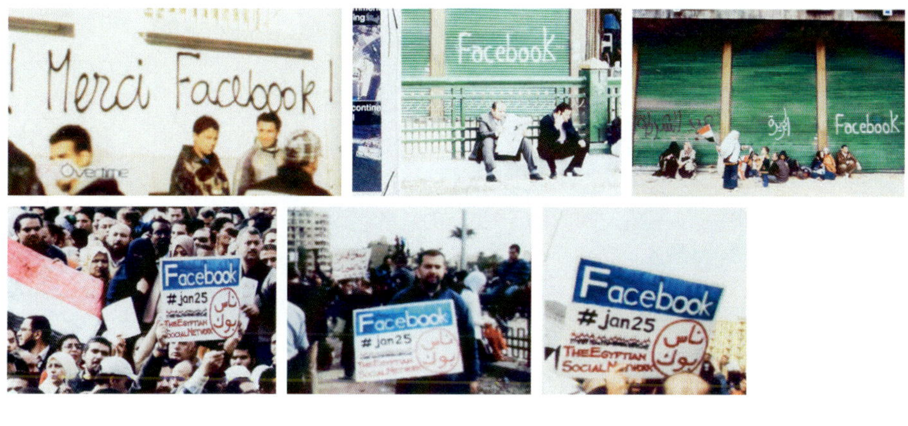

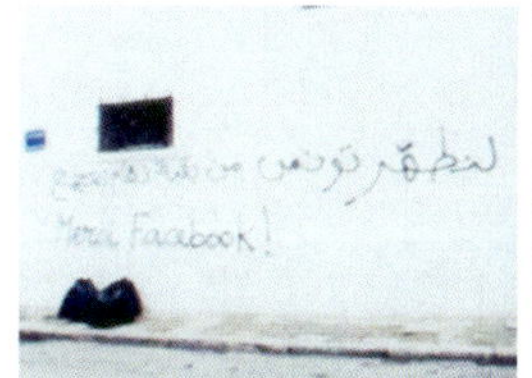

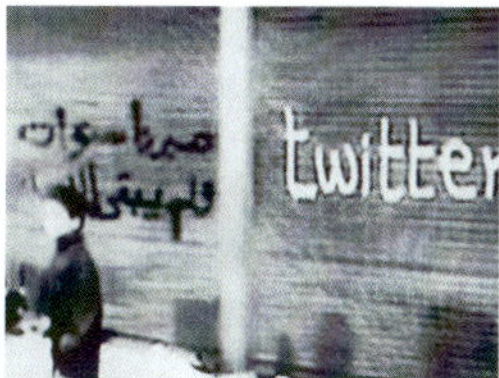

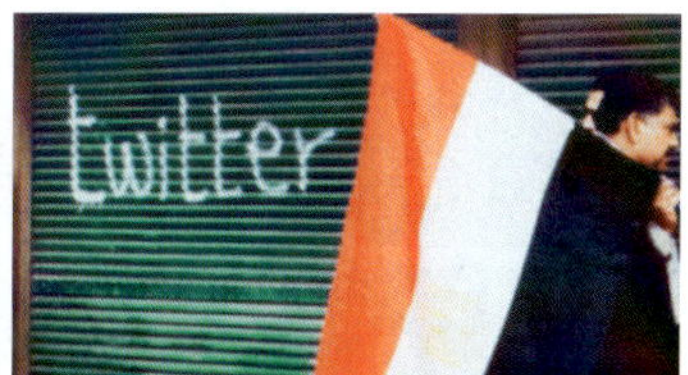

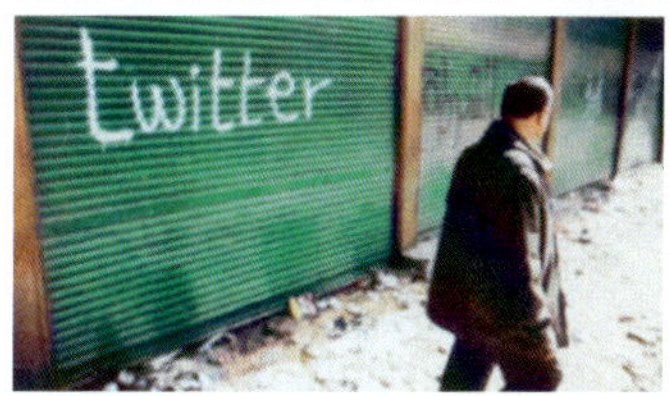

Auf großformatigen Papierbögen collagiert Saur Fotografien unterschiedlicher Provenienz und versieht sie handschriftlich mit Notizen, um sie zu erklären und zu verorten. Die Bilder werden mit Bleistiftlinien verbunden und gruppiert, überholte Fakten werden überklebt, ausradiert oder ergänzt. Der polyzentrische Aufbau liest sich wie ein indirektes Abbild der wolkenhaften Struktur des Internets – und so wie dieses uns ständig dazu zwingt, aus einer Flut von Bildern und Informationen auszuwählen, konfrontieren uns auch Saurs Collagen mit unzähligen Optionen, auf die wir unsere Aufmerksamkeit richten können.

In seiner Langzeitrecherche *Hope 2008–2017* kartografiert Saur Entstehung und Wandel des legendären „Hope“-Memes im Internet. Ein Meme besteht nie nur aus einem Bild, wie Limor Shifman hervorhebt,

***Facebook*, 2011, Details**

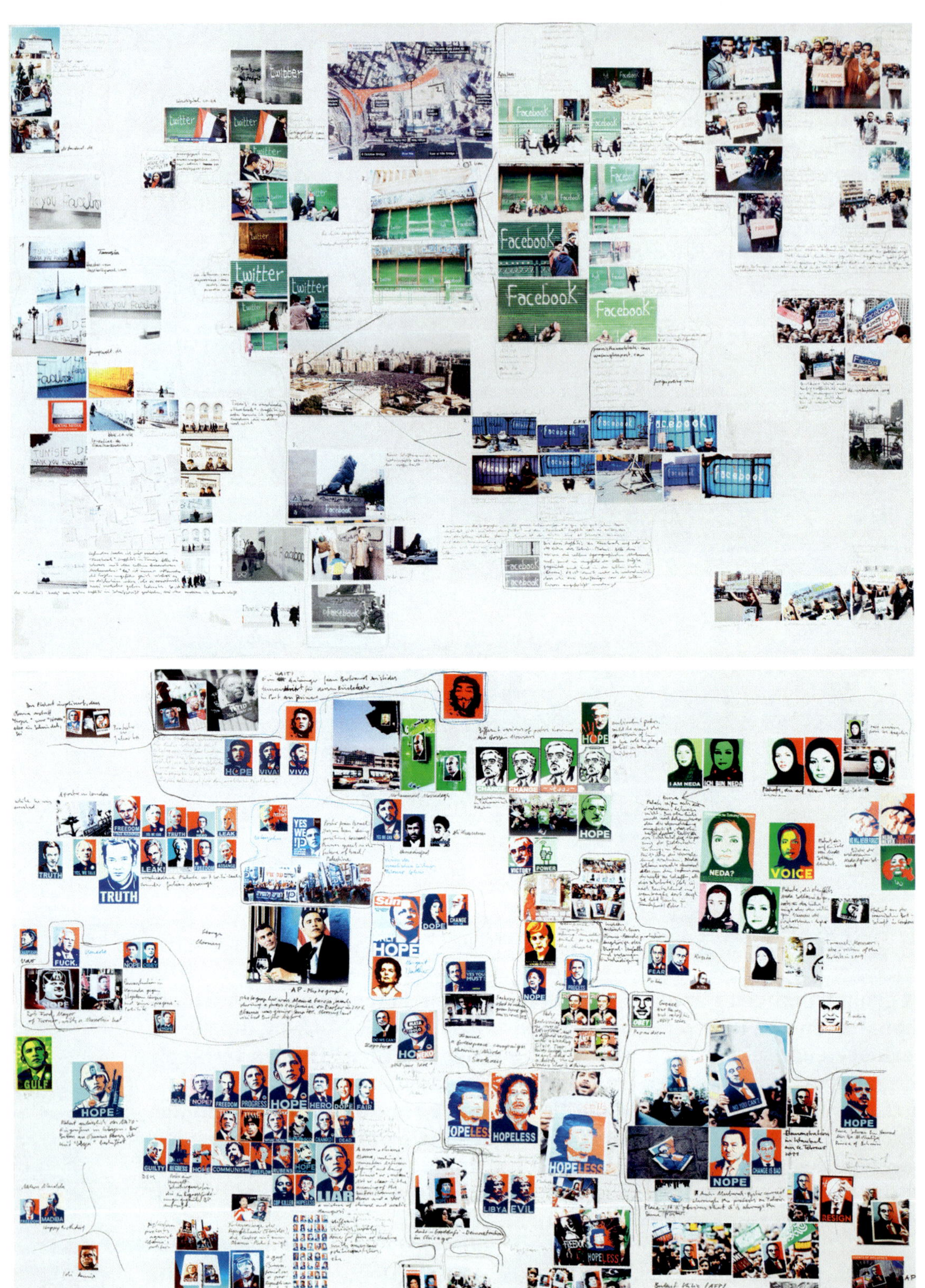

Facebook, 2011
Hope 2008–2011, 2011

sondern ist „eine bestimmte Manifestation aus einer Gruppe von Einheiten, die gemeinsam als Mem beschrieben werden kön"en“.[1]

Ausgehend von einer Pressefotografie und der darauf basierenden Grafik des Künstlers Shepard Fairey verfolgt Saur, wie sich das „Hope“-Plakat im Hinblick auf Farbgebung, Stil, Text und ikonografischen Gehalt, aber auch in seiner Bedeutung immer wieder veränderte. Waren die Derivate von Faireys Grafik zunächst noch Kommentare zum politischen oder popkulturellen Geschehen in den USA – sie zeigten unter anderem Osama Bin Laden, Edward Snowden, Donald Trump, Drohnen sowie Amy Winehouse und Michael Jackson – wurde das Template bald zur Ikone im Kontext von Revolutionen in arabischen Ländern sowie im Iran. Mit zunehmender Bekanntheit des Memes entstanden immer abstraktere Versionen, die ganze Sätze („I Am Neda“, „Angie-You-Can“) einbanden sowie andere Farben als Blau, Rot und Weiß kombinierten. Schließlich reichte das scherenschnittartige Porträt einer Person im Hochformat aus, um eine Verbindung zum „Hope“-Plakat und zu politischen Protestbewegungen herzustellen.

In der früheren Arbeit *Facebook* verfolgte Saur Graffitis der tunesischen

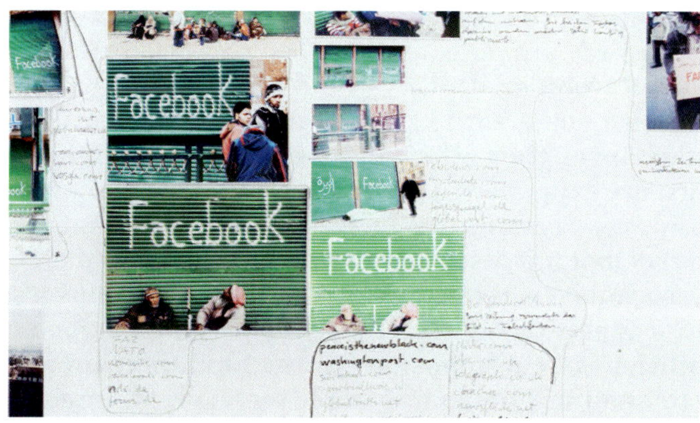

und ägyptischen Revolutionen, die sich auf Facebook oder Twitter bezogen. Was Saur hier zeigt, ist nicht der Gebrauch von Graffiti im arabischen Raum, sondern seine mediale Aufbereitung in der westlichen Welt. Von Schrift- und Sprachbarrieren entbunden, werden diese Graffitis überall verstanden, weshalb sie massenhaft von den Medien veröffentlicht und aufgegriffen wurden. Sie avancierten im Westen zu Ikonen der sogenannten „Facebook-Revolution“.

Saur macht deutlich, was „going viral“ eigentlich meint: Gleich biologischen Viren vermehren und verändern sich Bilder. Sie affizieren und stoßen dabei auf heftige Resonanz, die sich wiederum in der Produktion von immer neuen, veränderten Bildern in immer neuen Kontexten äußert. Ein Meme kann auf einen Blick erfasst werden und ist „prozessual, immer in Bewegung, aber auch ein lebendiges Zeugnis seiner eigenen Entwicklung, ein lebendiges Archiv“[2]. Jedes einzelne Bild funktioniert wie ein Aufhänger, der das Bewusstsein zurück zum Meme steuert. Diesen Zusammenhang von Aufmerksamkeitsdynamiken im Internet und Bewusstseinszuständen des menschlichen Gehirns illustrierte Daniel Dennett schon 1994 mit dem

Facebook, 2011, Detail

Starting with a press photograph and artist Shepard Fairey's graphic developed from it, Saur follows how the "Hope" poster has continually changed regarding colouring, style, text and iconographic content as well as meaning. Whereas the derivatives of Fairey's graphic were initially comments about political or pop cultural happenings in the USA—amongst others, they show Osama Bin Laden, Edward Snowden, Donald Trump, drones as well as Amy Winehouse and Michael Jackson—the template soon became an icon in the context of the revolutions in some of the Arabic countries and in Iran. As the meme acquires an increasingly high profile, ever more abstract versions emerge that include whole sentences ("I am Neda", "Angie-You-Can") and combine other colours than red, blue and white. Eventually, the paper-cut-out-like image of a person in portrait format was enough to create a connection to the "Hope" poster and to political protest movments.

In his earlier work, *Facebook*, Saur tracked graffiti from the Tunisian and Egyptian revolutions appearing on Facebook and Twitter. What Saur shows here is not the use of graffiti in Arab countries, but its media treatment in the Western world. These graffiti, freed from speech and language barriers, were understood everywhere and so were published and reused en masse in the media. They were promoted in the Western world to an icon of the so-called "Facebook Revolution."

Saur makes clear what going viral in fact means: like biological viruses, images propagate and change. They affect and thereby meet with intense reactions, which in turn are expressed in the production of ever new, altered images in ever new contexts. A meme can be understood at a glance and is "processual, ever in flux, but it is also a living testament of its own evolution, a living archive."[2] Each image is like a hook that steers consciousness back to the meme. This connection between the dynamics of attention on the Internet and the conditions of consciousness in the human brain was illustrated by Daniel Dennett in 1994 in his simple sentence, "Consciousness is an enormous complex of meme effects in the brain."[3] Not least, the case of Donald Trump reveals the incredible power memes can unleash in the formation of political opinion.

Saur designs his works in stark contrast to his subject: unlike the users on the Internet, the viewers of his images cannot modify them. They may be conceived as long-term investigations but are not, however, fed into new cycles of appropriation. As unimposing and tentative as Saur's collages appear at first glance, they are still counterpoints to the constantly changing websites. They are abiding records of an invisible network of "chains of communication"[4] on the Internet.

Linda Huke

1 Limor Shifman, *Meme. Kunst, Kultur und Politik im digitalen Zeitalter*, Berlin 2014, p. 57.
2 Boaz Levin, Fabian Knierim, *Kartografie eines lebendigen Archivs / Mapping A Living Archive: Zu D. H. Saurs Hope 2008–2017, 2017*, in: *Biennale für aktuelle Fotographie / Farewell Photography*, 2017 (addendum to *Camera Austria International*, issue 138, June 2017), p. 7.
3 Daniel Dennett, *Philosophie des menschlichen Bewusstseins*, Hamburg 1994, p. 277.
4 Levin, Knierim 2017, ibid.

einfachen Satz: „Das Bewusstsein ist also ein ungeheurer Komplex von Mem-Effekten im Gehirn.“[3] Nicht zuletzt der Fall Donald Trump zeigt, welch erstaunliche Kräfte Memes in Bezug auf politische Meinungsbildung entfalten können.

Saurs Arbeiten stehen in starkem Kontrast zu seinem Sujet: Anders als die User*innen im Internet können die Betrachter*innen seine Bilder nicht weiterentwickeln. Sie sind zwar als Langzeitrecherchen konzipiert, werden aber nicht in neue Appropriations-Kreisläufe eingespeist. So unscheinbar und vorläufig Saurs Collagen auf den ersten Blick auch daherkommen, sind sie doch Kontrapunkte zu den im stetigen Wandel begriffenen Webseiten. Sie sind bleibende Aufnahmen eines unsichtbaren Netzwerks von „Kommunikationsketten“[4] im Internet.

Linda Huke

1 Limor Shifman, *Meme. Kunst, Kultur und Politik im digitalen Zeitalter*, Berlin 2014, S. 57.
2 Boaz Levin, Fabian Knierim, *Kartografie eines lebendigen Archivs / Mapping A Living Archive: Zu D. H. Saurs Hope 2008–2017, 2017*, in: *Biennale für aktuelle Fotographie / Farewell Photography*, 2017 (Beilage zur *Camera Austria International*, Heft 138, Juni 2017), S. 6.
3 Daniel Dennett, *Philosophie des menschlichen Bewusstseins*, Hamburg 1994, S. 277.
4 Levin, Knierim 2017, ebd.

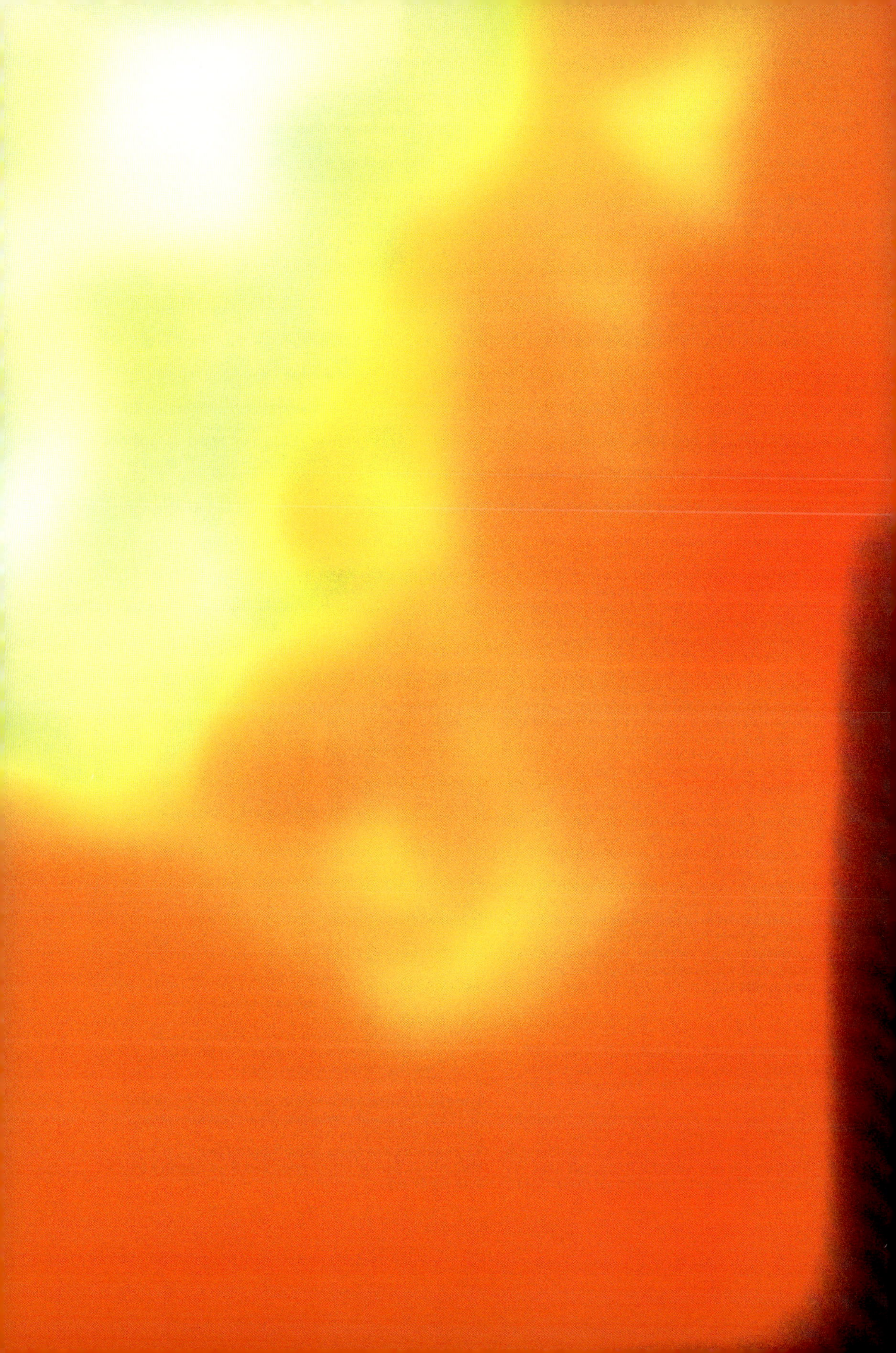

BILDINDEX
IMAGE INDEX

Cover

Adaption eines auf YouTube zirkulierenden anonymen Handyvideos, das eine Explosion zeigt.

Adaptation of an anonymous mobile phone video circulating on YouTube, showing an explosion.

JULIA HÖNER
KERSTIN SCHANKWEILER
Affect Me. Social Media Images in Art

18
19

Neda Agha-Soltan, 20. Juni 2009, Teheran, Videostills
Neda Agha-Soltan, 20 June, 2009, Tehran, video stills

www.youtube.com/watch?v=8zFslcGmZnM
© picture alliance/dpa

Das Handy-Video zeigt eine junge Frau, die in der Nähe des Revolutionsplatzes im Zentrum von Teheran auf der Straße ver-blutet sein soll. Die Studentin, deren Name im Internet mit Neda angegeben wird, soll am Samstag (19. Juni 2009) kurz zuvor bei einer Demonstration angeschossen worden sein. Es ist nicht festzustellen, ob dieser am Samstag ins Internet gestellte Film tatsächlich den Tod der jungen Frau zeigt. Bei Film- und Fotomaterial von den Demonstrationen im Iran ist sehr häufig mit unabhängigen Quellen nicht feststellbar, ob sie authentisch sind.

The mobile phone video shows a young woman who supposedly bled to death on the street near the Revolution Square in the center of Tehran. The student, who according to the Internet was named Neda, is supposed to have been shot shortly before, at a demonstration on Saturday (19 June, 2009). It is not clear whether this video posted on the Internet on Saturday actually shows the death of the young woman. It is often not possible to determine with independent sources, whether video and photo material from demonstrations in Iran are authentic.

20

Kerim Okten, Türkei Iran Ankara-Protest, 2009
Kerim Okten, Turkey Iran Ankara Protest, 2009

© picture alliance/dpa, Foto/photo: Kerim Okten

Während eines Protests gegen die Iranische Regierung in Ankara in der Türkei am 27. Juni 2009 halten iranische Protestierende Plakate mit den Aufschriften: „Ich bin Neda", „Hört auf Menschen zu töten" und „Wo ist meine Stimme?" in die Höhe. Irans Wächterrat sollte am 28. Juni 2009 sein Urteil zur Wahl bekannt geben, aber bereits am 26. Juni bestand ein Sprecher darauf, dass es keinen Wahlbetrug gegeben habe.

Iranian protestors hold banners that read "I'm Neda", "Stop Killing People", and "Where is my vote?" during a protest against the Iranian government in Ankara, Turkey on 27 June, 2009. Iran's powerful Guardian Council was supposed to give its final ruling on the election on 28 June, 2009, but on 26 June, 2009, a spokesman already insisted that there had been no election fraud.

Meme: Ein Boot mit Neda Agha-Soltans Gesicht, das LOST Iran zieht.
Meme: A boat with Neda Agha-Soltan's face on it dragging LOST Iran.

www.knowyourmeme.com photos/41092-lostiran
© Gepostet von Noure_Azadi auf Facebook. Angabe und Urheber*in konnten nicht verifiziert werden./Posted by Noure_Azadi on Facebook. Online source and author could not be verified.

Plakatierung des Künstlers ABCNT in Los Angeles als Ausdruck der Empörung über die Tötung von Neda Agha-Soltan in Teheran.
Images pasted in Los Angeles by artist ABCNT as an expression of outrage over the killing of Neda Agha-Soltan in Tehran.

www.unurth.com/ABCNT-Neda-Los-Angeles
© ABCNT

D. H. Saur, *Hope 2008–2011*, 2011, Details/details
Collage/collage
50 x 70 cm

Courtesy der Künstler/the artist

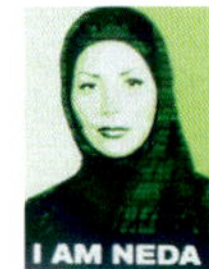

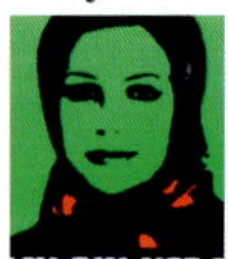
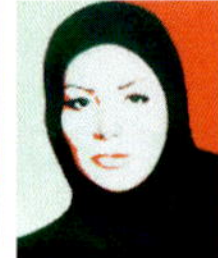
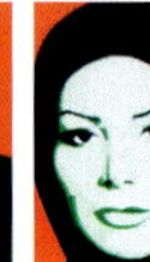

21

NEDA Meme

www.emilybennington.com/daily-grace/daily-grace-1/
© Angabe und Urheber*in konnten nicht verifiziert werden./Online source and author could not be verified.

Vorschlag, Neda Agha-Soltan zur Person des Jahres des *Time* Magazins zu küren, basierend auf einem Plakat des Künstlers ABCNT.
Proposal to elect Neda Agha-Soltan *Time* magazine's person of the year, based on a poster by artist ABCNT.

www.abcnt.wordpress.com/2009/11/26/make-neda-person-of-the-year/
© ABCNT

D. H. Saur, *Hope 2008–2011*, 2011, Details / details
Collage / collage
50 x 70 cm
Courtesy der Künstler / the artist

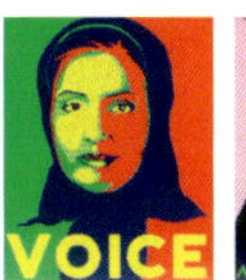

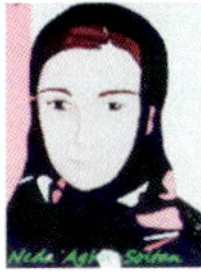

22
23

D. H. Saur, *Hope 2008–2011*, 2011, Details / details
Collage / collage
50 x 70 cm
Courtesy der Künstler / the artist

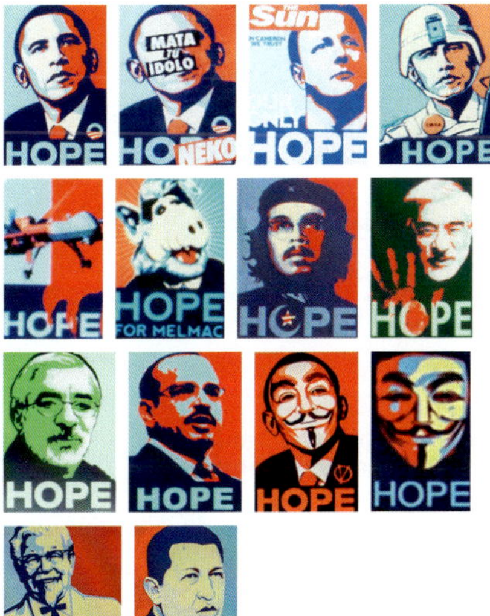

24

Passbild von Khaled Said, 2010
Passport photo of Khaled Said, 2010
https://en.wikipedia.org/wiki/File:Khaled_Mohamed_Saeed.jpg
© Angabe und Urheber*in konnten nicht verifiziert werden. / Online source and author could not be verified.

Khaled Said-Graffiti von Case (Andreas von Chrzanowski) auf der Berliner Mauer, September 2011, Schriftzug oben: „Khaleds Rechte sind Ägyptens Rechte“, unten: „Wir sind alle Khaled Said“, Kalligrafie von Mohamed Gaber.
Graffiti of Khaled Said on the Berlin Wall by Case (Andreas von Chrzanowski), September, 2011, writing at the top: “Khaled’s rights are Egypt’s rights”, at the bottom: “We are all Khaled Said”, calligraphy by Mohamed Gaber.
Mischtechnik mit Sprühdosenlack / mixed media with sprayed laquer
Hauptquartier der / headquarter of the Friedrich Ebert Stiftung, Berlin
https://commons.wikimedia.org/wiki/File:Khaled_Said_Graffiti_on_Berlin_Wall.jpg
© Foto / photo: Nora Shalaby

Stencil-Graffiti mit Porträt von Khaled Said und einem Vers aus einem Gedicht von Amal Donkol: „Würde mein Blut sich in Wasser zwischen deinen Augen verwandeln, würdest du meine blutbefleckten Kleider vergessen?“, Kairo 2011.
Stencil graffiti with portrait of Khaled Said and a vers of a poem by Amal Donkol: “Would my blood turn into water between your eyes, would you forget my clothes stained with blood?”, Cairo 2011.
https://commons.wikimedia.org/wiki/Category:Khaled_Mohamed_Saeed#/media/File:Mural_of_Khaled_Said.jpg
© Foto / photo: lilianwagdy

Wandmalerei mit Khaled Said in San Stefano, Alexandria, heute nicht mehr vorhanden.
Painting of Khaled Said in San Stefano, Alexandria, now painted over.
www.flickr.com/photos/60329285@N04/5694178383/
© Amro Ali, Foto / photo: lilianwagdy

Proteste in Melbourne, in Solidarität mit der Ägyptischen Revolution, 4. Februar 2011
Egypt Uprising solidarity protest Melbourne, 4 February, 2011
https://commons.wikimedia.org/wiki/File:Egypt_Uprising_solidarity_Melbourne_protest,_4_February_2011.jpg
© Creative Commons, Foto / photo: John Englart (@Takver)

Khaled Said auf fiktivem Geldschein
Khaled Said on a fictional banknote
www.facebook.com/ElShaheeed/photos/pb.104224996294040.-2207520000.1447668291./117946854921854/?type=3&theater, hochgeladen am 2. August 2010 / uploaded on 2 August, 2010.
© Angabe und Urheber*in konnten nicht verifiziert werden. / Online source and author could not be verified.

Stencil-Graffiti mit Porträt von Khaled Said, Kairo
Stencil graffiti with portrait of Khaled Said, Cairo
www.facebook.com/ElShaheeed/photos/pb.104224996294040.-2207520000.1447664664./424232494293287/?type=3&theater, hochgeladen am 5. Juni 2012 / uploaded on 5 June, 2012.
© Angabe und Urheber*in konnten nicht verifiziert werden. / Online source and author could not be verified.

25

Ein Demonstrant hält den Cartoon von Carlos Latuff in die Höhe.
Protester holding up the cartoon by Carlos Latuff.

https://latuffcartoons.files.wordpress.com/2012/06/khaled-said-cartoon-cairo-7-july-2012-reuters.jpg
© Carlos Latuff

Kimo Nour, I am Khaled Said—I Am Egypt.
http://justonereason.net/wp-content/uploads/2011/01/170988_10150090779907243_621222242_6072515_4827095_o.jpg
© 2010 We are all Khaled Said, www.elshaheeed.co.uk

Grafik mit Khaled Said, „Ich fordere mein Recht“.
Graphic with Khaled Said, “I demand my right.”
www.facebook.com/ElShaheeed/photos/pb.104224996294040.-2207520000.1447668464./115738538476019/?type=3&theater, hochgeladen am 24. Juli 2010 / uploaded on 24 July, 2010.
© Angabe und Urheber*in konnten nicht verifiziert werden. / Online source and author could not be verified.

Ammar Abo Bakr, Graffiti mit der Leiche von Khaled Said, Mohamed-Mahmoud-Straße, Kairo, heute nicht mehr vorhanden.
Ammar Abo Bakr, Graffiti showing the face of the corpse of Khaled Said, Mohamed Mahmoud Street, Cairo, now painted over.
www.urbanophil.net/kunst/streetartwochen-8-maertyrergalerie-in-kairo/
© Foto / photo: Felix Hartenstein

Carlos Latuff, Politischer Cartoon von Khaled Said und Hosni Mubarak, veröffentlicht während der ägyptischen Proteste 2011.
Carlos Latuff, Political cartoon of Khaled Said and Hosni Mubarak, published during the 2011 Egyptian protests.
https://commons.wikimedia.org/wiki/File:Khaled_Mohamed_Saeed_holding_up_a_tiny,_flailing,_stone-faced_Hosni_Mubarak.png
© Carlos Latuff

Carlos Latuff, Politischer Cartoon von Khaled Said mit der ägyptischen Flagge, veröffentlicht während der ägyptischen Proteste 2011.
Carlos Latuff, Political cartoon of Khaled Said with Egyptian flag, published during the 2011 Egyptian protests.
https://latuffcartoons.files.wordpress.com/2013/06/khaled-saeed-death-3-years-on.gif
© Carlos Latuff

40
41
42
43

Lara Baladi, *Alone, Together, … In Media Res,* 2012, Videostills / video stills
Dreikanalvideoinstallation / three-channel video installation, 42 Min
Maße variabel / dimensions variable
Courtesy die Künstlerin / the artist

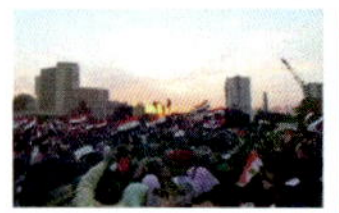
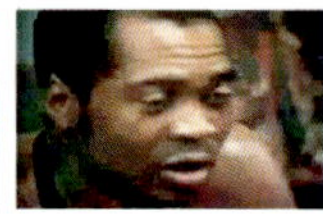
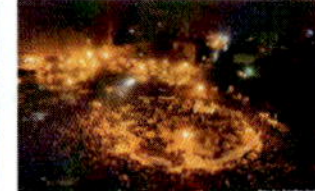

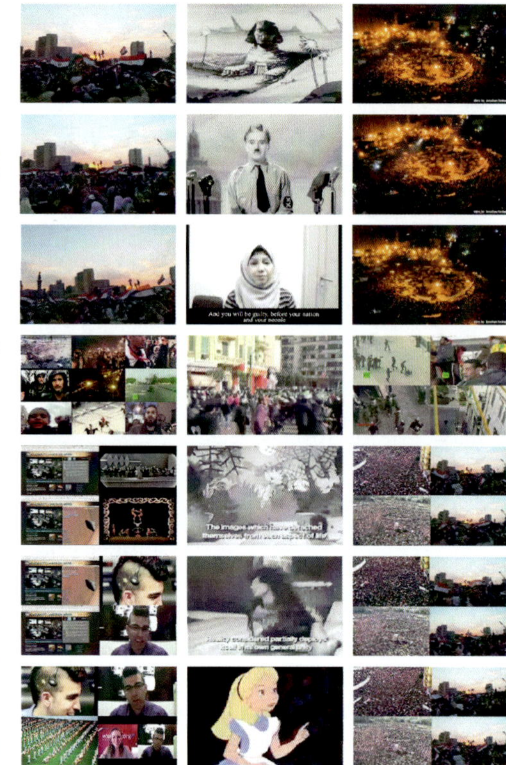

TOBIAS WENDL
Die Wiederkehr der Bilder: Zur Aneignung fotografischer Bildikonen in ausgewählten Künstlerprojekten zwischen 1945 und 2005
The Return of Images: Appropriations of Iconic Photographs in Selected Artists’ Projects from 1945 to 2005

56

Nilüfer Demir, Fotographie von Alan Kurdi, 2015
Nilüfer Demir, Photograph of Alan Kurdi, 2015
www.expressgazete.com/images/haberler/2016/11/nilufer_demir_in_cektigi_alan_kurdi_fotografi_tum_zamanlarin_etkili_fotograflari_arasinda_h13681_f0457.jpg
© picture alliance / dpa, Foto / photo: Dogan News Agency
Am Strand des Küstenortes Bodrum in der Stadt Mugla in der Türkei angespülter Leichnam eines Kindes, das am 2. September 2015 beim Versuch, auf die griechische Insel Kos überzusetzen, ertrunken ist. Mindestens elf syrische Flüchtlinge starben, als das Boot sank, nachdem es die Türkei verließ.

Washed up body of a child who drowned during a failed attempt to sail to the Greek island of Kos, at the shore in the coastal town of Bodrum, Mugla city, Turkey, 2 September, 2015. At least eleven Syrian

migrants died in the loss after leaving Turkey.

Pekka Jylhä, *Until the sea shall free him*, 2016
Verbundstoff, Glas und bemaltes Holz / composite material, glass, painted wood
177 x 36 x 46 cm
www.artfacts.net/exhibpics/743989.jpg
© picture alliance / dpa, Foto / photo: Martii Kainulainen
Die Skulptur *Until the sea shall free him* zeigt Alan Kurdi in einer gläsernen Box. Die Arbeit des finnischen Künstlers Pekka Jylhä wurde im März 2016 in der Ausstellung *We Have Inherited Hope—the Gift of Forgetting* in der Helsinki Contemporary Gallery in Finnland gezeigt.
Sculpture *Until the sea shall free him* by Finnish artist Pekka Jylhä showing Alan Kurdi in a glass box. The work was on display in march 2016 as part of the exhibition *We Have Inherited Hope—the Gift of Forgetting* at the Helsinki Contemporary Gallery in Finland.

Carlos Rodríguez Casado, Cartoon mit / with Ai Weiwei, 2016
www.elespanol.com/cultura/arte/20160206/100240146_0.html
© Carlos Rodríguez Casado

59

Iri und Toshi Maruki, *Hiroshima Panels, Panel 6: Atomic Desert,* 1952
Öl und Tinte auf Leinwand / oil and ink on canvas
180 x 720 cm
© Maruki Gallery

Salvador Dalí, *The Three Sphinxes of Bikini*, 1947
Öl auf Leinwand / oil on canvas
40,6 x 51,4 cm
Morohashi Museum of Modern Art, Fukushima
© VG Bild-Kunst, Bonn 2017

Mieczysław Berman, *Apoteoza*, 1947
Fotomontage / photomontage
31 x 20 cm
Muzeum Narodowe we Wrocławiu
© Muzeum Narodowe we Wrocławiu

Atombombentorte, Washington, November 1946
Mushroom cloud cake, Washington, November 1946
www.gettyimages.co/uk/Licence/71083487
© Harris & Ewing Studio, Foto / photo: Stock Montage / GettyImages
Von links: U.S. Navy Vizeadmiral W.H.P. Blandy (1890–1954), seine Frau und Konteradmiral Frank J. Lowry (1888–1955) beim Anschneiden einer Torte in der Form eines Atompilzes anlässlich eines Empfangs für die Operation Crossroad – einem U.S. Nuklearwaffentestprogramm – in Washington D.C., 6. November 1946.
From left: U.S. Navy Vice Admiral W.H.P. Blandy (1890–1954), his wife, and Rear Admiral Frank J. Lowry (1888–1955) cut a cake in the shape of a mushroom cloud at a reception for Operation Crossroad, a U.S. programme that tests nuclear weapons, in Washington D.C., 6 November, 1946.

60

Roy Lichtenstein, *Atom Burst*, 1965
Acryl auf Holztafel / acrylic on wood panel
61 x 61 cm
Modern Art Museum of Fort Worth, The Benjamin J. Tillar Memorial Trust
© Estate of Roy Lichtenstein/DACS 2017, VG Bild-Kunst, Bonn 2017

Andy Warhol, *Atomic Bomb*, 1966
Siebdruck auf Leinwand / silkscreen print on canvas
264 x 204,5 cm
© 2017 The Andy Warhol Foundation for the Visual Arts, Inc. / Licensed by Artists Rights Society (ARS), New York

64

Eddie Adams, Fotografie von Nguyễn Văn Lém, 1. Februar 1968
Eddie Adams, Photograph of Nguyễn Văn Lém, 1 February, 1968
www.newseum.org/wp-content/uploads/2015/05/News_podcast_pulitzer_1969-e1431460840302.jpg
© picture alliance / AP Photo, Foto / photo: Eddie Adams
Das Archivfoto vom 1. Februar 1968 zeigt den südvietnamesischen Leiter der Nationalpolizei General Nguyễn Ngọc Loan in dem Moment, in dem er den Việt Cộng-Angehörigen Nguyễn Văn Lém auf einer Straße in Saigon zu Beginn der Tet Offensive erschießt. Der Fotograf Eddie Adams gab später zu Protokoll, dass Loan nach der Erschießung auf ihn zugekommen sei und sagte: „Sie töteten viele meiner Landsleute und auch die Ihren" und dann wegging.
In this file photo from 1 February, 1968, General Nguyễn Ngọc Loan, South Vietnamese chief of the national police, shoots the Việt Cộng official Nguyễn Văn Lém into the head. The photo was taken in the streets of Saigon in the beginning of the Tet Offensive. Photographer Eddie Adams reported that after the shooting, Loan approached him and said, "They killed many of my people, and yours too". Then he walked away.

Wolf Vostell, *Miss America*, 1968
Collage, Siebdruck, Lasurfarbe auf Leinwand, Foto / collage, silkscreen print, transparent colour on canvas, photo
200 x 120 cm
Museum Ludwig, Köln / Cologne, Inv.-Nr. ML 01152, Zugang 1976.02.23
© VG Bild-Kunst, Bonn 2017, Foto / photo: Rheinisches Bildarchiv, rba_c004388

Jerry Kearns, *Madonna and Child*, 1986
Montage auf Azetat / montage on acetate
71 x 58 cm
© Jerry Kearns

65

Nick Út, *The Terror of War*, 1972
© picture alliance / AP Foto, Foto / photo: Nick Út
Das Archivfoto vom 8. Juni 1972, aufgenommen von Huỳnh Công „Nick" Út, zeigt Kinder, darunter die neunjährige Kim Phúc in der Mitte, die in entsetzlicher Angst die Route 1 (nahe Trang Bang) nach einem Napalm-Luftangriff auf mutmaßliche Việt Cộng-Verstecke herunterrennen. Sie werden gefolgt von südvietnamesischen Soldaten. Nachdem Nick Út das Foto gemacht hatte, legte er die Kamera beiseite und gab dem mit schweren Verbrennungen verletzten Mädchen Wasser zu trinken und goss es auf ihre Wunden. Dann fuhr er sie gemeinsam mit weiteren Kindern zum nächsten Krankenhaus. Dort weigerte sich der Arzt zunächst, Kim Phúc aufzunehmen mit der Begründung, sie habe zu schwere Verbrennungen, um sie zu retten. Nick Út zeigte seinen Presseausweis und erklärte, dass dann bereits am folgenden Tag Fotos von ihr überall auf der Welt veröffentlicht würden, zusammen mit einem Bericht wie das Krankenhaus Hilfe verweigerte.
In this 8 June, 1972, file photo taken by Huỳnh Công "Nick" Út, South Vietnamese forces follow terrified children, including 9-year-old Kim Phúc in the center, as they run down Route 1 near Trang Bang after an aerial napalm attack on suspected Việt Cộng hiding places. After making the photo, he set aside his camera, gave the badly burned girl water, poured more on her wounds, then loaded her and others into his van to take them to a hospital. When doctors refused to admit her, saying she was too badly burned to be saved, he angrily flashed his press pass. The next day, he told them, pictures of her would be displayed all over the world, along with an explanation of how the hospital refused to help.

Zbigniew Libera, *Nepal, from the Positives series*, 2003
C-Print / c-print
120 x 154,6 cm
© Raster Gallery, Warschau / Warsaw

Judy Chicago & Donald Woodman, *Im/Balance of Power, Holocaust Project*, 1991
Acryl gesprüht, Ölfarbe und Foto auf Leinwand, Siebdruck und Stoff auf Leinwand / sprayed acrylic, oil paint, and photography on canvas, silkscreen print and fabric on canvas
196,22 x 241,94 cm
© Judy Chicago & Donald Woodman, Foto / photo: Donald Woodman

70

Sam Nzima, Fotografie von Hector Pieterson, 1976
Sam Nzima, Photograph of Hector Pieterson, 1976
www.saha.org.za/youth/the_death_of_hector_pieterson.htm
© SAHA collection AL2547, Foto / photo: Sam Nzima

Str, *Safrica Reenactment*, 2003
© picture alliance / dpa, Foto / photo: Str
Am 16. Juni 2003 stellen Jugendliche während der Feierlichkeiten zum Jugendtag in Soweto, Johannesburg, Südafrika, den Tod von Hector Pieterson nach. Am 16. Juni 1976 wurde Hector Pieterson dort während Anti-Apartheids-Protesten von der Polizei erschossen.
On Monday, 16 June, 2003, the National Youth's day in South Africa, youths in Soweto, Johannesburg reenact the death of Hector Pieterson. On 16 June, 1976, Hector Pieterson was shot there by the police during anti Apartheid protests.

Mangena, Cartoon mit / with Hector Pieterson, 2015
https://pbs.twimg.com/media/CHn4l9k-WoAA6hmc.jpg
© Mangena

ERNST VAN ALPHEN
"Poor Images" and the Affect of Exhibitionism
„Poor Images" und der Affekt des Exhibitionismus

86
87

Thomas Hirschhorn, *Subjecter (Katastrophé)*, 2010
Atelieransichten / studio views & Details / details
Schaufensterpuppe, Brautkleid, Collage, Klebeband / mannequin, wedding dress, collage, adhesive tape
180 x 250 x 350 cm
Courtesy Privatsammlung / private collection
© VG Bild-Kunst, Bonn 2017, Foto / photo: Thomas Hirschhorn

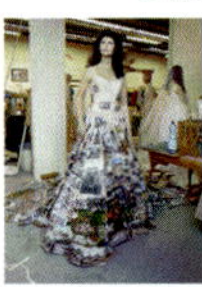
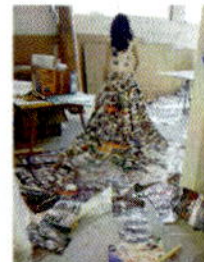
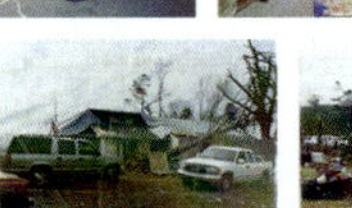
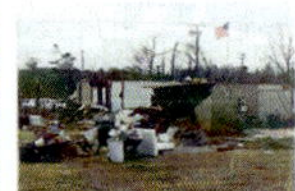
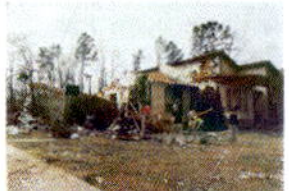
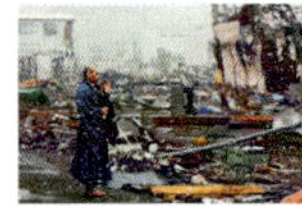
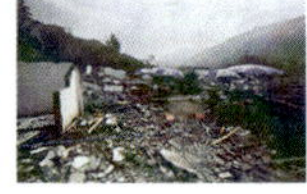

90

Thomas Ruff, *Nudes cs02*, 2011
C-Print / c-print
157 x 110 cm
Courtesy der Künstler / the artist & Konrad Fischer Galerie
© VG Bild-Kunst, Bonn 2017

91

Thomas Ruff, *Nudes vg02*, 2000
C-Print / c-print
147 x 110 cm
Courtesy der Künstler / the artist & Konrad Fischer Galerie
© VG Bild-Kunst, Bonn 2017

94

Andy Warhol, *Empire*, 1964, Filmstill / film still
16 mm Film, schwarz / weiß, ohne Ton, 16 Bilder pro Sekunde / black and white, silent, 16 frames per second, 8:05 h
© 2017 The Andy Warhol Museum, Pittsburgh, PA, a museum of Carnegie Institute; 2017 The Andy Warhol Foundation for the Visual Arts, Inc. / Licensed by Artists Rights Society (ARS), New York

95

Andy Warhol, *Sleep*, 1963, Filmstill / film still
16 mm Film, schwarz / weiß, ohne Ton, 16 Bilder pro Sekunde / black and white, silent, 16 frames per second, 5:21 h
© 2017 The Andy Warhol Museum, Pittsburgh, PA, a museum of Carnegie Institute; 2017 The Andy Warhol Foundation for the Visual Arts, Inc. / Licensed by Artists Rights Society (ARS), New York

Andy Warhol, *Empire*, 1964, Filmstill / film still
16 mm Film, schwarz / weiß, ohne Ton, 16 Bilder pro Sekunde / black and white, silent, 16 frames per second, 8:05 h
© 2017 The Andy Warhol Museum, Pittsburgh, PA, a museum of Carnegie Institute; 2017 The Andy Warhol Foundation for the Visual Arts, Inc. / Licensed by Artists Rights Society (ARS), New York

LARA BALADI

108
109

Lara Baladi, aus der Serie / from the series *Ana Masri (I am Egyptian)*, 2010–2017
Fotografien von / Photographs by Lara Baladi
Courtesy die Künstlerin / the artist
© Fotos / photos: Lara Baladi

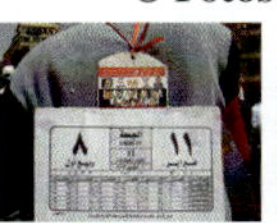
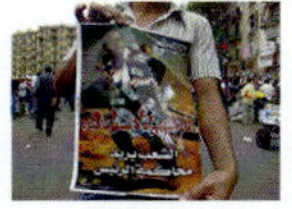
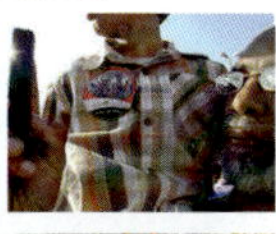
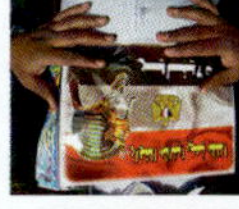
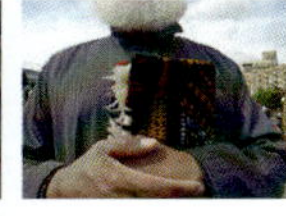
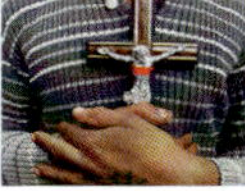
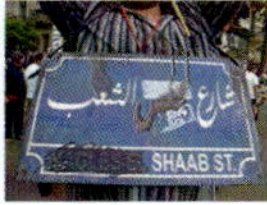

110
111

Lara Baladi, *Vox Populi, Archiving a Revolution in the Digital Age*
Studie für die interaktive web-basierte Timeline der ägyptischen Revolution 2011. Fortlaufendes Projekt seit 2011. / Study for the interactive web based timeline of the 2011 Egyptian revolution. Ongoing Project since 2011.
Courtesy die Künstlerin / the artist
© Lara Baladi

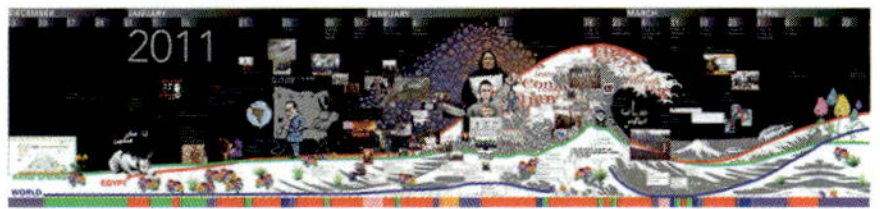

Lara Baladi, Video mit dem Papierprototyp für die Timeline *Vox Populi, Archiving a Revolution in the Digital Age*, 2015, Videostills
Paper prototype video for the timeline, *Vox Populi, Archiving a Revolution in the Digital Age*, 2015, video stills
http://tahrirarchives.com/timeline
Courtesy die Künstlerin / the artist
© Lara Baladi

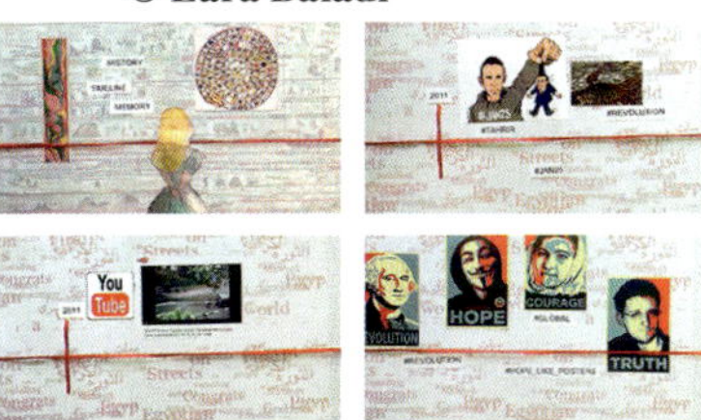

112
113

Lara Baladi, *Be Realistic, Ask for the Impossible*, 2017
Studien für ein Wandgemälde in KAI 10 / Studies for a mural in KAI 10
Graffiti artist Salma Samy Ahmed Elbalouty
Courtesy die Künstlerin / the artist
© Lara Baladi

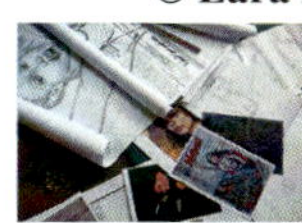
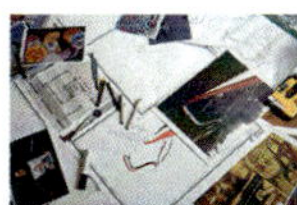

IRENE CHABR

114
115

Irene Chabr, nachfolgend Einzelbilder aus dem Projekt / listed below images from the project *Wandernde Gesten,* 2015–2017 (work in progress), mit gelöschten Slogans, Hashtags und Quellenangaben / including slogans, hashtags, and sources
Courtesy die Künstlerin / the artist

#LET'S KISS IN IRAN #MY STEALTHY FREEDOM
#LetsKissInIran #MyStealthyFreedom #FatemehEkhtesari #MehdiMousavi
www.facebook.com/hashtag/letskissiniran

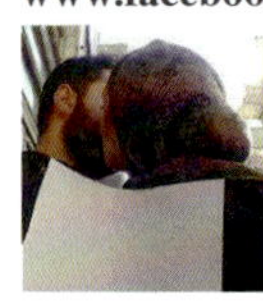

I MAKE A $60K A YEAR + BENEFITS. I HAVE A MINIMAL DEBT & NO HEALTH PROBLEMS. MY LIFE IS GOOD. I STILL THINK WASHINGTON & WALL STREET ARE BROKEN! I AM THE 99%.
#WeAreThe99% #OccupyWallstreet
www.wearethe99percent.tumblr.com

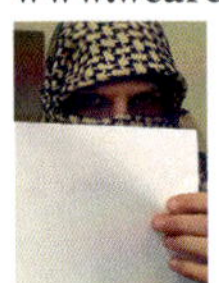

#SIRTIMIZI DÖNÜYORUZ
#SırtımızıDönüyoruz #WeAreTurningOurBacks #TurkeyElections #Erdoğan #Feminizm
www.twitter.com/hashtag/sırtımızıdönüyoruz

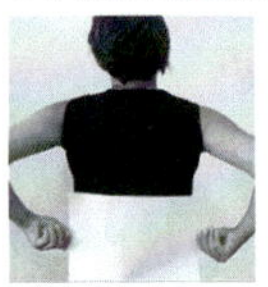

AMERICAN DREAM? MORE LIKE AMERICAN NIGHTMARE. I'M FOR A 99% WITHOUT A FEAR FOR THEIR FUTURE. WE ARE THE 99%. OCCUPY WALL STREET.
#WeAreThe99% #OccupyWallstreet
www.wearethe99percent.tumblr.com

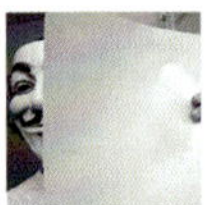

GREETINGS FROM SPAIN. YOUR FIGHT IT'S OUR FIGHT. # WE ARE THE 99%.
#WeAreThe99% #OccupyWallstreet
www.wearethe99percent.tumblr.com

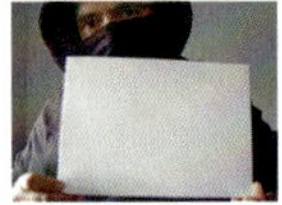

#StopA4WaistChallenge #FuckYourBeautyStandards #BodyPositivity #Facepalm
www.instagram.com/explore/tags/a4waist/

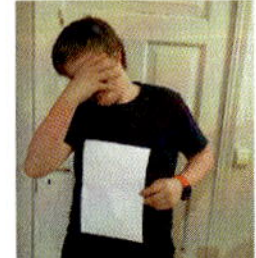

#FREE CHEN
#FreeChenGuangcheng #DarkGlasses #China
www.ichenguangcheng.blogspot.ch

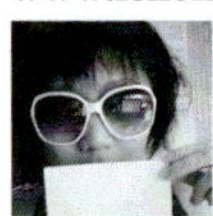

A SECURITY OFFICER WHO IS TAKING BRIBES WILL NOT INSURE MY SAFETY!!!
#KenyaIMNotATerrorist #AntiTerrorLaws #Ethnic#Profiling #Refugees
www.kenyaimnotaterrorist.tumblr.com

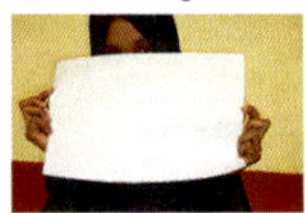

I NEED FEMINISM COZ SOMETIMES WE DO NOT REALISE THAT WE ARE BEING CONTROLLED OR THAT WE OURSELVES ARE CONTROLLING A "LOVED" ONE!
#WhoNeedsFeminism #INeedFeminism
https://www.twitter.com/WNFeminism

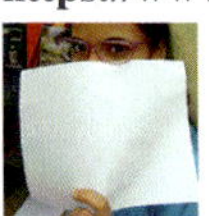

MUTTER, PFLEGEFACHFRAU, GESCHÄFTSSTELLENLEITERIN, VORSTANDSMITGLIED. N., 42 JAHRE.
#UeliDasBinIch #StopSexism #Feminism #Switzerland
http://www.20min.ch/schweiz/news/story/Frauen-zeigen-Ueli-Maurer--wer-sie-wirklich-sind-27913425

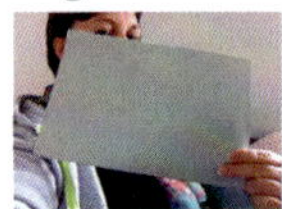

I'M WITH THE UPRISING OF WOMEN IN THE ARAB WORLD BECAUSE I AM AN EMPLOYEE AND SUPPORT FINANCIALLY MY YOUNGER BROTHERS. HOWEVER, I AM STILL TREATED WITH THE DISCRIMINATION, AS A WOMAN I HAVE TO HIDE MY FACE AND REPORT MY MOVEMENTS.
#TheUprisingOfWomenInTheArabWorld
www.uprisingofwomeninthearabworld.com

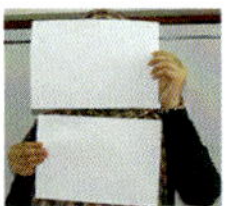

DON'T HIDE BEHIND A PIECE OF PAPER! YOU'RE BEAUTIFUL!
#StopA4WaistChallenge #IMMoreThanMyWaist #FuckYourBeautyStandards #BodyPositivity
www.instagram.com/explore/tags/a4waist/

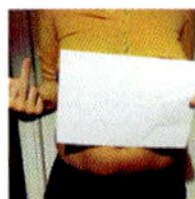

I AM A FULL TIME COLLEGE STUDENT. I WAS FIRED FROM MY SERVING JOB (WHICH PAYS MY RENT + GROCERIES) BECAUSE I WOULDN'T DROP A CLASS TO WORK MORE SHIFTS. I AM THE 99%.
#WeAreThe99% #OccupyWallstreet
http://www.wearethe99percent.tumblr.com

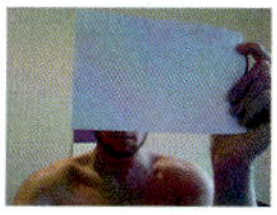

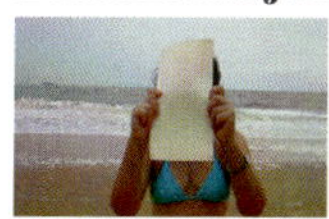

LIBERTÉ ÉGALITÉ POUR TOUTES ET TOUS!
#OpBlueBra #BlueBraGirl #WeAreAllBlueBraGirl #Tahrir #ArabSpring
irc.telecomix/join#opBlueBra

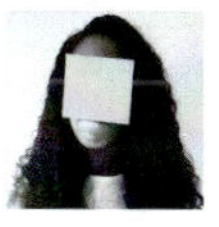

#BRING BACK OUR GIRLS
#BringBackOurGirls #ChibokGirls #Nigeria
https://www.instagram.com/explore/tags/bringbackourgirls/

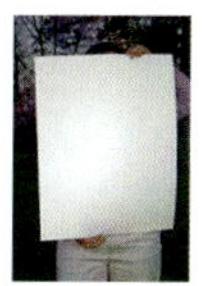

WE ARE FAMILY FARMERS. ONE OF US KEEPS A SECOND JOB SO THAT WE CAN HAVE HEALTH CARE. WE'RE NOT BIG ENOUGH TO QUALIFY FOR SUBSIDIES. HOW WILL WE FEED OUR CHILDREN? HOW WILL WE FEED OURSELVES? HOW WILL WE FEED YOU? WE ARE THE 99%.
#WeAreThe99% #OccupyWallstreet
www.wearethe99percent.tumblr.com

#SPEAK BEAUTIFUL
#SpeakBeautiful #SelfEsteem #RealBeauty #BodyPositivity #Dove #Unilever
https://www.twitter.com/hashtag/speakbeautiful

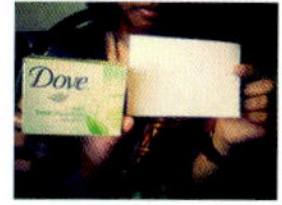

I WORK ON WALL ST. I AM LIVING, BREATHING AFFIRMATION OF THE FACT THAT WHERE AND TO WHOM WE ARE BORN MATTER THE MOST. FUCK THAT. I AM THE 1%. I STAND WITH THE 99%.
#WeAreThe1% #WeStandWithThe99% #OccupyWallstreet
www.westandwiththe99percent.tumblr.com

I AM THE LAST ONE STANDING AT WORK. I'M SO GRATEFUL TO HAVE A JOB WITH INSURANCE TO COVER MY CUSTOM ORTHOPEDIC SHOES, THAT THE 12 HOURS DAYS JUST FLY BY AND I ALMOST FORGET THAT I CAN BARELY STAND OR WALK. I AM THE 99%.
#WeAreThe99% #OccupyWallstreet
www.wearethe99percent.tumblr.com

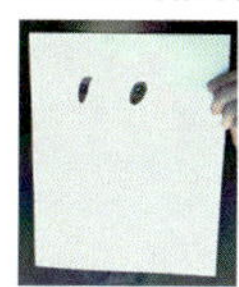

116
117

Irene Chabr, *Wandernde Gesten I*, 2015
Tintenstrahldrucke, wiederverwendete Sperrholzplatten, Papierstapel mit Bildreferenzen, Slogans und Hashtags / inkjet prints, re-used plywood boards, stack of paper with image references, slogans and hashtags
Verschiedene Maße / dimensions variable
Ausstellungsansicht / installation view Station 21, Zürich, 2015
Courtesy die Künstlerin / the artist
© Foto / photo: Flurin Bertschinger

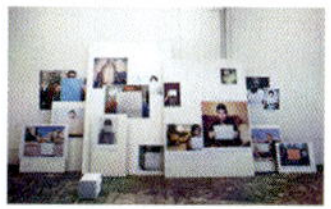

Irene Chabr, *Wandernde Gesten I*, 2015, Detail / detail
Courtesy die Künstlerin / the artist
#BRING BACK OUR GIRLS
MichelleObamaBringBackOurGirls.jpg
www.upload.wikimedia.org/wikipedia/commons/f/f3/Michelle-obama-bringbackourgirls.jpg

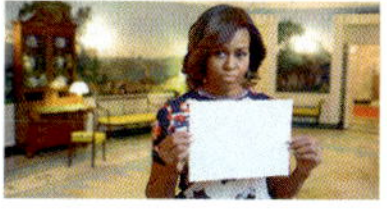

Irene Chabr, *Wandernde Gesten I*, 2015, Detail / detail
Courtesy die Künstlerin / the artist
JE SUIS CHARLIE. ALEPPO, SYRIA.
#JE SUIS CHARLIE
2015-01-11-B66xzMDCMAEkd7.jpglarge667x499.jpg
www.zaina-erhaim.com/je-suis-charlie/

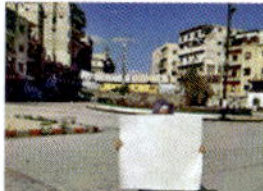

118
119

Irene Chabr & Noëmie Stähli, *Harraga (www.youtube.com/watch?v=TT2ijWrTUr4; www.youtube.com/watch?v=eWvvRF3Y-S8; www.youtube.com/watch?v=36kbTfnVkg)*, 2013, Videostills / video stills
Zweikanalvideoprojektion / two-channel video projection, 3:26 Min, endless loop
Courtesy die Künstlerinnen / the artists

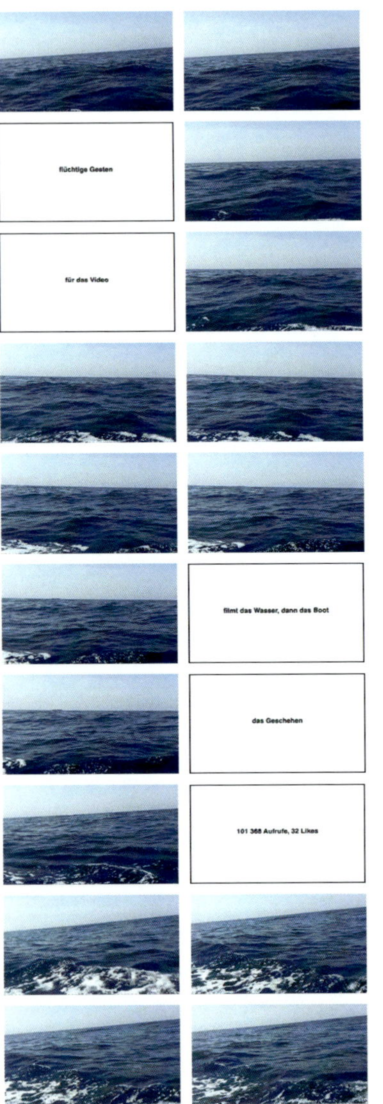

FORENSIC ARCHITECTURE

124
125

Forensic Architecture, *Air Strike Atimah*, 2015
3D-Pulverdruck eines Wolkenmodells, CNC-gefräster Hartschaum / powder bed fusion 3D print of cloud model, CNC base milled from high density foam
25 x 70 x 80 cm
Courtesy Forensic Architecture
© KAI 10 | Arthena Foundation, Foto / photo: Alexandra Höner

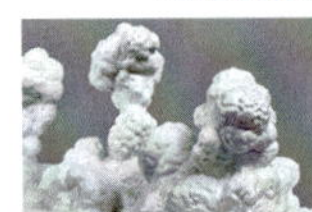
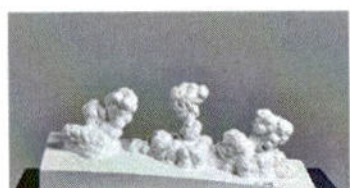

126
127
128
129

Forensic Architecture, *Air Strike Atimah*, 2015, Videostills / video stills
Video, Farbe, Ton / video, colour, sound, 2:43 Min
Maße variabel / dimensions variable
Courtesy Forensic Architecture

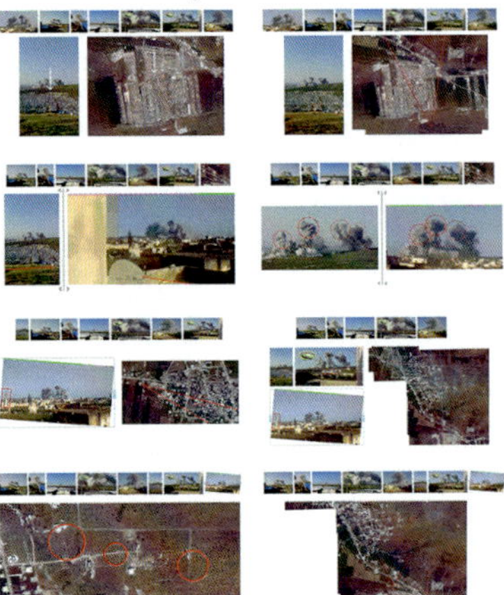

LYNN HERSHMAN LEESON

130

Lynn Hershman Leeson, *Big Hoodie*, 2016
Archivarischer Digitaldruck / archival digital print
40 x 74,91 cm
Courtesy die Künstlerin / the artist & Waldburger Wouters, Brüssel / Brussels

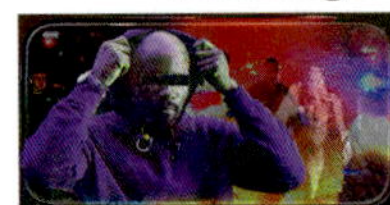

131

Lynn Hershman Leeson, *Image Capture on Discarded Broken Cell Phone after Trayvon Martin Riots*, 2012
Archivarischer Digitaldruck / archival digital print
129,2 x 76,2
Courtesy die Künstlerin / the artist & Waldburger Wouters, Brüssel / Brussels

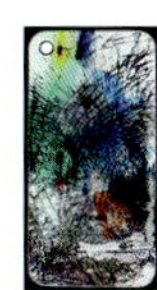

132

Lynn Hershman Leeson, *Final water is rising*, 2016
Archivarischer Digitaldruck / archival digital print
25,4 x 22,32 cm
Courtesy die Künstlerin / the artist & Waldburger Wouters, Brüssel / Brussels

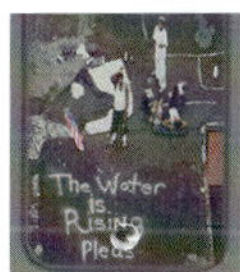

133

Lynn Hershman Leeson, *Cyclops of the anthropocine 1*, 2016
Archivarischer Digitaldruck / archival digital print
25,4 x 20,4 cm
Courtesy die Künstlerin / the artist & Waldburger Wouters, Brüssel / Brussels

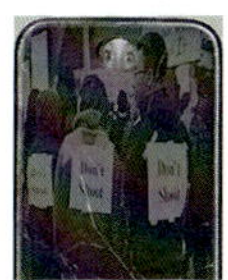

134
135

Lynn Hershman Leeson, *iPhone Crack (August Moon)*, 2014, Videostills / video stills & Installationsansichten / installation views
iPhone, Beamer, Sockel, technische Vorrichtung / iPhone, beamer, pedestal, technical devices
120 x 45 x 35 cm
Courtesy die Künstlerin / the artist & Waldburger Wouters, Brüssel / Brussels
© Installationsansichten / Installation views KAI 10 | Arthena Foundation, Foto / photo: Alexandra Höner

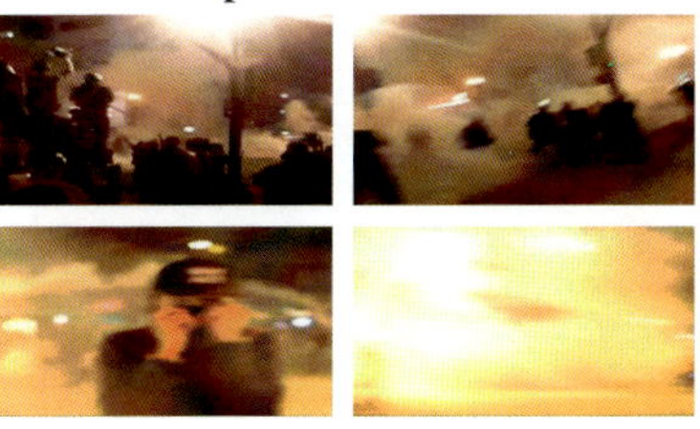

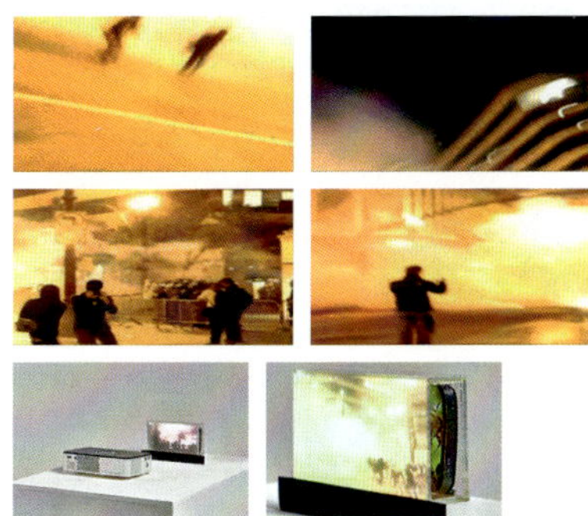

THOMAS HIRSCHHORN

136
137
138

Thomas Hirschhorn, *Subjecter (Katastrophé)*, 2010, Installationsansichten / installation views & Details / details
Schaufensterpuppe, Brautkleid, Collage, Klebeband / mannequin, wedding dress, collage, adhesive tape
180 x 250 x 350 cm
Courtesy Privatsammlung / private collection
© VG Bild-Kunst, Bonn 2017, Fotos / photos: Thomas Hirschhorn

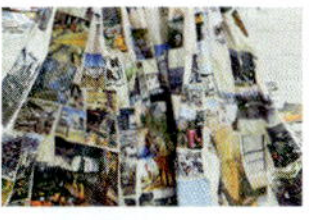
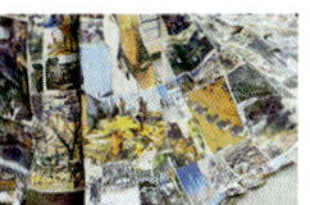

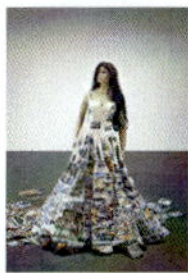

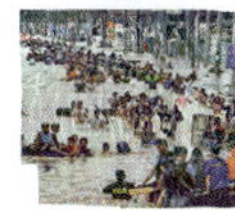
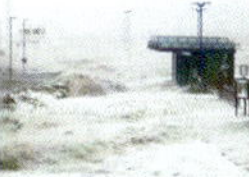

RANDA MAROUFI

145
146

Randa Maroufi, *Le Park*, 2015, Fimstills / film stills
Film, 14 Min, produziert von / produced by Le Fresnoy, Studio national des arts contemporains
Courtesy die Künstlerin / the artist & Le Fresnoy, Studio national des arts contemporains

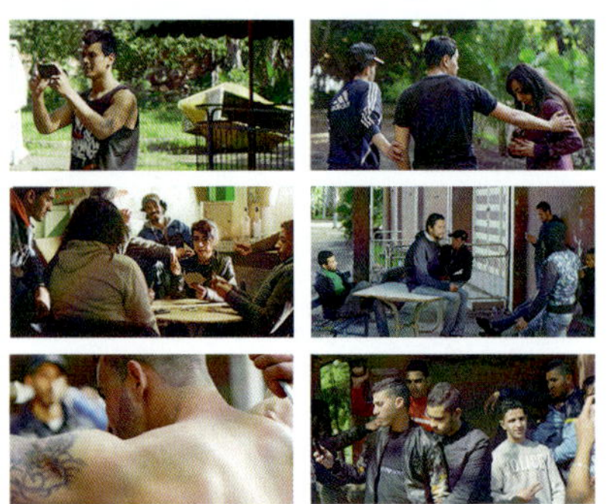

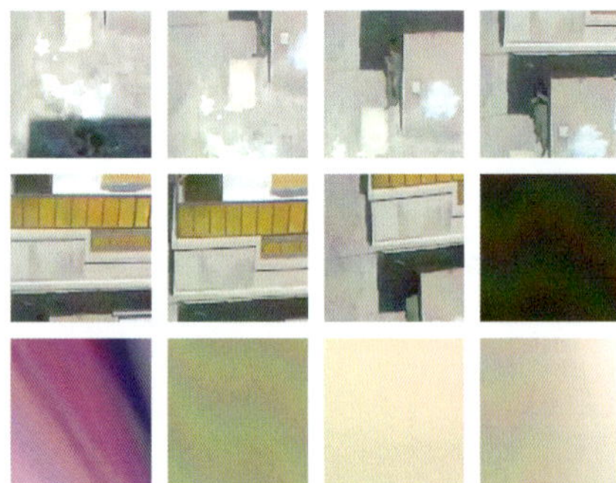

RABIH MROUÉ

148
149

Rabih Mroué, *The Pixelated Revolution*, 2012,
Part 1 of the series *The Fall of a Hair*, 2012,
Videostills / video stills
Video, Farbe, Ton / video, colour, sound,
21:58 Min
Courtesy der Künstler / the artist &
Sfeir-Semler Gallery, Beirut & Hamburg
© Rabih Mroué

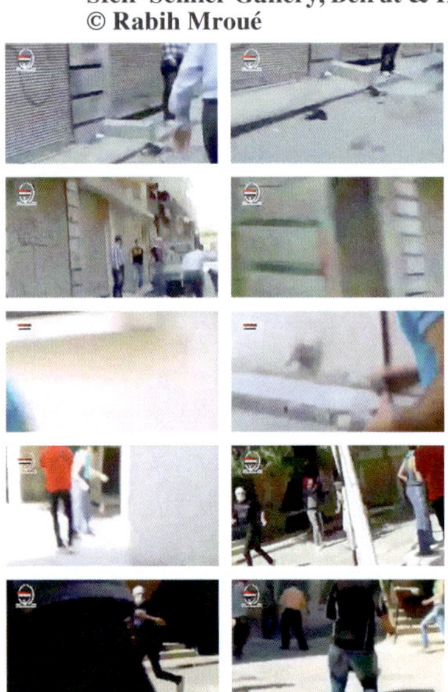

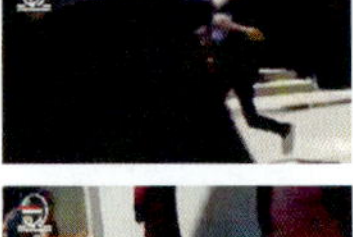

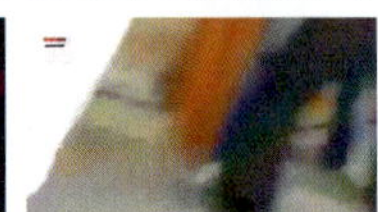

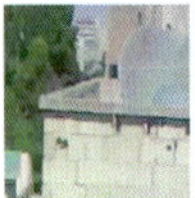

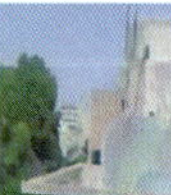

154

Rabih Mroué, *Blow Up 3*, Part 3 of the series
The Fall of a Hair, 2012
Lightjet-Drucke auf Hochglanzpapier / lightjet
prints on high gloss paper
131 x 90 cm
Courtesy der Künstler / the artist &
Sfeir-Semler Gallery, Beirut & Hamburg
© Rabih Mroué

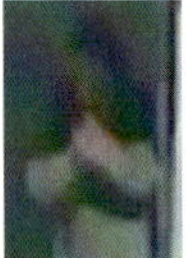

155

Rabih Mroué, *Blow Up 4,* Part 3 of the series
The Fall of a Hair, 2012
Lightjet-Drucke auf Hochglanzpapier / lightjet
prints on high gloss paper
131 x 90 cm
Courtesy der Künstler / the artist &
Sfeir-Semler Gallery, Beirut & Hamburg
© Rabih Mroué

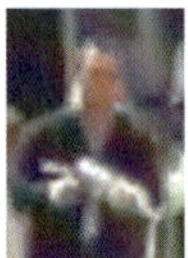

156

Rabih Mroué, *Blow Up 5*, Part 3 of the series
The Fall of a Hair, 2012
Lightjet-Drucke auf Hochglanzpapier / lightjet
prints on high gloss paper
131 x 90 cm
Courtesy der Künstler / the artist &
Sfeir-Semler Gallery, Beirut & Hamburg
© Rabih Mroué

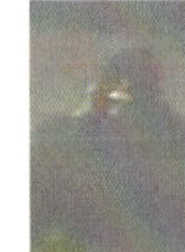

157

Rabih Mroué, *Blow Up 7*, Part 3 of the series *The Fall of a Hair,* 2012
Lightjet-Drucke auf Hochglanzpapier / lightjet prints on high gloss paper
131 x 90 cm
Courtesy der Künstler / the artist & Sfeir-Semler Gallery, Beirut & Hamburg
© Rabih Mroué

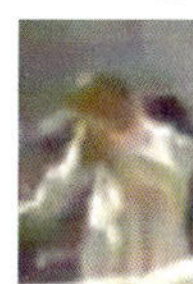

THOMAS RUFF

160

Thomas Ruff, *jpeg ny14,* 2006
C-Print / c-print
253 x 185 cm
Courtesy der Künstler / the artist & Konrad Fischer Galerie, Düsseldorf & Berlin
© VG Bild-Kunst, Bonn 2017

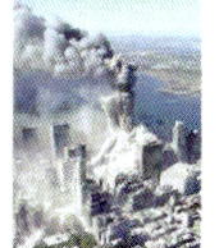

161

Thomas Ruff, *jpeg ny02*, 2004
C-Print / c-print
269 x 364 cm
Courtesy der Künstler / the artist & Konrad Fischer Galerie, Düsseldorf & Berlin
© VG Bild-Kunst, Bonn 2017

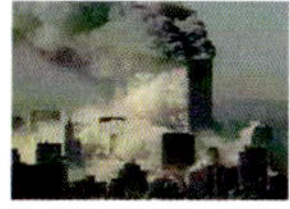

162

Thomas Ruff, *jpeg ny01*, 2004
C-Print / c-print
256 x 188 cm
Courtesy der Künstler / the artist & Konrad Fischer Galerie, Düsseldorf & Berlin
© VG Bild-Kunst, Bonn 2017

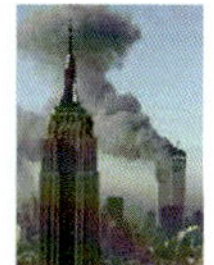

163

Thomas Ruff, *jpeg ny11*, 2006
C-Print hinter Diasec / c-print, diasec face mount
193 x 193 cm
Courtesy der Künstler / the artist & Konrad Fischer Galerie, Düsseldorf & Berlin
© VG Bild-Kunst, Bonn 2017

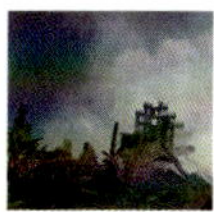

D. H. SAUR

164
165

D. H. Saur, *Facebook*, 2011, Details / details
Collage / collage
70 x 100 cm
Courtesy der Künstler / the artist

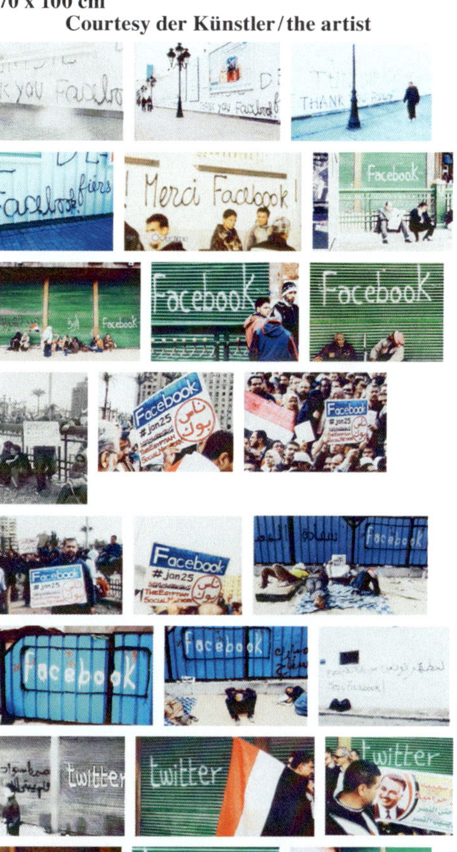

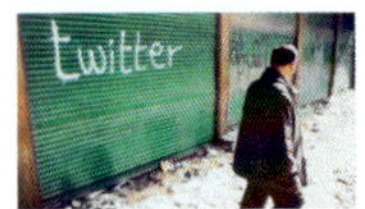

166

D. H. Saur, *Facebook*, 2011
Collage / collage
70 x 100 cm
Courtesy der Künstler / the artist

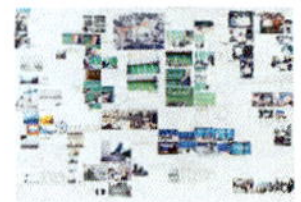

D. H. Saur, *Hope 2008–2011*, 2011
Collage / collage
50 x 70 cm
Courtesy der Künstler / the artist

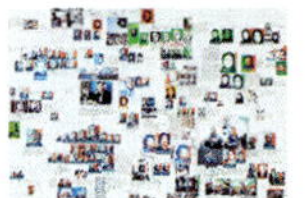

167

D. H. Saur, *Facebook*, 2011, Detail / detail
Collage / collage
70 x 100 cm
Courtesy der Künstler / the artist

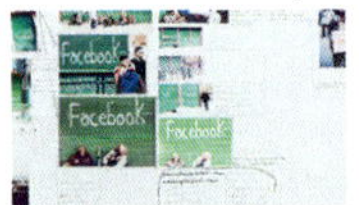

WERKLISTE
LIST OF WORKS

Lara Baladi
*1969, Libanon / Lebanon
lebt und arbeitet / lives and works in Boston & Cairo
http://tahrirarchives.com

Be Realistic, Ask for the Impossible, 2017
Multimediainstallation, bestehend aus Wandgemälden, LED-Laufschrift und drei Videoinstallationen: / multimedia installation, consisting of murals, LED ticker, and three video installations:

Alone, Together, … In Media Res, 2012
Dreikanalvideoinstallation / three-channel video installation, 42 Min

Ana Masri (I am Egyptian), 2010–2017
Fotografien von / Photographs by Lara Baladi, endless loop

Vox Populi, Archiving a Revolution in the Digital Age
Web-basierte Timeline der ägyptischen Revolution 2011, fortlaufendes Projekt seit 2011 / web based timeline of the 2011 Egyptian revolution, ongoing project since 2011
Maße variabel / dimensions variable
Courtesy die Künstlerin / the artist

Irene Chabr
*1983, Schweiz / Switzerland
lebt und arbeitet in Zürich / lives and work in Zurich
www.chabr.ch

Wandernde Gesten II, 2017
Inkjet- und Laser-Prints, Kartonwabenplatten / inkjet and laser prints, honeycomb paperboard panels

Irene Chabr & Noëmie Stähli

Harraga (www.youtube.com/watch?v=TT2ijWrTUr4; www.youtube.com/watch?v=eWvvRF3Y-S8; www.youtube.com/watch?v=36kbTfnVkg), 2013
Zweikanalvideoprojektion / two-channel video projection, 3:26 Min, endless loop
Maße variabel / dimensions variable
Courtesy die Künstlerinnen / the artists

Forensic Architecture
Gegründet / founded in 2011
Sitz am / based at Goldsmiths, University of London
www.forensic-architecture.org

Air Strike Atimah, 2015
3D-Pulverdruck eines Wolkenmodells, CNC-gefräster Hartschaum / powder bed fusion 3D print of cloud model, CNC base milled from high density foam
25 x 70 x 80 cm
Courtesy Forensic Architecture

Air Strike Atimah, 2015
Video / video, 2:43 Min
Maße variabel / dimensions variable
Courtesy Forensic Architecture

Lynn Hershman Leeson
*1941, USA
lebt und arbeitet / lives and works in San Francisco
www.lynnhershman.com

iPhone Crack (August Moon), 2014
iPhone, Beamer, Sockel, technische Vorrichtung / iPhone, beamer, pedestal, technical devices
120 x 45 x 35 cm
Courtesy die Künstlerin / the artist & Waldburger Wouters, Brüssel / Brussels

Big Hoodie, 2016
Archivarischer Digitaldruck / archival digital print
40 x 74,91 cm
Courtesy die Künstlerin / the artist & Waldburger Wouters, Brüssel / Brussels

Final water is rising, 2016
Archivarischer Digitaldruck / archival digital print
25,4 x 22,32 cm
Courtesy die Künstlerin / the artist & Waldburger Wouters, Brüssel / Brussels

Cyclops of the anthropocine 1, 2016
Archivarischer Digitaldruck / archival digital print
25,4 x 20,4 cm
Courtesy die Künstlerin / the artist & Waldburger Wouters, Brüssel / Brussels

Image Capture on Discarded Broken Cell Phone after Trayvon Martin Riots, 2012
Archivarischer Digitaldruck / archival digital print
129,2 x 76,2 cm
Courtesy die Künstlerin / the artist & Waldburger Wouters, Brüssel / Brussels

Thomas Hirschhorn
*1957, Schweiz / Switzerland
lebt und arbeitet / lives and works in Paris
www.thomashirschhorn.ch

Subjecter (Katastrophé), 2010
Schaufensterpuppe, Brautkleid, Collage, Klebeband / mannequin, wedding dress, collage, adhesive tape
180 x 250 x 350 cm
Courtesy Privatsammlung / private collection

Randa Maroufi
*1987, Marokko / Morocco
lebt und arbeitet / lives and works in Paris & Tanger
www.randamaroufi.com

Le Park, 2015
Film, 14 Min, produziert von / produced by Le Fresnoy, Studio national des arts contemporains
Courtesy die Künstlerin / the artist & Le Fresnoy, Studio national des arts contemporains

Rabih Mroué
*1967, Libanon / Lebanon
lebt und arbeitet / lives and works in Berlin
www.sfeir-semler.com/gallery-artists/rabih-mroue

Blow Up, 2012
Part 3 of the series *The Fall of a Hair*, 2012
Nr. / No. 1, 3, 4, 5, 7 (von insg. 7 Drucken / out of 7 prints)

Lightjet-Drucke auf Hochglanzpapier / lightjet prints on high gloss paper
je / each 130 x 90 cm
Courtesy der Künstler / the artist & Sfeir-Semler Gallery, Beirut & Hamburg

The Pixelated Revolution, 2012
Part 1 of the series *The Fall of a Hair*, 2012
Video, Bildschirm mit Countdown, Farbe, Ton / video, countdown screen, colour, sound, 21:58 Min
Maße variable / dimensions variable
Courtesy der Künstler / the artist & Sfeir-Semler Gallery, Beirut & Hamburg

Thomas Ruff
* 1958, Deutschland / Germany
lebt und arbeitet / lives and works in Düsseldorf
www.konradfischergalerie.de/artists/thomas-ruff

jpeg ny11, 2006
C-Print hinter Diasec / c-print, diasec face mount
193 x 193 cm
Courtesy der Künstler / the artist & Konrad Fischer Galerie, Düsseldorf & Berlin

D. H. Saur
* 1983, Deutschland / Germany
lebt und arbeitet / lives and works in Berlin

Hope 2008–2017, 2008–2017
Zwei Collagen / two collages
150 x 320 cm, 50 x 70 cm
Courtesy der Künstler / the artist

Facebook, 2011
Collage / collage
70 x 100 cm
Courtesy der Künstler / the artist

AUTOR*INNEN
AUTHORS

Ernst van Alphen

ist Professor für Literaturwissenschaften an der Universität Leiden. Aktuelle Buchpublikationen sind *Art in Mind: How Contemporary Images Shape Thought* (University of Chicago Press), *Staging the Archive: Art and Photography in Times of New Media* (Reaktion Books) und *Failed Images: Photography and its Counter-Practices* (Valiz, im Druck).

is Professor of Literary Studies at Leiden University. Recent book publications are *Art in Mind: How Contemporary Images Shape Thought* (University of Chicago Press), *Staging the Archive: Art and Photography in Times of New Media* (Reaktion Books), and *Failed Images: Photography and its Counter-Practices* (Valiz, in press).

Marion Eisele

ist Kunsthistorikerin und arbeitet als Projektleiterin in KAI 10. Dort hat sie 2016 das Performance Projekt *Take Up Your Space* (mit Julia Schleis) realisiert. Sie war u.a. für das NRW KULTURsekretariat und die Günther-Peill-Stiftung am Leopold-Hoesch-Museum Düren tätig und kuratierte 2017 die Gruppenausstellung *Genius Loci V* in der Setareh Gallery, Düsseldorf.

is an art historian and project manager at KAI 10, where she realized the performance project *Take Up Your Space* (together with Julia Schleis) in 2016. Amongst others, she has worked for the NRW KULTURsekretariat and the Günther Peill Foundation at the Leopold-Hoesch-Museum Düren and curated the group show *Genius Loci V* at Setareh Gallery in Düsseldorf in 2017.

Julia Höner

studierte Kulturwissenschaften in Hildesheim und London und arbeitet als Kuratorin in KAI 10. Dort hat sie u.a. die Ausstellungen *Vom Eigensinn der Dinge* (2013) und *Less is a Bore* (2016) realisiert. Sie war Mitglied der Fachjury zur Jungen Szene der Kunststiftung NRW und unterrichtet im Wintersemester 2017/2018 an der Hochschule Düsseldorf im Master Kultur, Ästhetik und Medien.

studied aesthetics and cultural studies in Hildesheim and London and works as a curator at KAI 10. Amongst others, she has realised the exhibitions, *The Stubborn Life of Things* (2013) and *Less is a Bore* (2016). She was a member of the expert panel for Kunststiftung NRW's Junge Szene and will teach at the University of Applied Science in Düsseldorf in the Master's programme Culture, Aesthetics and Media during winter semester 2017/2018.

Linda Huke

studiert Kunstgeschichte im globalen Kontext an der Freien Universität Berlin und ist studentische Hilfskraft am Sonderforschungsbereich *Affective Societies*. Im Rahmen ihres Studiums beschäftigt sie sich primär mit der zeitgenössischen Kunstproduktion in den arabischen Ländern.

is studying Art History in a Global Context at Freie Universität Berlin and is a student assistant for the Collaborative Research Centre *Affective Societies*. The focus of her studies is contemporary art from the Arab world.

Tasja Langenbach

ist Kunsthistorikerin und Kulturwissenschaftlerin und arbeitet seit 2004 als freie Kuratorin. Sie war Jurymitglied u.a. für den Förderpreis für junge Künstler*innen des Landes NRW, das *European Media Art Festival* Osnabrück und den Medienkunstpreis Marl. Im Sommersemester 2017 unterrichtete sie an der Hochschule Düsseldorf im Master Kultur, Ästhetik und Medien. Seit 2012 ist sie künstlerische Leiterin der *Videonale – Festival für Video und zeitbasierte Kunstformen* in Bonn.

is an art historian and cultural scientist and works as a freelance curator since 2004. She was a member of the expert panel for the Förderpreis für junge Künstler*innen des Landes NRW, the *European Media Art Festival* Osnabrück and the Medienkunstpreis Marl. She teached at the University of Applied Science in Düsseldorf during summer semester 2017. She has been directing the *Videonale – Festival für Video und zeitbasierte Kunstformen* in Bonn since 2012.

Katja Müller-Helle

ist Kunsthistorikerin und arbeitet als Postdoktorandin in der Kollegforschergruppe *BildEvidenz. Geschichte und Ästhetik* an der Freien Universität Berlin. In ihrem aktuellen Buchprojekt beschäftigt sie sich mit der Destruktion von Musikinstrumenten in der Kunst und Popkultur im Lichte einer Theoriegeschichte der Transgression seit 1950.

is an art historian and currently postdoctoral researcher at the Center for Advanced Studies *BildEvidenz. History and Aesthetics* at Freie Universität Berlin. Her recent book project deals with the destruction of musical instruments in art and popular culture in light of a history of transgression since 1950.

Kerstin Schankweiler

ist Kunsthistorikerin und arbeitet als Postdoktorandin am Sonderforschungsbereich *Affective Societies* der Freien Universität Berlin. Ihr aktuelles Forschungsprojekt beschäftigt sich mit Bildzeugenschaft und den affektiven Dynamiken von Bildern in Zeiten der sozialen Medien.

is an art historian and currently postdoctoral researcher in the Collaborative Research Centre *Affective Societies* at Freie Universität Berlin. Her current research project deals with image testimonies and the affective dynamics of images in times of social media.

Stefanie Stallschus

lehrt und forscht als wissenschaftliche Mitarbeiterin (Postdoc) zur Geschichte der Gegenwartskunst an der Technischen Universität Berlin. Ihr aktuelles Forschungsprojekt untersucht den Mythos der Nacht in seiner Bedeutung für die künstlerische Arbeit mit den technischen Medien.

teaches and conducts research on the history of contemporary art at Technische Universität Berlin. Her current research project examines the myth of the night in its importance for artistic work with technical media.

Verena Straub

ist Kunsthistorikerin und arbeitet als wissenschaftliche Mitarbeiterin am Sonderforschungsbereich *Affective Societies* der Freien Universität Berlin. In ihrer Dissertation beschäftigt sie sich mit Videotestamenten von Selbstmordattentäter*innen im Nahen Osten, sowie den Aneignungen dieser Bilder in der zeitgenössischen Kunst.

is an art historian and works as a research assistant in the Collaborative Research Center *Affective Societies*, at Freie Universität Berlin. Her dissertation focuses on the video testaments of suicide bombers in the Near East and the adoption of such images in contemporary art.

Tobias Wendl

ist Professor am Kunsthistorischen Institut der Freien Universität Berlin und der Inhaber der Alfried Krupp von Bohlen und Halbach-Professur für Kunst und visuelle Kulturen Afrikas. Er ist Gründungsmitglied des Sonderforschungsbereichs *Affective Societies*.

is Professor at the Institute of Art History at Freie Universität Berlin, where he holds the Alfried Krupp von Bohlen und Halbach Chair for African Arts and Visual Cultures. He is a founding member of the Collaborative Research Centre *Affective Societies*.

IMPRESSUM
IMPRINT

Dieser Katalog erscheint anlässlich der Ausstellung
This catalogue is published on the occasion of the exhibition
Affect Me.
Social Media Images in Art
Lara Baladi, Irene Chabr, Forensic Architecture, Lynn Hershman Leeson, Thomas Hirschhorn, Randa Maroufi, Rabih Mroué, Thomas Ruff, D.H. Saur

11.11.2017–10.3.2018
KAI 10 | Arthena Foundation, Düsseldorf

AUSSTELLUNG
EXHIBITION

Kuratorinnen
curators
Julia Höner, Kerstin Schankweiler

Koordination der Ausstellung
exhibition coordination
Marion Eisele, Julia Schleis

Assistenz
assistance
Sabine Allroggen, Susanne Kalf-Muhtaroglu, Birgit Popien, Nadine Jeddeloh

Gefördert durch
supported by

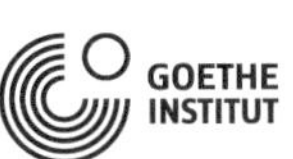

schweizer kulturstiftung
prohelvetia

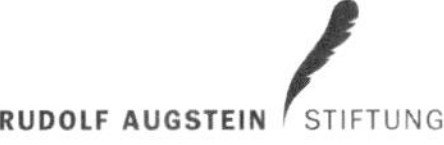

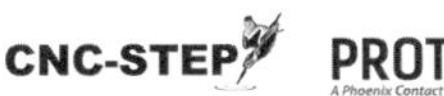

PROTIQ
A Phoenix Contact Company

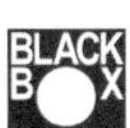

PUBLIKATION
PUBLICATION

Herausgeber*innen
editors
KAI 10 | Arthena Foundation, Düsseldorf; Sonderforschungsbereich 1171 Affective Societies, Freie Universität Berlin; Julia Höner; Kerstin Schankweiler

Redaktion
editing
Marion Eisele, Julia Höner, Kerstin Schankweiler

Bildredaktion
image editing
Marion Eisele, Linda Huke, Susanne Kalf-Muhtaroglu

Gestaltung
design
Krispin Heé, Berlin/Zürich
Studio Daniel Rother, Berlin

Vorwort
foreword
Monika Schnetkamp, Birgitt Röttger-Rössler

Texte
texts
Ernst van Alphen, Marion Eisele, Julia Höner, Linda Huke, Tasja Langenbach, Katja Müller-Helle, Stefanie Stallschus, Verena Straub, Kerstin Schankweiler, Tobias Wendl

Übersetzung
translation
Heather Allen: Vorwort/foreword, Essay von/by Tobias Wendl, Künstlertexte zu/artists texts on Irene Chabr, Lynn Hershman Leeson, Randa Maroufi, Rabih Mroué, D.H. Saur
Barbara Lang: Essay von/by Julia Höner & Kerstin Schankweiler, Künstlertexte zu/artists texts on Lara Baladi, Forensic Architecture, Thomas Hirschhorn, Thomas Ruff
Wilhelm Werthern: Essay von/by Ernst van Alphen

Lektorat
copyediting
Marion Eisele, Julia Höner, Linda Huke, Barbara Lang, Kerstin Schankweiler, Julia Schleis

Lithografie
lithography
Henning Krause

Fotonachweis
photo credits
Siehe Bildindex ab Seite 172/see image index starting page 172

Produktion
production
Spector Books

Druck
print
Fritsch Druck GmbH, Leipzig

Buchbinderei
book bindery
Müller Buchbinderei GmbH Leipzig

Die Deutsche Nationalbibliothek verzeichnet diese Publikation in der Deutschen Nationalbibliografie; detaillierte bibliografische Daten sind im Internet über http://dnb.dnb.de abrufbar.

The German National Library lists this publication in the German National Bibliography; detailed bibliographic data is available on the Internet at http://dnb.dnb.de.

Vertrieb
distribution

Germany, Austria: GVA, Gemeinsame Verlagsauslieferung Göttingen GmbH & Co. KG, www.gva-verlage.de

Switzerland: AVA Verlagsauslieferung AG, www.ava.ch

France, Belgium: Interart Paris, www.interart.fr

UK: Central Books Ltd, www.centralbooks.com

USA, Canada, Central and South America, Asia, Africa: ARTBOOK | D.A.P. www.artbook.com

Australia, New Zealand: Perimeter Distribution, www.perimeterdistribution.com

1. Auflage/first edition
Printed in Germany
ISBN 978-3-95905-190-3

Erschienen bei/published by:
Spector Books OHG
Harkortstr. 10
04107 Leipzig
www.spectorbooks.com

Dank an
thanks to

alle Autor*innen/all authors, alle Künstler*innen/ all artists, Mai Mahmud Abdelfatah Shucry Ayyad, Michael Carter, Salma Samy Ahmed Elbalouty, Inas El-Wakil, Ralf Gaertner, Matthias Grotevent, Günter & Aaron & Lieselotte, Mark Hellar, Jan Hoeft, Frank Hylewicz, Johanna Keller, Tony Lutter, Max & Emil & Clara, Sarah Nankivell, Maik Prus, Thomas Reul, Fabienne Rosenbach, Ana Siler, Noëmie Stähli, Patrick Waldburger, Dieter Warlies

Eine Kooperation von KAI 10 | Arthena Foundation, Düsseldorf und dem Sonderforschungsbereich 1171 Affective Societies, Freie Universität Berlin.

A cooperation of KAI 10 | Arthena Foundation, Düsseldorf and the Collaborative Research Center 1171 Affective Societies at Freie Universität Berlin.

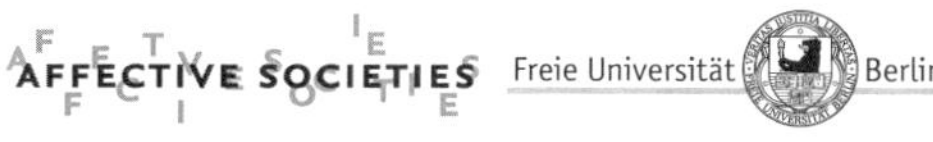

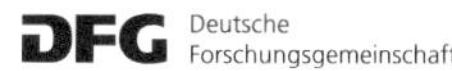

KAI 10 | Arthena Foundation
Kaistraße 10
40221 Düsseldorf
Tel. +49 (0) 211 99 434 130
Fax +49 (0) 211 99 434 131
info@kaistrasse10.de
www.kaistrasse10.de

Vorsitzende
chairwoman Arthena Foundation
Monika Schnetkamp

Künstlerischer Direktor
artistic director
Zdenek Felix

Kuratorin
curator
Julia Höner

Projektleitung
project management
Marion Eisele, Julia Schleis

Wissenschaftliche Mitarbeiterin
research assistant
Susanne Kalf-Muhtaroglu

Restaurierung
conservation
Sabine Allroggen

Haustechnik
facility management
Paul Rosenthal

Freie Universität Berlin
Fachbereich Politik- und Sozialwissenschaften
SFB 1171 Affective Societies
Habelschwerdter Allee 45
14195 Berlin
www.sfb.affective-societies.de

Sprecherin
speaker
Prof. Dr. Birgitt Röttger-Rössler, Institut für Sozial- und Kulturanthropologie

Geschäftsführung
management
Dr. Katharina Metz

Leitung des Teilprojektes *Affektive Dynamiken von Bildern im Zeitalter von Social Media*
Head of Project *Affective Dynamics of Images in the Era of Social Media*
Prof. Dr. Tobias Wendl, Kunsthistorisches Institut, Abteilung Kunst Afrikas

Wissenschaftliche Mitarbeiterinnen
research assistants
Dr. Kerstin Schankweiler, Verena Straub

Studentische Hilfskraft
student assistant
Linda Huke